GAME WRITING HANDBOOK

GAME WRITING HANDBOOK

RAFAEL CHANDLER

Charles River Media
A part of Course Technology, Cengage Learning

COURSE TECHNOLOGY
CENGAGE Learning™

Australia • Brazil • Japan • Korea • Mexico • Singapore • Spain • United Kingdom • United States

Game Writing Handbook
Rafael Chandler

Cover Designer: Tyler Creative Services

© 2007 Course Technology, a part of Cengage Learning.

For product information and technology assistance, contact us at
Cengage Learning Customer & Sales Support, 1-800-354-9706

For permission to use material from this text or product,
submit all requests online at **cengage.com/permissions**
Further permissions questions can be emailed to
permissionrequest@cengage.com

Library of Congress Control Number: 2007005313
ISBN-13: 978-1-58450-503-7
ISBN-10: 1-58450-503-6

Course Technology
25 Thomson Place
Boston, MA 02210
USA

Cengage Learning is a leading provider of customized learning solutions with office locations around the globe, including Singapore, the United Kingdom, Australia, Mexico, Brazil, and Japan. Locate your local office at:
international.cengage.com/region

Cengage Learning products are represented in Canada by Nelson Education, Ltd.

For your lifelong learning solutions, visit **courseptr.com**
Visit our corporate website at **cengage.com**

Printed in the United States of America
2 3 4 5 6 7 11 10 09 08

For Heather.

You are my sunshine.

Contents

Acknowledgments

I would like to thank my wife (and fellow author) Heather for her support and dedication during the creation of this book. Her experiences as a game developer and writer were extremely helpful.

I am very grateful to my editor, Jenifer Niles, for her encouragement and support, and for the excellent advice.

A big thank you goes out to all the game developers who agreed to be interviewed for this book.

Special thanks go to Susan O'Connor, who was the technical editor of this manuscript. Her advice and feedback were invaluable and deeply appreciated.

Finally, I want to thank my personal trainer, Scott Anspach of Health Fitness Designs, for turning me into a lean mean writing machine.

Preface

The *Game Writing Handbook* is about the process of creating game narrative. Many excellent books have been written on the subject, but most of these books have dealt with the theoretical implications of story in games or with the elements of narrative that guide the writing process. By contrast, the *Game Writing Handbook* focuses on the day-to-day work of the game writer from beginning to end. It includes sample spreadsheets, checklists, and nuts-and-bolts information about the development process.

This book is geared toward game writers, designers, and creative directors, but is a useful tool for any developer whose work impacts the development of a game's story content.

A number of veteran game developers were interviewed for this book. Their advice, insights, and shared experiences will prove useful for the aspiring game writer.

I've used several projects as examples in this book: *Rise of Merlin, King Arthur: Fall of Camelot, Justice Unit,* and *Odin: Nine Runes.* All games are fictional.

This book is a stake in the ground. My primary motivation was to document the work of the game writer as I have known it. I realize that the information presented herein is, in great part, informed by my own experiences in the industry and that writers at other companies will have learned different methods. Therefore, please understand that some of this material may differ from your own experiences as a game writer. The principles are, nonetheless, universal. Though you may not wind up directing the voice actors on your project or creating a flipbook animatic, someone else probably will, and your knowledge of the process will make you a more valuable member of the team.

If you write a game, I hope that this book helps you. Let me know.

Rafael Chandler

writer@rafaelchandler.com

About the Author

During his seven years in the game industry, Rafael Chandler has worked as a writer for Electronic Arts, SouthPeak Games, 1C, Ubisoft, and NHN. He's written story lines, dialogue, design documents, and marketing materials for over 35 titles, including *Monster Madness: Battle For Suburbia*, *Ghost Recon™: Advanced Warfighter*, *Rainbow Six™: Lockdown*, and various unannounced next-generation projects. Chandler is the author of Screen/Play, a regular feature at Gamasutra.com, and he has lectured on game narrative and design at the Russian Game Developers Conference and the Game Writers Conference. In addition to his work in the video game industry, Chandler is also a published author of horror fiction, and was the writer of *Dread: The First Book of Pandemonium*, a table-top role-playing game of horror-action. For more information, visit *www.rafaelchandler. com*.

1 Writing A Game

In This Chapter

- The Industry
- Context
- Screenwriting Transition
- Documentation
- Game Writing

How do you write a game? It's not a linear narrative construct like a novel or movie script or TV show teleplay. Instead of developing a story that will be observed and appreciated, you're writing a document whose content will be affected by the audience. Furthermore, the work that you do will not be printed and published like a book or article. It will be adapted and integrated into a complex software program, often through collaboration between dozens of game developers.

As a game writer, you will be delivering the context for an interactive entertainment experience, and you'll create a series of documents detailing the nonlinear interactions of people whose gameplay strategies will vary wildly. The dialogue won't be sequential. In one instance, the player may run around the corner and open fire, resulting in screams of panic from the enemy guards. Another player might crouch and listen, eavesdropping on the enemy conversations before deciding to find a way to sneak past them. The game writer understands all of these potential outcomes and creates story content that accommodates all of these scenarios. Understanding how to make it work is the focus of this book.

THE INDUSTRY

The game industry is bigger than ever. The evolution of technology has resulted in platforms such as the Nintendo® DS™, PlayStation® 3, PSP™, Wii™, and Xbox® 360, and, of course, the PC remains a strong platform for game development.

Game settings are myriad, but many of them parallel the genres of movies and television programs: western, science fiction, fantasy, cops and robbers, martial arts, espionage, and even romance and comedy. Game genres continue to develop, including such standbys as the first-person shooter, the platform, the racing game, real-time strategy, sports, and flight simulation. This continued expansion and evolution has resulted in a steady growth in sales, in the number of game developers and publishers, and in the number of jobs for game writers.

TRENDS

The next generation of consoles affords us more opportunity for story in games, and the maturation of the game industry has resulted in titles that feature a narrative depth that wasn't possible before. Games like the *Final Fantasy*® series and the *Metal Gear Solid*® series are known for sweeping story lines delivered in gorgeous prerendered cinematics. Other games, such as *The Elder Scrolls IV*®: *Oblivion*™, furnish narrative without the use of cinematic sequences, instead providing player-authored story lines that branch into numerous directions with the player's input.

As our audience shifts, so too does the demand for mature storytelling. The core audience for video games is older than it was in the heyday of the Nintendo Entertainment System® and the Sega® Genesis™. Adult gamers demand complex, polished story lines, similar to those found in feature films and novels.

Character development has become important; games now feature characters that evolve through the course of a game series, such as Sam Fisher™, the protagonist of the *Splinter Cell*™ games. The series' fourth installment, *Double Agent*, features a darker, more cynical Fisher than the previous installments. Cloud Strife, one of the main characters in the *Final Fantasy* series, begins as an aloof and uncaring antihero but eventually becomes a hero and a leader. The protagonist of *Panzer Dragoon*™ *Saga*, a young man named Edge, loses his idealism and becomes obsessed with revenge against the military leaders who betrayed him. Over time he falls in love with a beautiful mystery woman named Azel and learns of a threat to the entire world, and he puts aside his bitterness in his quest for peace and harmony.

This evolution in the depiction of central characters has resulted in a shift in the landscape of game writing. Emotion is now a design goal. The evolution of graphics in games makes it possible for games to amuse, frighten, awe, and thrill the player. In-game characters, such as Alyx from *Half-Life*® *2*, have become lifelike and realistic in their demeanor, and voice acting has improved drastically from the early days of games like *Resident Evil*®.

Games routinely feature emotional story lines featuring betrayal (*Grand Theft Auto*™ *3*), romance (*Max Payne*® *2*), paranoia (*Half-Life 2*), and darker themes such as abuse and murder (*Silent Hill*® *2*). These complex themes are played out over the course of a 10- or 20-hour game experience that immerses a player in another world. Unlike a movie or book, the player gets to experience these elements while engaged in an interactive experience, putting the audience in the role of author to some extent.

RECOGNITION

These changes have not gone without recognition. The Academy of Interactive Arts and Sciences awards games for excellence, including an award for Outstanding Achievement in Character or Story Development. The Game Developers Choice Awards offers an award for Excellence in Writing. Prior to 2000, the ceremony was known as The Game Developers Spotlight Awards and featured recognition for Best Script, Story, or Interactive Writing. The Canadian Awards for the Electronic and Animated Arts features a category for Best Writing for a New Media Production. These awards indicate that the industry as a whole now places a premium on quality scriptwriting and story development and that game writing is a valuable contribution to the development process.

IMMERSION

Game writing also serves to contextualize the action of the player on-screen and contributes to the immersion factor. If, in a game of medieval fantasy with photo-realistic graphics and detailed character models whose hair and clothing move in a realistic manner, the characters speak with modern accents and idioms, the immersion is ruined. When your character is walking through a forest in a rainstorm, you expect to hear the sound of rain and the sound of leaves being crunched underfoot. If the sound doesn't match the visuals, then the spell is broken and the player is reminded that it's just a game. If the dialogue and voice acting don't match the characters depicted on-screen, something is lost, and the impact is diminished.

Good writing can deepen the game experience, which is why game writers are often hired on the basis of past credentials (such as film, television, or book experience).

PROGNOSIS

Essentially, the bar has been raised. Games like *God of War*™ and *Halo 2* feature high-quality story lines, dialogue, and voice acting, which means that in order to remain competitive, other game writers must improve their techniques. This also impacts games currently being developed, as many studios pride themselves on their storytelling. Studios like BioWare® have created specific methods for telling great stories in games, and publishers like Electronic Arts™ are creating games by asking questions like, Can a video game make you cry?

What this means for game writers is that there is a demand for their work. While many studios still hand scriptwriting duties over to game designers or other members of the team, it's more and more common to see advertisements for positions for narrative designers, story designers, or writers on studio Web sites. Some writers are employed in-house and may even work on game design or production. Other writers may be hired as freelancers or may be tasked with creating the dialogue and nothing else.

Given the growing need for writers, it is only natural that game studios will look to TV and movie writers to fulfill that need, but that influx of outside talent is not without its downside. If writers enter the industry and work on games in the same way that they work on television programs, novels, or movies, their work will be unsuitable and will only create additional work for the other developers. They may complicate matters, resulting in editing, rewrites, or the hiring of additional writers.

In any case, it's crucial for game writers entering the industry to understand how games are created and how this process affects their work (as well as how they, in turn, will impact the development of a game). Writing a game screenplay in the same way that a TV show or novel is written will not work. Games aren't passive media, to be observed and appreciated by a passive audience. As an active media, whose key experience is user interaction, games require a unique form of documentation, which will be different from project to project. So game writers must study game design and production to understand what they'll be contributing to a game's development. It's not just a plot synopsis or a story line or a few thousand lines of dialogue. Game writers create context.

CONTEXT

In the early days of video and computer games, context was furnished outside of the game environment (see Figure 1.1). For example, *Pong*®, for the Atari® 2600, featured the image of a man holding a ping-pong paddle on the box. The name, *Pong*, also echoed the name of the game of ping-pong, to further contextualize the experience. When the user began to play the game, the context had been established, and the two rectangles on either side of the screen were then recognized as ping-pong paddles. The white square that moved back and forth was obviously a ping-pong ball.

The same was true for many other games. To establish some kind of context for the arbitrary images on-screen (bouncing circles, slow-moving squares, oddly shaped polygons that followed the movement of the controller or joystick), box art, marketing materials, and user manuals explained the context for the game. The player was a heroic knight, an intrepid space explorer, a pirate, a dragon. This lent meaning to the game and gave the player some explanation for his or her interaction with the game.

It didn't add much to the game. If, while playing *Combat* on the 2600, the user was told that the shapes represented tanks, or dragons, the gameplay was the same: fire at the enemy and destroy it, without being hit by the enemy's fire. Nonetheless, it was important enough to warrant inclusion in the game's materials.

Content	Explanation for action, core concept for the game
Context	Material created during production, like character models

FIGURE 1.1   The difference between context and content.

EVOLUTION OF CONTEXT

As games became more complex, their context matured as well. Clearly recognizable characters, such as Mario, enabled users to grasp more complicated contexts while playing a game. For example, instead of a fairly simple situation (two tanks on a battlefield are fighting one another), games could present relatively complex scenarios (an Italian plumber is called into action when a princess is captured by a malevolent reptile and must fight an army of walking mushrooms and flying turtles on his quest to save her).

While this context could be delineated in some detail via the marketing materials or user manual, a great deal of information could be delivered on-screen. Mario was a recognizable figure, down to his suspenders and moustache, and his adversaries were clearly identified as mushrooms with feet, turtles with wings, and reptilian monsters that breathed fire.

The early 1980s was therefore a period of some expansion of storytelling techniques in the game industry, as technological improvements made it possible to deepen the narrative constructs that drove gameplay. It wasn't necessary to explain the nuances of the story line in the user manual, as the player could gather all of the information by playing the game.

The landscape of games was changing. Coin-operated systems, whose primary goal was to divorce players from their quarters, generally featured endless loops in which the difficulty increased until the player walked away. Unbeatable games like *Space Invaders*™, *Asteroids*™, and *Centipede*™ all employed context as a static means of defining the user experience: you are a bounty hunter, you are a spaceship pilot, you are a guy who shoots at giant centipedes. These situations were static, in that there was never any real resolution to the situation: the centipedes were never defeated, the invading space monsters were never repelled. The action continued until the player walked away, and the story never ended.

Home systems provided a paradigm shift: the endless loop wasn't nearly as lucrative as the game that could be beaten. If you could beat a game, you could scratch that achievement off your list and then go out and purchase a new game. Certainly, many games had replay value, but it was still customary to play a game until it was beaten and then to pursue a new challenge. This resulted in games whose contexts were presented and then resolved by player action. The princess was kidnapped, the hero set out to rescue her, and the game concluded with her safe return (and with the defeat of the villain).

Between the cartoonish graphics, the technological parameters (little or no voice, limited space for text on-screen), and the medium's perception in the mass market as a toy for children, there wasn't much demand for game writers at the time.

MODERN CONTEXT

As the console market continued to develop, resulting in more advanced hardware and graphics, the stories continued to evolve. Today, consoles such as the PS3, Xbox 360, and Wii all offer graphical power and memory that are leaps and bounds beyond their predecessors. Consequently, the context for the gameplay is also quite evolved from its roots.

Voice acting is performed by professionals, and the characters move like real people because their motions have been captured through the use of special body-suits and computer programs. The story lines are often slick and polished, featuring adult subject matter and complex interactions between characters.

Of course, production values vary from project to project, and many games are published with hackneyed dialogue, convoluted or nonexistent story lines, and stereotypical characters. Not all game developers take advantage of the possibilities that technology affords them, and often, the context for a game is mediocre in comparison to the graphics or gameplay.

Part of the reason for this is that many developers and publishers put a premium on gameplay or visual elements but think of story and dialogue as minor details that can be furnished by anyone on the development team, regardless of writing ability. Nonetheless, enough studios believe in the power of game narrative to hire professional writers to create the context for their games.

ACTORS

Many games are propelled by digital actors, who are as easily recognizable as real-world Hollywood actors. Some are adapted likenesses, and some are created likenesses. Each has its challenges and advantages.

Adapted likenesses are game characters whose images are derived from existing characters, be they comic book heroes or famous film characters. James Bond, Spider-Man, Harry Potter, and Neo are all examples of adapted likenesses. Their resemblance to the source material varies, depending on considerations such as source format and game platform.

The format of the source material can result in differing interpretations of an adapted likeness. For example, *Ultimate Spider-Man*™ featured a cel-shaded hero who resembled the comic book likeness of Spider-Man®. However, *Spider-Man 2* was designed to look like the character played by Tobey Maguire in the feature film of the same name. If your source material is a novel, as in the case of *The Lord of the Rings: The Fellowship of the Ring*, your artists are likely to base the character models on their own concept art. However, the source material for *The Lord of the Rings*™: *The Two Towers*™ was the second installment in the film trilogy, so the character models were based on the actors who played the characters in the movie.

Game platform can play a determining factor in the appearance of an adapted likeness. Harry Potter's avatar may look a lot like Daniel Radcliffe in a next-gen console version of the game, but on a handheld, the features won't be as crisp or accurate and their depiction will probably be more stylized or cartoonish.

Created likenesses are characters developed by game companies who become so iconic that they take on a life of their own. For example, Lara Croft, heroine of the *Tomb Raider*™ games, is one of the most famous female game characters. Her attitude and accent and attributes are all recognized as part of her persona. Another well-developed character, Alyx Vance, one of the main characters in *Half-Life 2*, is cited as one of the first "digital actors."

Whether adapted or created, there are certain expectations for the character in question, and this creates additional parameters for a game writer. You can't just write dialogue for a character like Spider-Man or Harry Potter or James Bond—it's important that you understand the character and that you are familiar with the story components of the work that you're going to be adapting. While working on a James Bond title, for instance, you might write dialogue for the actor currently playing Bond (Daniel Craig at the time of this writing), you might work on a game that's based on a classic Bond film (such as the 2005 *From Russia With Love*™, which featured the voice of Sean Connery, along with an adapted likeness based on the 1963 film), or you might work on a game set in the Bond universe but not based on any movie (such as *Everything or Nothing*™, an original story that featured the likeness and voice of Pierce Brosnan).

Research is the key, as there will be expectations from your fellow developers and your audience. To deliver the style and feel that the game requires, you must familiarize yourself with the source material, and it must be the correct material. Studying the gritty and mature films by Sam Raimi will not help you if you're writing a game based on the wacky, fast-talking Spider-Man of the cartoon series.

SCREENWRITING TRANSITION

It can be challenging to make the transition from passive media, such as films or TV, to active media like interactive games. In passive media the producers and directors and writers have complete control over the experience; for the most part, everyone watching a film is going to see the same movie. Films that play with perception or timeframe, such as *Memento* and *Rashomon*, may cause some debate among viewers about what really happened, or what it was really about. However, these films are the exception, not the rule.

Games place a great deal of control in the hands of the player. The amount of linearity in a game varies. Some games are extremely linear, and present the player with a single corridor through the entire game, whether the player is in the woods, in the streets of a city, or walking through an office building. The developers can control which doors can be opened and which doors will always be closed. Obstructions such as barricades, overturned furniture, and crashed cars can be used to close off avenues of escape or investigation, meaning the player will perceive that, ultimately, there's only one way to advance.

Other games are quite nonlinear, such as the *Elder Scrolls* games, most notably *Morrowind*® and *Oblivion*. In both games the player begins the game in a small town that he or she can explore at great length. Gradually, the player realizes that the town is only one small corner of a massive world whose environs can be investigated in any way that the player chooses. The developers have used few (if any) artificial barriers to fence in the player; instead, the world is an open sandbox that the player can interact with as desired. Other nonlinear titles include the infamous *Grand Theft Auto 3* and *Grand Theft Auto: San Andreas*™, in which the player is a criminal who can walk and drive through a large city without being forced to choose a specific path.

DOCUMENTATION

The first thing to understand when writing a game is that game documentation is a unique and evolving process. Every studio documents story content in a different way, but it's rarely similar to the format employed by filmmakers and novelists. There is only one area of overlap, and that is the passive media that drives story content in some games. To clarify this, let's take a look at the differences between passive and active media (see Figure 1.2).

Passive media	Appreciated or observed, but not influenced by the player, such as cinematics	Intro to Final Fantasy X
Active media	Story content that's presented in-game, during the action	Intro to Half-Life 2

FIGURE 1.2   The difference between passive and active media.

Passive Media

Some of the story content in video games can be defined as passive media. This is content that is appreciated or observed, but not influenced, by the player. For example, many games begin with a prerendered cinematic sequence, a computer-generated movie that introduces main characters, settings, and the game's key conflict or scenario. These cinematics aren't always prerendered; sometimes, they're scripted sequences that run in-game.

Passive media is just like a movie, in the sense that the player has no control over what's going on. It's a static presentation of content, and there's no interaction. This gives the developer complete control over the story elements that are presented, making it possible to create dramatic or revealing sequences that wouldn't necessarily be possible in game. It's also less likely that the player will miss some key piece of information, because the player won't be focusing on the gameplay. Most passive media can be skipped by the player with a push of the button, but then the game's setting and scenario may not make much sense.

The documentation of passive media varies, depending on where you work. However, many studios employ the standard Hollywood script format, because it is familiar and accessible.

This kind of media may feel familiar to writers who have experience with other passive forms such as film, television, and books. However, many developers avoid passive media. Ubisoft™, for example, has recently indicated that in the future they will not employ any cinematic elements in their games.

Active Media

Active media is story content that's presented in-game, during the action. This content is affected by the player. For example, in *Half-Life 2*, characters such as Barney and Alyx frequently talk to the player, giving orders and information. The townspeople in *The Elder Scrolls IV: Oblivion* walk to and from work, and the player can stop them in the street and ask them questions. This kind of story content is interactive, because the player retains control over the experience and can even initiate it in many cases.

Some active media is optional, because the player can choose to avoid it altogether while playing the game. In *Doom® 3* various emails are found on discs, which the player can choose to access or ignore. The same is true for the journals and memos found in the *Resident Evil* series. For the most part, these items provide flavor material that adds to the experience. They can be passed over because they don't offer critical information.

In essence, active media is story content delivered during gameplay. When you're playing the game and you learn something new about your situation, that's active media.

The degree of control the developer has over content delivered during gameplay varies wildly from project to project. Some games are tightly scripted and linear and offer the player very little room to maneuver while playing. For example, there is only one corridor that cuts through the office building or sewer system or space station. In that way, the developer can ensure that the player is exposed to the correct kind of information and that the player experience is very close to what the developer had in mind.

This kind of control must be tightly polished in order to work, because if the player can't figure out what the developer wants, the experience is frustrating. The active media must therefore be polished and tightly scripted as well. If the player is supposed to go through a certain door to reach a control station, the information must be given to the player in a way that won't be misinterpreted. For example, the player might receive a radio transmission telling him to enter the door at the end of Sector B. If the transmission is played during the middle of a firefight, however, the player might not hear his commanding officer because he's busy unloading a machine gun at the enemy. After the firefight, he's going to be confused.

Documenting active content is an ever-developing challenge. It's easy to write content when you know that the material is linear: one person speaks, another responds, someone enters the room. But in a situation where every action taken by the player results in some change to the narrative structure, it can be difficult to predict the order in which voice cues will be played.

The Hollywood screenplay format will not work for active media, because the document was created for a passive medium. Furthermore, the very format of the Hollywood screenplay is impractical given the constraints of game development. Consider the margins and the liberal use of white space that are typical of a shooting script. These are intended as areas where notes and corrections can be made during filming, a process that has no counterpart in game development. The centered text, the huge font, the white space—these elements don't help game writers. In fact, they can serve as an enormous hindrance. Bear in mind that the rule of thumb is that one page of a script equals one minute of film time. Imagine applying that to a video game. Most single-player experiences range from 10 to 20 hours. Try carrying a 600- to 1200-page screenplay to a meeting. Or reading through it. Or looking for a specific line of dialogue. It just isn't feasible.

STORY DOCUMENTS

The documentation must fit the medium, so the story document must be formatted in an appropriate fashion. Subsequent chapters will discuss the process of developing a game and will outline a specific method for documenting story and dialogue content. For now, let's take a look at some of the core characteristics of game story documents.

CONTEXT

When designing a game, it's important to document the context—the explanation or justification for the events that transpire on-screen. Each game is defined by a setting, a genre, and a rising action that compels the character to act in some way: the earth is invaded by aliens, the hero's village is burned to the ground by an evil sorcerer's army, the town is overrun by flesh-eating zombies. Regardless of the specifics, each game's context must be defined early in the development process.

The process of creating a context can take many forms. For instance, the writer may start with a synopsis that outlines the core events and major characters in the story. Once this document has gone through the necessary approval stages, the next step might be the creation of a more detailed story outline that provides a detailed description of all of the missions or segments in a game, including information about locations, major events, and key moments. The story synopsis might consist of a few paragraphs, whereas the story outline might be several pages long.

A further extension of this document would be a mission document that outlines the story content for an individual mission, quest, or scenario. Alternatively, depending on the type of game, there might be a series of documents outlining the key regions in a game or the planets on which the space traveler can land and explore.

Characters drive story and dialogue, so a document that outlines all of the major characters in the game is a powerful tool early in the project. These documents can delineate a character's personality, background, appearance, speech patterns, accent, educational level, friends and family, attitudes toward other characters in the game, and so on. The more detailed the description, the easier it will be to write dialogue for the character later on. This document will also prove useful when creating concept art or character models.

These documents are all intended for a specific audience: your fellow developers. The point is to furnish information that will enable them to create content for a game, be it code, audio components, or art assets. To that end, the documents should be easy to read and content-driven, not humorous or over-written. In essence, this is an exercise in technical writing, intended to make the team's job as easy as possible.

Because it is so familiar, and so easy to access, a standard word-processing program such as Microsoft® Word is the easiest way to create context documents. This subject is discussed in more detail in Chapter 3, Documenting the Story.

DIALOGUE

Depending on the degree of player freedom in a game, documenting dialogue can be extremely confusing. Consider this scenario, culled from a fairly linear action game. The player begins in a hallway and is carrying a pistol. As the player approaches the corner ahead, his commanding officer comes in over the headset. She tells the player that there are two hostiles headed his way. The player turns around and starts running the other way, looking for a way out. Of course, there's nothing there, so the CO tells the player that he needs to turn around, but if the player instead runs around the corner and kills both enemies, she congratulates him on neutralizing the enemy.

Try visualizing the documentation for that particular exchange. Now add another variable to the equation. Now add a few hundred more. Even the most linear game features choice at nearly every step of the way, because the player can always choose to NOT do something. The player can choose to avoid a firefight or go the wrong way or drop a crucial item. To keep the player on track, many games employ voice cues or text on-screen to tell the player what he's doing wrong.

Processing all of this content is a challenge for the game writer. It gets more complicated when more variables are added. For example, games like *Grand Theft Auto 3* offer a world that the player can explore in all directions. The world isn't infinite; it's just very large and not constrained by artificial barriers. The world is the street, and the player can walk the streets of the city in any direction before reaching the edge of the map (a river or some other obstacle). When writing dialogue for a game as wide open and nonlinear as *Oblivion* or *Gun*™ or *True Crime*®, the writer can't rely on linear documentation methods.

Interestingly enough, the writer's best friend is an accounting tool.

SPREADSHEETS

To document the dialogue for a game, many writers employ spreadsheets such as Excel®. The benefits of a spreadsheet are outlined in more detail in Chapter 7, Organizing Dialogue. For now, let's go over the basics.

Spreadsheets feature columns that can be used to divide content into sections, for example, speaker, dialogue, inflection, location, effects, and filename. When documented in a spreadsheet, this is much easier to read and process than a line of text on a page.

Spreadsheets allow the user to manipulate large quantities of text quickly and easily. The writer can highlight a column and move it to either side of the page or delete it altogether. Using filters, the writer can select only one type of content (such as all dialogue spoken by a specific character). It's possible to sort content alphabetically or by chronological order.

Spreadsheets are ideal because they allow developers to create and deliver information with a minimum of complication.

GAME WRITING

Now that we've talked about context and documentation, we can begin to explore the process of how a game is actually written. We'll begin by exploring the stages of game development. Then we'll talk about some of the people you might interact with on your development team.

DEVELOPMENT STAGES

Preproduction

This stage typically lasts for a few weeks or months. Numerous decisions are made during the preproduction stage of development (see Figure 1.3). First, the developers must define the gameplay experience. What is the genre? Is this a shooter, a flight sim, or a turn-based strategy game? What is the setting? Western, science fiction, or survival horror? What kind of look and feel will define the game?

Pre-production	Period of evaluating and decision-making; core concept established
Production	Storyline, characters, and events are written and designed
Post-production	Game testing and polish, postmortem and legacy documentation

FIGURE 1.3   Preproduction, production, and postproduction.

The developers will need to define some of the marketing strategy. There are numerous considerations during this part of preproduction, given the way that marketing drives sales in the game industry; these decisions have a serious impact on story design. Depending on their publishing situation, the developers may just make a note of some of the game's key selling points, or they may prepare a full-blown marketing overview. It's important to at least consider the brand. Are the story line, plot, and concept all appropriate for the brand? *Sonic the Hedgehog*™ is a fun, lighthearted series, and the brand just doesn't lend itself well to dark or complex story lines. By the same token, the *Silent Hill* games are gruesome and sinister, with little room for humor or irreverence.

While discussing the marketing strategy, it's also important to look over the game's characters. The marketing department may have some input about the number of characters in the game or the way the characters should appear in the game. They may also want to apply a specific rating to the game or include certain items, events, or scenarios in the story line. This all affects the work of the game writer.

During preproduction a discussion of the game's rating will also probably ensue. Depending on a game's rating, certain elements will be permitted, while others will be forbidden to the game writer. For example, nudity and gore are not possible in an E- or T-rated game. On the other hand, just because a game is rated M for mature doesn't mean that all bets are off. Many games are rated M because they feature violence, but they don't include any nudity or language. Before including adult subject matter in your story documents or game script, ensure that such content is appropriate for the game.

During the preproduction phase of a licensed game, it's important to evaluate the impact of that license on the game's content. The game and the licensed property should be as coherent as possible to avoid confusion. If the game is based on a movie, novel, or comic book, the writer should do the appropriate research to determine the style, characters, and story line of the source material. This can take many forms. Some games, such as *Star Wars*® *Episode III: Revenge of the Sith*™, actually feature scenes from the movie and allow the player to interact with characters from the film. Other games, such as *The Chronicles of Riddick™: Escape From Butcher Bay*, serve as prequels or sequels to licensed properties (in this case, the prequel to the movie *Pitch Black*). Naturally, licensing a book or movie will also affect the dialogue that's written. The game writer will want to study the source material for the speech patterns of the protagonists, so that the sound is consistent.

After all of this research and discussion has concluded, the developers can begin to structure the actual concept of the game. While the game writer and his collaborators have been discussing story line, characters, dialogue, and settings, the programmers have been talking about code and engine, and the artists have been discussing art direction and concept art. The game's concept is approved and documented, and work can now begin.

Production

During the production phase, the game writer develops the story line, characters, and events. While these were all created during the concept phase, their development can take months or years. Generating page after page of documentation, the game writer outlines the scenarios, their impact on the story, the characters' backgrounds and biographies, and the major events that will be depicted in prerendered or scripted cinematics.

In addition, the writer will create dialogue, sometimes thousands of lines of it. *Halo 2* featured over 15,000 lines, and *Call of Duty® 2* boasted over 20,000. This is atypical, but in any case, the creation of dialogue will require months of work, including writing, critique, and numerous revisions. If the game features prerendered cinematics or scripted cut scenes, these will require documentation and dialogue. Working with concept artists and cinematic artists, the game writer will create screenplays for these passive media elements and may even participate in the process of creating animatics (detailed in Chapter 8, Creating Cinematics).

Once the dialogue has been written, the developers will cast voice actors. If the game writer has furnished detailed notes about the voices needed for the game, this process will flow more smoothly. Once the voice actors are cast, the dialogue will be recorded over a series of voice shoots, and the voice cues will then be placed in the game.

After all of the elements have been created and integrated, the process of testing and refinement will begin. The quality assurance department's testers will play through the game, documenting bugs found in the story elements. By this time, the testers will already have begun the testing process for other, more critical areas of the game, such as functionality and hardware compatibility. Therefore, testing of the story and dialogue may not be a high priority for the game.

As a result, the game writer may take it upon himself to test game content and ensure that the voice cues are playing at the appropriate time and that the story material is of sufficiently high quality. It might be necessary to use alternate voice cues or to record new voice cues altogether.

Postproduction

The testing process continues during the stage of postproduction. The game's ship date looms, and everyone on the team is pulling in the same direction, trying to haul the game out the door in time for the street date. Bugs are being fixed, and the game is being polished by dozens of hands.

Again, the focus will be the game's smooth execution. Crash bugs and unplayable areas will receive the lion's share of attention, as opposed to lines of dialogue that don't play when they're supposed to. Generally, problems with dialogue are not taken as seriously as problems with the game's executable (and with good reason). Again, the writer may wind up addressing many of these issues personally.

DISAMBIGUATION

At this point, it's necessary to differentiate between three terms that are used throughout this book: script, screenplay, and Screen/Play. The confusion between some of these terms can complicate discussions, so for the purposes of this book, the following definitions will be used.

Script

Scripting is the process of placing objects in-game and assigning behaviors to them. This is usually achieved through the use of scripting tools or editors, such as UnrealEd. A scripter may need to know a scripting language, such as Lua, or the scripting tool that the scripter uses may consist of a series of easily accessed drop-down menus. The scripting process, as it pertains to story design, is discussed in Chapter 11, Integrating Dialogue.

Screenplay

A screenplay is a story document. It can include dialogue, camera angles, special effects, sound effects, or other forms of context. Screenplays take many forms, including Word documents, spreadsheets, and proprietary software systems.

Screen/Play

The Screen/Play format is one example of active documentation. Screen/Play is a spreadsheet designed to streamline the process of documenting story content, including dialogue, context, filename, and location. More information is available in Chapter 7, Organizing Dialogue.

SUMMARY

Ultimately, the more groundwork is laid during the early stages of a game, the easier the later stages will be. If the writer anticipates the challenges of production and postproduction and tries to preemptively solve them during the preproduction stage, the game's story and dialogue will benefit.

DEVELOPER INTERVIEW

Chris Avellone, Creative Director, Obsidian Entertainment
Planescape: Torment, Star Wars: Knights of the Old Republic II™

ENTERING THE FIELD

If I were to boil down the most important lessons for a game writer entering the field, I'd start with the simple premise that you're working on a game first, and everything else, including the narrative, is secondary to the game—maybe even lower down the totem pole than that, as much as I hate to admit it. The game mechanics, the gameplay, the fun factor is the meat of the game, and the story needs to complement it and cater to it, not override it. The player cares about the things he can do, not always the context, if that makes any sense.

Second of all, attention to detail and documenting your work is probably the one of the most valuable skills to learn and practice. Unlike comics, novels, and to a lesser extent, tabletop RPGs, computer game designers can omit nothing about the camerawork of a scene, the tone and background of a character you need to voice-cast, the layout of the environment, the systems for interaction, exactly who can say what to who and when, character behavior, townsfolk schedules, or anything down to the items the people of the world are carrying. A computer game writer has to be aware of this level of detail and what the parameters are in order to effectively do their job—any game writer should familiarize themselves with not only the game genre and characters, but the toolset and scripting system that brings those characters to life. It aids in creating meaningful interactions and cinematic sequences that make use of the resources that already exist rather than forcing new assets to be created (or worse,

→

having the sequences you need to deliver the story cut or removed because they don't work in the engine that you're writing for).

Third, games are progressing toward a movie-style brevity in scripts and interactions, especially for action games—and preferably, these interactions should never stop the player's action at all. Practice word economy in your scripts, and while not all the rules for writing for movies apply, there are some script formatting and plot pacing practices you can take from movies and apply to games equally.

Fourth, contract writing is a challenge. If possible, it's better to be part of a game development team full-time from day one. I feel that stories often suffer when they are integrated after the foundation of the game has been laid out, and I think a lot of the disconnect between stories and game mechanics often arise because the story's left until too late. Get on board early, and do whatever you can to stay all the way to the end, especially during the voice acting and the bug-fixing stage of the game—those stages are just as important as the beginning of a game.

CHALLENGES OF GAME WRITING

Aside from having to learn the mechanics of the game and the world you're writing for, one of the unique challenges—at least for the style of RPGs Obsidian does—is that you have to reflect that the "story" is usually many stories all in one. Depending on how you define the personality of your characters, the player may experience different reactions or parts of the story completely out of order for how the writer may have envisioned it.

For example, in *Neverwinter Nights™ 2* we have an "influence" setting with the people in your party that reflects how much they trust or hate you, and depending on what that setting is (which is affected by your actions over the course of the game), it changes how much of their background information they share with you, how much they're willing to risk their lives for you, or how helpful they are at key points in the game. If that influence level gets too low, they either hate you, rebuke you, or eventually, in some cases, leave your party entirely. Obviously, each of these factors can adjust the pacing of the story and change how certain events play out, and as a writer and designer, you have to accommodate these potentially random events so that these things can happen, yet the player's experience in the game world is still strong.

Also, the player isn't usually static in role-playing games. In *Neverwinter Nights 2* the player may be evil, good, or be a different profession (fighter, bard, rogue), and any of these qualities may allow them to interact with other characters in the game world differently. As an example, when someone in the game

→

world asks you for help, a game writer has to create different branches for how the player can respond to the character (and vice versa), including branches for how you accomplish the quest (evil, good, diplomatically) and all the while make sure that each branch is satisfying and feels "reactive" for the world the player is in. Phew.

New Opportunities

Interactivity. In essence, the player is not passively absorbing the experience and the events like they would in a novel or comic (or even a movie or TV show). They are able to interact with it and make it react in different ways, which I think immediately makes the game narrative more immersive than it would otherwise be. But this transitions into the next question.

Pitfalls

One of these pitfalls is the interactivity. You give up a streamlined, focused flow of a story line or narrative for the sake of letting the player adjust their own pacing, depending on the nature of the game. Especially for role-playing games, you need to construct your narrative in such a way that complements the events around it. The story isn't a chapter—it's an area or mission that could have any of a number of events or timing the player may be able to explore or encounter in any order.

A Good Experience

I suppose the product I'm most proud of is *Planescape: Torment*, a *Dungeons and Dragons*™ game set in the Planescape universe. The universe had an interesting set of parameters; the license was built around "mental real estate," the idea that if enough people believed in something strongly enough (say a religion, idea, or a god), they could bring it into being, so there was a constant war being waged—not for territory, but for ideas and the power of belief. Furthermore, the setting of the game was completely open-ended—the player was allowed to have access to the planes, where just about any environment or creature you could imagine existed. It was a setting that really encouraged the imagination and it was a pleasure to write for.

So let's see, what went right about it? First off, an excited team. Some of us (including me) were very new to the product cycle, and we had a lot of enthusiasm. Second of all, the license was a liberating one, and it actually complemented the plotline of the game we had envisioned—but the third most

→

important thing is that the story didn't require you know anything about the license to enjoy it. It could stand on its own, and it didn't exclude people that didn't know about the setting. I usually find one of the truest tests of a game story is if it could stand by itself outside of the license and still be strong. If the story requires an intimate knowledge of the game setting for people to appreciate it, I think that ends up being a barrier to accessibility.

Also, if there's anything I would encourage writers to practice it's the following—learn to sell your story, sell your ideas, not just to the team, but to the publishers as well. Talk to your teammates, tell them the cool points in the story, talk to the area designers, the modelers, tell them the context for each encounter, why it's going to be cool for the character and so on. You'll see the results in the end.

Lastly, try to interweave the story for the game mechanics, as I think the story gets stronger as a result. You're writing for a game, and the more the gameplay is actually woven into the story, the stronger both become. For example, on *Planescape: Torment*, one of the protagonist's (many) "problems" is that he's immortal, solely a story choice. But if you take that story choice, and then weave it into the game mechanics so (1) there's no death and (2) he wakes up in a new location every time he is knocked unconscious, then you actually create a whole new game experience for the player—one, you've prevented the character from reloading their game (which I would argue is a strength), and two, you've introduced a puzzle mechanic in the game, where there may be instances where the player may be able to get past a lethal obstacle by failing rather than destroying it (we used this to great effect for sneaking in and out of areas by "dying," as well as solving certain deathtrap puzzles in the game).

Streamlining the Process

There are a few things—one, try to keep the leads and the producer consistent. Nothing can change the direction of a game more than switching horses in midstream. Also, it's a tendency for many developers I know that when they "inherit" an idea, system, or a section of code from someone else, their first desire is to rewrite so it makes sense to them, and this just causes delays, and more often than not, bugs. If you have the time to make it better, great, but changing a working idea for the sake of change is not always the best option.

Overcoming Challenges

Try to hold on to your leads—and there's a variety of tactics for this, but it's not always the province of the game writer. For the inheritance problem, the only

$\rightarrow$

thing you can do is take enough time for self-examination to check yourself (and have others check you) when you may be doing work that is ultimately unnecessary and possibly dangerous for the product.

Some of the hardest lessons to learn are (1) you can't do it all by yourself, you need to share and you need to delegate—and provide good documentation to the people you're delegating to. (2) You need to have a detail-oriented mindset. You can't leave anything up in the air or for someone else to figure out later; if you do, you're asking for trouble down the line. (3) You need to be mindful of scope and the resources you have at your disposal and reevaluate frequently. If your story calls for 9 levels in a game, you have 18 months, and looking at the schedule, you notice each level takes the team 2 months to do, you need to edit yourself—be mindful of the schedule, check the estimated work loads, and adjust accordingly. It's better if you make cuts yourself rather than be forced to do it later on.

LICENSED PROPERTIES

[It's] stressful, and even though I love the licenses, it still can be a little claustrophobic working in someone else's universe—and intimidating waiting for the fan reaction. At times, it's hard to get the tone of someone else's voice (say, Lucas or Greenwood) just right to make it happen. Fortunately, both these universes have enough freedom in them to allow for good stories, narratives, and characters. They're expansive, with plenty of adventure locales and cool factions and themes, so it's hard not to find something to get excited about and draw upon.

Also, I think Obsidian's been lucky in this instance, but working with the content quality folks for Forgotten Realms™ on *Neverwinter Nights 2* and again with the LucasArts® folks in *Stars Wars: Knights of the Old Republic II: The Sith Lords*, the approval process went very smoothly for many aspects of the stories for these games. Part of it I think was the work Obsidian invested in making sure we knew the genre we were writing for, and the second was simply just keeping the lines of communication open on changes and the universe.

OVERCOMING OBSTACLES

I'll try to cite RPGs as my basis, simply because that's what I've worked on for most of my career—although I can't imagine there's a huge difference in other game genres, only that their word count and story is probably a lot less branching than most of the RPGs that Obsidian makes (or the ones Black Isle Studios™ used to do).

$\rightarrow$

For old school RPGs, it's "localization" (translating the game into other languages). Much of the narrative comes across from interactions and text exchanges with others. Translating words is expensive, and when you're doing it for nine (or more) languages that's a lot of translator time, and a lot of management to make sure that all of it is getting translated and into the game correctly. The president of Interplay, Brian Fargo, actually had many strong words (and rightfully so) to share with me concerning the word count on *Planescape: Torment*, and we almost had to cut many of the interactions with the companions in the game because there were simply too many words in the game, making it too expensive to manage and translate. It was a rough lesson to learn, but it sure helps you edit yourself in the future, trust me.

When it comes to more modern-day RPGs, the audio/voice-casting budget actually ends up being a bigger issue. Doing voice-overs for role-playing games can get very expensive, and even worse, they often need to be done before the game has been thoroughly tested and any issues with quests or exposition have been ironed out. Some of these things may result from levels being cut, characters being cut, and so on, that are just part of the bug-fixing and finalization of the game. You may suddenly discover that you're going to lose two cut scenes or one main quest-giver character who was intended to give a critical piece of information.

As a result, you have to be very detail-oriented in your story and make sure you have "back-ups" in play in case you need to make changes. For example, when we were doing *Fallout*™ *2* (and its sister title), we tried to make sure a number of the key characters and quest-givers in the game were expressly not voice-acted, so we had more time to edit them at the end of the project if the testers were encountering bugs with them.

THE WORKING WRITER

Writers should familiarize themselves with the genre and scripting and matinee tools for the game engine. Writers need to learn how to be designers, and designers need to learn how to write (mostly script writing). Both should be able to set up their own cut scenes and cinematics in the game or, at the least, understand how it's done so they know exactly how to structure their requests and edit the requests to fit what the engine can do rather than "blue skying" it.

Also, equally important, they should always sit in on the voice-casting and voice-acting sessions. If not, something is in danger of being lost in translation, some critical word or phrase mispronounced (especially in a fantasy title), or having someone miscast for a part. Nothing undermines a dramatic sequence

→

quite like discovering the lines that you intended to be delivered by a hard-bitten soldier is are being spoken by someone who sounds like they're 12 years old and have just taken a deep breath of helium to boot.

Good game writers should study and, if possible, practice game design. They should know the toolset of the game they're writing for, how to set up quests, how areas are built, what AI you can assign to enemies and allies, and how conversations and cut scenes are implemented in the engine. They should make efforts to learn all of this as soon as possible. It will cause their work to be stronger because their work then complements what the game engine can actually do. It also allows them to communicate the narrative and its implementation to the team members doing it more effectively (if the writer isn't doing it themselves).

As for the creative director and producer, game writers should either (1) make sure they understand exactly what the creative director and producer want from the writer, what kind of experience they're trying to invoke, and (2) if this is lacking, provide this direction to them.

LAST WORDS OF ADVICE

A few things, especially for people looking to break into the field of games. Be persistent. Keep sending your resume out, even to places with no job postings. Find the email addresses of some of your favorite designers and ask them for advice, or just to set up a dialogue—they'll probably have some good advice to share. Work on implementing your stories into game editors in your spare time and use that as demos of your work. Obsidian's *Neverwinter Nights 2*, for example, comes with a game editor you can use to build your modules and put your stories into those. Release that to the community, get feedback, improve, iterate, and keep trying. Some of the best resumes we've gotten are from people who set up their own mods or adventures, and it was well-received by others in the community.

That's all I have to say at the moment. Thanks for the opportunity. For now, I have to get back to hammering away on our next RPG.

2 Creating the Concept

In This Chapter

- The Working Writer
- The Game Concept

Now that we've covered a basic overview of the game-writing process, let's delve a little more deeply into the process of creating a game's concept. This process, undertaken during the preproduction phase, will define the ideas behind the game. Much ink will be spilled during this stage, but most of the ideas will be discarded upon evaluation. The concept phase is an opportunity for brainstorming and collaboration, a chance to throw out great ideas that may or may not prove feasible when the other pieces of the puzzle (such as gameplay and market positioning) have been determined.

THE WORKING WRITER

Between marketing, design, direction, production, and management, there are many cooks in the kitchen, and it is rare that a writer will be tasked with making significant decisions. In fact, the writer is sometimes handed a list of needed voice cues and asked to write dialogue for each one. "Wounded female cries out in distress." "Police officer radios for backup." "Evil wizard threatens hero character, then cackles maniacally." The writer's job in this case is simply to fill in the blanks with dialogue and then submit the work for approval.

The working writer is not usually responsible for creating an idea from whole cloth. Some movie scripts are written and pitched to studios, and many novels are written and then submitted to publishers. The game-writing process is different. In the game industry, ideas are cheap, and plentiful, and the studio usually doesn't hire a writer because it needs ideas or game pitches. Generally, a triple-A title (the industry's equivalent of a summer blockbuster) is already conceptualized by the time the writer is brought in.

The game writer doesn't work in a vacuum. Frequently, key components of the story line and characters are determined through a collaborative process with the other developers. The core vision of a game is determined by numerous external factors as well.

FRANCHISE

A sequel that is consistent in tone with its predecessors will probably feature similar characters, dialogue, story line, and narrative techniques. A radical shift in style is rare. *Resident Evil 4* was notable in that it abandoned many of the hallmarks of the franchise (zombies, the T-Virus, the Umbrella Corporation, and the location of Raccoon City) in favor of a completely new milieu (Spain, demented villagers, and cults). Despite these changes, and the significant changes to the gameplay, the game was a success. However, as a general rule, the apple does not fall far from the tree. While games in a series may evolve technologically, as a general rule, their format tends to change very slowly over time. The numerous games in the *Metal Gear Solid* line all feature similar espionage-based action and story lines. All four *Silent Hill* games feature eerie, unsettling story lines that revolve around the small ghost town of Silent Hill. In a way, this can make a writer's work easier. Rather than try to fabricate an entire narrative saga out of whole cloth, the writer can concentrate on developing a story line that fits within the series' parameters.

PUBLISHER

The game developer's relationship with a publisher is also a determining factor in the kind of writing that will be required. Often, if a developer is owned by a publisher, the story and characters will be heavily influenced by decisions made by the publisher. Because the publisher will be distributing and marketing and possibly even bankrolling the game, they may want to exert creative influence over the game's concept. The game writer may have to satisfy the developer and publisher, who will not always have overlapping goals for the project. As a general rule, the larger the game, the less control the game writer will have.

GAMEPLAY

The game design will probably be the biggest influence over the work of a game writer. It is relatively uncommon for the story to influence the gameplay, and attempts to design a game in this fashion are not usually successful.

The gameplay is developed by the design team, which can include a lead designer, creative director, designers, level designers, and scripters. While the process of documenting a game's gameplay varies from studio to studio, the writer's input is typically minimal at best. More often than not, the core decisions are made, and the writer works within those parameters. The game's lead designer or creative director may already know precisely what kind of writing he expects from the writer. "It's kind of hard-boiled, like a film noir." "It's majestic, lofty, *Lord of the Rings*–type stuff. Real serious." "We're hoping for something that's funny like *Ace Ventura*, but kind of sick like *Reservoir Dogs*."

Core elements of the game design that can have a serious effect on the game writer's job include cast, levels, pace, linearity, tools, and cinematics.

Cast

Part of the game's design is a delineation of the game's major characters. If, for example, you're working on a medieval fantasy game about a trio of champions who do battle against an evil wizard, then some of the core dynamics of the story line and dialogue have already been determined. If the player controls one character, while the other two are controlled by artificial intelligence, one avenue has already opened up: character development and exposition can be provided by conversation between the hero characters between battles. On the other hand, if the game design requires the player to select one character at the beginning of each scenario, and there are no teammates, the background chatter is no longer possible, and the writer must find another way to convey the story material.

Levels

The level design of a game has a direct impact on the kind of narrative that can be used. For example, to continue the aforementioned scenario, if the hallway leading into the Fortress of Perdition is long and winding, then the banter between the AI teammates is a viable way to develop their personalities and to reveal information about the story line. Of course, this conversation must be play-tested to ensure that the characters aren't still talking when they reach the end of the hallway and begin to fight the monsters inside the fortress. If, on the other hand, the hallway leading into the Fortress of Perdition is short, there won't be time for a conversation between the two characters in question.

The waters are muddied when a game's design changes during production. It may be decided that the level has too many polygons, and the lead artist determines that the only solution is to cut the hallway altogether and just start the characters in the main chamber of the fortress. This also makes it impossible for the characters to talk among themselves, as they will be attacked by monsters almost immediately. The problem with this scenario is that the writer has already written the dialogue, and the voice actors may have already recorded it in the studio. At this point, the content must be discarded, but if the writer is familiar with the rest of the level, she may be able to find another place to use it, perhaps in another hallway later on.

Pace

A fast-paced game leaves little time for dialogue or other story materials. While zipping through a high-speed shooter like *Serious Sam*™, the player doesn't really have time for story elements. *Serious Sam*'s primary form of narrative context is NETRICSA, an artificial intelligence implanted into his brain that delivers some in-game tips and hints, as well as occasional snippets of story content. On the other hand, a game like *The Elder Scrolls III: Morrowind* moves at the player's pace and features a wealth of manuscripts, conversations with nonplayer characters, and other story elements to hold the player's interest. Since *Morrowind* isn't a game whose primary thrust is surviving endless waves of rapidly moving enemies, it's possible to spend a great deal of time exploring the narrative content.

Tools

In addition to in-game dialogue and cut scenes, there are also various gameplay-dependent tools that can facilitate story development in games. For instance, games in modern or futuristic settings often employ headsets and walkie-talkies as methods for communication between the player and a nonplayer character. For example, in *Metal Gear Solid*, the player character Solid Snake communicates with Mei Ling, his systems analyst, via radio. This exchange permits the developers to shed some light on Snake's personality and allows for exposition and story advancement.

Cinematics

Through the use of prerendered and scripted cinematics, the game designer can set aside a specific time and place for the delivery of certain kinds of story content. This can include plot development, "wow moment" visuals (such as explosions and fight scenes), glory shots (such as characters walking toward the screen in slow motion), character development, or context for upcoming gameplay. The content for the individual cinematics may be written out in the design document, leaving the writer to write the dialogue, or the content may be defined in a bulleted list without specific instructions, leaving the writer to pitch ideas to the design team (or producer or management or whomever).

MARKETING

The marketing department may have an effect on the game writer's job during the concept phase. One of the most interesting dichotomies in the video game industry is the recurrence of the mantra, "We don't need story in games." This is the claim of many developers, who assert that gameplay is far more important than story and that story is superfluous at best and an impediment at worst. However, it is interesting to note that marketing materials frequently begin with a story synopsis. Consider the back of the box, the press release, or the web copy. More often than not, the story materials are presented before the list of features. Clearly, the marketing department, responsible for inspiring audience interest in the product, perceives the story elements to be a strong selling point.

That being said, the marketing department may have their own ideas about narrative, which typically focus on the look and sound of the main characters. For example, marketing may want the main character to be voiced by a celebrity voice actor, or they may even want to use that actor's likeness in the game. It's also possible that they will want to exert some influence over the characters' personas and appearances to make them more marketable. After all, the main characters in the game are most likely going to be part of the ad campaign, and it's natural to want the characters to be as appealing as possible. This can become a tricky minefield if the lead character is a professional soldier and the marketing department suggests a busty redhead in a halter top. Fortunately for the game writer, such decisions typically rest in the hands of decision-makers like producers, managers, and directors, leaving the game writer in the position of furnishing feedback and suggestions.

FRANCHISE

When working on a series of games, the writer may find that certain restrictions are carried over from previous installments to provide continuity throughout the series. This continuity can take the form of ratings, references to previous games, character histories, and the overall game experience.

Ratings

A game's rating can determine a great deal about its story content and presentation. Usually, games in a series tend to garner the same rating, so that fans of the series can rely on a specific kind of content. The game writer needs to understand what kind of rating the series has earned and why.

An M-rated game can cross a number of lines, and it's possible to write extremely mature content (featuring many of the same story elements that drove R-rated films such as *The Godfather* and *The Silence of the Lambs*). It's also possible to write content that's driven solely by gratuitous gore, heavy profanity, and strong sexual content, without any attention given to a well-thought-out story line. All bets are off with the M rating, although if the line is crossed too many times, it's possible to earn the Adults Only (AO) rating. Most stores do not carry AO-rated games on their shelves.

The T-rated game, roughly equivalent to a PG-13 film rating, may feature some degree of violence or profanity, but the story content must also be appropriate. Merely cutting the gore out of *Silent Hill 2* would not suffice, as the subplot concerning sexual abuse would still put the game in M-rated territory.

The E-rated game, which is somewhere between a G and PG rating, means that adult subject matter is completely out of the question. Think *Sesame Street*.

References

Games in a series often feature recurring characters or situations. Many of the *Resident Evil* games feature the Umbrella Corporation and their mutagenic T-Virus, for example. The *Splinter Cell* games feature terrorist groups that must be thwarted by the agents of the Third Echelon, and so on.

The game writer needs to understand what has already transpired in the previous iterations of a franchise, so that story lines are not repeated and so that past events can be alluded to in-game.

Characters

Of course, in a series of games, characters appear in sequels down the line. Sometimes, a character's return is a surprise. Other times, the characters are connected by some kind of relationship. Heather, the protagonist of *Silent Hill 3*, was the daughter of the player character from the first *Silent Hill*.

Killing a character is a tricky proposition. Often, if the character is a major one, this is something that must be decided in a series of meetings with producers and directors. Many game series are developed by multiple studios; killing off a major character in one game could impact the development of a game thousands of miles away, so it's a complex decision to make.

Game Experience

Ultimately, games are developed for the players. Those who will be playing the games are often the harshest critics, and if a favorite character is portrayed in an unacceptable way by the game writer, the fans will be furious. It's important to devote some attention to the fan base, to at least understand what it was about the previous installments that they enjoyed so much.

Licensing

When working on a licensed property such as a book or film, the game writer must adhere to certain conventions of the source material. Even in the case of an original story line and concept, such as *007: Everything Or Nothing*, the game writer must study and understand the movies that inspired the game was inspired.

Coherence

The game writer will work to ensure that the story and dialogue are appropriate for the license as well. In addition, the premise of the game's story line must make sense in relation to the source. For example, even though *The Lord of the Rings: The Third Age™* features an all-new cast and scenarios, the events in the game still intersect with the scenes from the film trilogy from time to time. This, combined with certain set pieces such as the ruins of Osgiliath, creates a consistency with the source material that justifies the use of the license.

Character Restrictions

Similar to a franchise title, the licensed game features a cast that must be handled carefully. There's no point in killing a major character who clearly lived through the movie, and it's unlikely that a game writer will be successful if he tries to do this. In addition, there may be restrictions on the depiction of the characters in the game. Some actors will give permission for the use of their voice and likeness, whereas others will not. For instance, *Buffy the Vampire Slayer*® featured most of the cast of the TV show, but the lead actress declined, so the game featured a sound-alike, and the likeness didn't bear a close resemblance to Sarah Michelle Gellar.

Major events

In the case of many licensed games, the player is interested in reliving key events from the source material. Often, during the development of a licensed game, the schedule matches that of the material being filmed, which can result in complications. The film won't necessarily be shot and produced on a timetable that suits the game developer's needs, resulting in the sloppy or rushed work of many tie-in games. It's sometimes difficult to match key events in the film with counterparts in a game if the developers aren't even sure what the scene will look like.

COMPETITIVE ANALYSIS

Throughout the development process, members of the development team are going to be playing other studios' games. It's a necessary kind of research, and it's also a good way for the team to blow off some steam after hours while playing multiplayer titles. The game writer can learn a great deal from the competition, and it's particularly useful to check out other games during the preproduction phase. After all, during production, work has begun, and the addition of new features is much riskier.

Competitive analysis isn't really gameplay per se; it's more of an examination of the other company's games and a systematic evaluation of what works and what doesn't. The writer listens to the voice acting, considers the dialogue, and observes the way that the game delivers story content to the player.

Style and execution vary wildly from project to project. When analyzing a game, the writer should consider the level of polish and ask himself how it was obtained. Why are the cinematics so effective? Why does the voice acting sound good? Or, if the execution is lacking in some way, the writer must consider what the developers did wrong. Does the voice acting sound unprofessional, or is it just a case of badly written dialogue? What is it about the dialogue that doesn't fit? Why don't the character animations look good?

It's also important to consider the game's pacing. Does it feel like the story content has been integrated into the game properly or does it feel haphazard? Perhaps the game features a huge introductory cinematic, followed by bland, near-silent gameplay, followed by another cinematic whose characters barely resemble the in-game character models. If there's a disconnect, the game writer should strive to document precisely what isn't working about the game's story content.

Naturally, the writer will want to analyze the story and characters as well. Is the story interesting, or is it a rehash of existing elements? Is it a new take on an old theme? How is that accomplished, specifically? Are the characters interesting? Do their actions match the personalities that have been created for them? Can you relate to the characters, or do their actions seem childish or arbitrary? Do they really belong in the game?

Competitive analysis is an investigative process, driven by questions that lead to more questions. Impressions and opinions ("I didn't like it") are utterly useless at this stage, as they do not provide concrete information that will help other developers or drive meetings forward.

Sometimes competitive analysis degenerates into a game-bashing session where developers take turns pointing out what they don't like about a game. This is typically a bad sign, indicating a lack of commitment to the process. To analyze a game is to study its tools and techniques and to specifically isolate which were successful, which were not, and which could be implemented (regardless of the other studio's success with that particular technique). For instance, if the game writer analyzes a game that features an aggravating robot sidekick that makes wisecracks and comments during firefights, it's not necessarily true that the talking robot sidekick is a bad idea; it might have been successful, had the dialogue been restricted to valuable in-game information. Consider the successful use of the fairy Navi in *The Legend of Zelda®: Ocarina of Time®*. The idea might be worth exploring.

THE GAME CONCEPT

Once much of the preliminary work has been done and possibilities have been ruled out, the game writer can begin work on the actual concept for the game. The process remains collaborative, and the writer is in all likelihood working with a group of designers, project leads, and directors.

CORE VISION

The goal at this stage is to create a series of documents outlining the game's creative direction, as well as certain key elements that will make the game stronger and more competitive in the eyes of the publisher and the consumer.

MAJOR SELLING POINTS

A typical game box includes a series of bulleted selling points on the back, such as "jaw-dropping photorealistic graphics" or "enemy A.I. that hunts and attacks players intelligently." The game writer may be involved in the drafting or rewriting of selling points for presentation in the concept materials. In addition, many games allude to the compelling story line or fully realized characters in the bulleted list. This will require input from the game writer, who will be able to best explain the story line and characters to the team.

Memorable Sequences

Many developers put a premium on memorable moments whose spectacle, complexity, or significance make an impression on the player. For example, the moment when the player first lays eyes on one of the massive enemies in *Shadow of the Colossus* is a very dramatic sequence. A classic example would be the revelation that Samus Aran, protagonist of the original *Metroid®* (1986), is actually a woman. This twist ending came as a shock to many gamers, at a time when most female characters existed to be rescued by male protagonists.

Strong First Impression

Some game developers take great pains to ensure that the first few moments of a game are packed with as much content and impressive material as they can fit into the sequence. The idea is that the average gamer doesn't play a game all the way through, so the first few moments are the only guaranteed exposure that the developer really has. In order to ensure that the game makes a good first impression and that it satisfies those who have borrowed or rented the game (so as to get good word-of-mouth or even to entice them into buying the game for themselves), some developers design the first mission to be a showcase for everything that the game presents.

The game writer is going to be laying the groundwork for a story line at this time. Characters will appear, scenarios will be presented, and a nemesis of some kind will probably be identified. A strong first impression for the narrative content is also worth exploring at this time. How will the characters be introduced? Via a credit sequence, like a TV show or movie? Via in-game action? Through a cinematic intro? How will the plot be developed? Will it be presented in full, giving way to the action sequence, or will it be revealed slowly, over the course of hours of gameplay?

The game writer needs to consider the way exposition takes place, and this is not merely an aesthetic consideration. The question of exposition is a game design issue that must be discussed with the other developers on the project.

Imagine a game writer contributing story content for a real-time strategy game with no central character; instead, armies clash on a battlefield, and the player assumes the role of a godlike commander who shifts troops around and issues orders through an interface. The context for a game like this generally takes the form of cinematic sequences between missions, which serve to contextualize the action to follow. In such a case, the exposition is delivered in short blasts of information, processed by the player and then switched off to allow for the continuance of gameplay.

On the other hand, an action game about a group of medieval warriors who hunt an evil wizard in a demon-infested castle might lend itself to a more integrated form of exposition. The history of the world, the personalities of the characters, and the nature of the conflict might all be parsed out through conversation, manuscripts, and cinematic sequences, resulting in an exposition that is gradual and molded by the pace and flow of the gameplay.

There are as many methods as there are games, in that each game presents the writer with unique challenges and opportunities. The purpose of the concept phase is to begin the construction of a sound strategy that is aligned with the game's design and direction.

Presentation

The key vision document takes many forms. In some cases it is a PowerPoint® presentation that is shown to studio management, marketing, and/or corporate management. The slideshow presents the core game experience, including a synopsis of the story line and the main characters. It's not unusual for such a presentation to be augmented by the use of video components, such as video capture of films with a similar look and feel or of games with a similar style or genre.

The key vision document might also take the form of a text document that lists the components of the game experience, each of which will in some way incorporate the work of the game writer.

STORY LINE

The process for writing a story line is dependent on the type of game being developed and on the development team responsible for creating the game. It is entirely possible that the game writer will be tasked with choosing between a nonlinear narrative with multiple endings or a three-act story with a rising action and climax or a player-authored sandbox-type game with hundreds of side quests and missions. The writer in this case would be in charge of, or at least involved in, making large-scale decisions about the game's design and direction.

However, it is also possible that such decisions will be in the hands of the game's producer, designer, or director, and that the writer will simply be informed of the decision: "We're making a linear shooter with fifteen minutes of prerendered cinematics spread out over a twelve-hour single-player game." The writer's interaction with the game concept, and with the rest of the team, is dependent on the project.

The structure of the game's story line can take many forms. Some developers rely on a three-act story whose rising action, reversal, and climax are modeled on classical structure. Others present a series of short 10–20 minute story arcs that encompass a segment of gameplay. The player watches a short intro and then plays through a level. During that time, story content is presented incrementally, building up to the completion of the level, and perhaps a short "outro," or the intro to the next gameplay sequence. There's probably a save point here and an opportunity to set the controller down and grab a drink.

Wide-open games like *Gun* present the game writer with a challenge: how to ensure that the player is exposed to the story content. In the case of *Gun*, the player is free to roam around in the Old West, getting into gunfights and taking on assignments. However, certain key missions are clearly delineated as story missions, and completion of these tasks will lead to further evolution of the story line. This process is described in more detail in Chapter 6, Structuring the Narrative.

LOCATIONS

The decision process for determining locations in a game can be based on a variety of sources. For instance, the art department may be tasked with researching and proposing interesting locations for action sequences in the game. If the game is a medieval action title, they may search the Internet for images of castles, moats, and villages. Part of the reason for the research is historical accuracy and part of it is a quest for inspiration. Striking images and architecture will no doubt be favored by this approach.

The locations in a game may instead be determined by the story line. If the writer has drafted a story overview whose action takes place on a Martian colony, aboard a space cruiser, and on the blistering surface of Mercury, then these will be the locations where the game is set. This approach tends to result in a series of locations that facilitate the flow of the story line.

The game's design may also play a large role. For example, if the game features a ninja character who operates in tight spaces, sneaking up and assassinating enemies stealthily, then the game's locations will need to support this gameplay mechanic. Corridors, shadows, and multiple entry points will all contribute to the player's experience in this kind of game, whereas wide-open plains will not.

During the concept phase, the variety of locations are often discussed. To avoid repetition, many games involve a series of radically different levels so that the player feels that progress is being made and that the game world is evolving in response to the action. For example, if the first mission takes place in a dark, claustrophobic cavern, the next mission may be set in a brightly lit desert environment. *Halo 2* begins on board a metallic space station and then puts the player on the surface of a futuristic Earth. The shift in color palette, architecture, and ambient sound all contribute to the variety.

The effect of location choice on a player is usually a part of the concept phase. For example, horror games such as *Resident Evil* and *Silent Hill* typically employ devastated ruins to create a feeling of tension and dread in the player. In games like *Super Mario Bros.*®, the locations are cheerful and feature the heavy use of primary colors and reassuringly simple shapes. There are no sharp edges or dark colors until the player reaches the dreaded castles of Bowser or the cartoonishly sinister Ghost Houses. The *Quake*™ and *Doom* games alternate between demonic fortresses, reminiscent of hell, and the menacing derelict space-station look of movies like *Alien*. This helps establish a certain mood for the game, augmenting the story line and gameplay that the player experiences.

CHARACTERS

Depending on the type of game being developed, the characters may already be created. The writer's job may consist of merely determining their character arcs and major events for this installment of the series. If the writer is hired with the purpose of creating characters for the game, there are a number of factors to take into consideration.

Different game characters have different attributes. This doesn't just mean that some are male and some are female, some are humans and some are robots or elves or dragons. It means that some characters are mute, and others have personalities and voices. Some are customizable avatars that look however the player wants them to look, and some are carefully crafted icons, like Lara Croft or Master Chief. When the writer begins work on the hero's background, personality, voice, and appearance, the question must be asked: is this appropriate for the game? This is explored in more detail in Chapter 5, Creating the Characters.

SUMMARY

Each project presents the game writer with a different set of parameters. By learning to anticipate these, the writer can effectively integrate a strong narrative into his game. In this chapter we considered the ideas that will guide the writer during the concept creation phase, including licensing, marketing, competitive analysis, publisher requirements, and gameplay.

DEVELOPER INTERVIEW

Mary DeMarle, Narrative Designer, Ubisoft
Myst® V: End of Ages, Myst IV: Revelation

GETTING STARTED

I first started working with Presto Studios, who had acquired the *Myst* license, so the first thing that I had to do was to get to know the *Myst* license inside and out. I had played the first *Myst* game, but I hadn't actually played *Riven®*, so first thing I did was to play *Riven* all the way through.

→

I also got really familiar with the source material, because buying the game is one thing, but getting to know the *Myst* community, and getting to know the fan base, there's a lot of information that exists outside of the game that you're not often aware of. Some of the research was with getting to know the people at Cyan, who had developed the first game, including Rand, the creator, and Richard Watson, who was the historian for all the D'Ni and *Myst* world lore. A lot of research consisted of meetings with them, and of reading the several books that had been set in the *Myst* universe. The fans had accumulated a great deal of knowledge as well, so reading the history and the lore that they had put on the fan sites was also helpful.

LICENSED GAMES

When you work on a licensed property, you don't always have time to devote to research. If you're lucky, you're able to do some during the preproduction stage.

Since you're writing the story, it's one of your priorities to gather information about the background and setting, but at the same time, you're starting to generate various ideas for the story line and for the game itself. For a couple of months, I was generating seven or eight story concepts, and we were also generating a lot of gameplay ideas, trying to see what was the most interesting story. The gameplay was pretty standard for the *Myst* license, so there wasn't as much focus on gameplay as there would have been if we had been working on a new game.

GAME WRITING CHALLENGES

You often hear that writing is still the area of game development that is the least developed in terms of expertise, and I think within the industry itself we're still trying to determine what the writer's role is. In my experience, I find that there are different categories of writing jobs that you can get into. A lot of times, beginning writers are just hired to write the script and dialogue. The story has been figured out, and the game designers have a clear idea of what they want, and they're directing the writer to write this or that scene or dialogue. For people just starting out in the industry, that's a good way to get experience in the field. If you don't really know much about game development, and you're not familiar with the production process, then if you're lucky enough to just be hired to write the dialogue, then I think that's one task that's a good introduction.

When I worked on *Myst III*, I'd never worked on a game before, and one of the first things that I had to come to terms with was the concept of the linear story line versus the nonlinear gameplay. I would write a story document, or

$\rightarrow$

propose an idea, and the game designer would ask, "What if the player doesn't do that? What if the player doesn't go there?" It was a question of grappling with that concept. There were numerous possibilities to consider, and I had to focus on honing my story and dialogue to ensure that I wasn't too specific with the dialogue, just in case the player didn't behave the way that I anticipated.

CONTRACT WRITING

I worked for several years as a contract writer. For example, I was a contract writer on *Homeworld 2*. I worked closely with the game designers to develop the story. They had a concept, and they came to me with it, and I worked with the lead designer on that to develop and strengthen the story: "If we did it like this, that would make it more interesting and compelling." Basically, taking their initial idea and fleshing it out with them. Then they took it in-house and tweaked it and developed it, and then came back to me and said, "Okay, here's our script with the dialogue written by the designers. Can you rewrite the script?"

I really enjoyed the freedom of the contract writing, but personally, I didn't have enough control over the story design. As a contract writer, you're often hired to put words on the page and make it sound good or to come up with ideas and nudge the story in a better direction, but the critical decisions are made in-house.

You can work on a project for a month or so, but then you won't hear back from them. The game is taken in-house for a while, and when they come back, they'll say, "We had to change the story." Now that I'm in-house, and I'm on the other side of the process, I know that I've done that to the contract writers that I'm working with. I feel like this is a better position for me, because I'm part of the overall game design process, and I'm making those decisions about how the story changes and evolves. The only position that really allows you to do that is the narrative design position.

NARRATIVE DESIGN

As a narrative designer, I am a game designer on the team, so I'm integral to the game's mechanics and the episodes and levels. The narrative designer creates the story line and integrates it into the design. For instance, I'll set the initial conditions for the story, giving purpose to the gameplay. You can enjoy gameplay for its own sake, and just play the game for fun, but the story tells you what you're doing and why. If you can make that interesting, and blend that narrative with the game's mechanics, you'll have a richer experience.

→

Part of my job is to initially set the objectives for every episode, and then as the design team works out the logistics of the level, to work the story into that structure. What comes from that process is that the story is getting honed and tweaked, and the ideas that you had at first are often getting thrown out the window. Once it's all kind of laid out, you're then executing the vision. You're creating the scenes, the scripts, the dialogue, and all within the conditions of the game. For example, this scene has to convey these five objectives. You also have to convey the characters and the emotional connection that you want to have with these characters, all within 30 seconds.

On the project I'm currently on, because there's so much work involved, we do have a contract writer, and the writer is creating the dialogue. I'm saying, here's the scene, this is what has to happen. The writer is then sending the dialogue to us, and I'm working as the editor. I'll say, okay, you're not hitting the emotional beat the way that we want here, or you're not building the player interest in this area. I direct the scriptwriter to ensure that he's delivering the most dramatic content, essentially. Then, of course, you get to the point where you have the content you want, but it's two minutes long, so you have to start cutting. Ultimately, I'm doing the final pass, in that case, so I am doing an awful lot of dialogue writing. But it's based on the initial base that the scriptwriter has given me.

THE FUTURE OF STORYTELLING IN GAMES

We're exploring a new medium. What we're doing in games is redefining how a story is told. It's like when films first started; there was no language of film. They basically set up cameras and filmed plays. It was some time before they discovered editing and the close-up and the language of film. This changed the way that stories were told, but essentially, they were still told in a passive, linear fashion. With games, we're rediscovering what story is. Is it just a narrative, with characters and a plot? Or is it the experience of the player as he discovers these elements?

We don't know quite how to tell a story in-game, and we're still experimenting with our techniques, so some of our work is also discovering the process of creating and integrating the narrative writer into a game design team.

I think that part of our challenge is the skill set that needs to be discovered within writers and designers themselves. You can't just know how to tell a story if you're working as a game writer. You have to know how to create a game, and you need to have game design skills. For the project I'm on right now, I'm working with the AI programmers, the animators, the sound department, and the

$\rightarrow$

scriptwriter, and I'm coordinating the efforts of all four groups in order to create a dialogue engine that will be realistic. As a writer, I know very little about AI programming or animation, but I'm now in a situation where I'm learning a lot. Now, I'm using all of those tools to appropriately tell a story.

Writers have to learn more than just how to write. They have to understand the variables that arise during game development, so that their writing can better reflect what's needed.

3 Documenting the Story

In This Chapter

- Context Delivery
- Technical Writing

Game writing isn't just a creative discipline. To create a compelling game narrative also requires technical writing skills and an understanding of the core principles of effective communication. Hastily written or ill-considered dialogue is easily recognizable as such, but sloppy documentation only reveals itself when it causes complications. By considering the way story content is delivered, and by applying the fundamental concepts of technical writing, the game writer can make the most of the planning stage, furnishing the rest of the development team with design documents that are useful and effective. In this chapter we'll cover the fundamental elements of game story and then take a look at some guidelines for document creation.

CONTEXT DELIVERY

Depending on the type of game that's being played, the platform that it's being played on, and the goals of the developers, the story can be communicated in a number of ways. Story is more than just cut scenes; it also includes in-game dialogue, text on screen, and art assets. By understanding the development process of each component, the writer can learn to anticipate problems and to make the most of the game's narrative.

CINEMATICS

The cinematic is a computer-generated movie that is either prerendered or created in-game, through the use of scripting tools. A cinematic can serve numerous functions. As a story device, it can communicate plot and character information. It can also be used as a player reward, a marketing tool, and a pacing device. Cinematics are often encountered at the beginning of a game but can also appear between missions, or at the end of the game. There are two types of cinematic: prerendered and scripted (see Figure 3.1).

Prerendered	Scripted
Created using specialized program	Created using scripting editor
Graphics superior to in-game	Graphics same as in-game
May be developed in-house or by an external vendor	Created by game designers

FIGURE 3.1   The difference between prerendered and scripted cinematics.

Prerendered

Prerendered cinematics are created and recorded and then inserted into the game. Often the cinematic is recorded using a computer program with sophisticated graphics and processing power, meaning that the cinematic is clearly better-looking than the gameplay. This can be jarring, because the drop-off in graphic quality is immediately noticeable when the cinematic ends and the game loads.

The prerendered cinematic may be created in-house, or it can be outsourced to a specialized studio. In either case, it's possible that the cinematic developers will use the character models and other art assets from the game. However, this requires that those components be created first, which can cause delays. For this reason, and because custom-built character models and objects can boast a higher polygon count, prerendered cinematics rarely use art assets from the game.

Cinematics can feature incredibly elaborate and spectacular sequences. For example, in the opening cinematic for *Onimusha™ 3* a vast army of gigantic monsters moves towards an unseen target. A ninja attacks the army, clashes with dozens of undead warriors, and then engages in a stunning swordfight with a demon, culminating in a series of explosions and special effects. Dozens, possibly hundreds, of monsters are visible on-screen at once, and individual hairs on the protagonist's head are clearly visible. None of this is possible in-game, given the limitations of the PlayStation 2's technology.

Scripted

Scripted cinematics, sometimes known as in-game cinematics, are created (and sometimes recorded) using the game engine. Through the scripting process, designers create short cinematic sequences using art assets from the game in real-time. The distinction here is that the scripted cinematic uses the game engine, not another program. This means the graphics, models, and levels seen in the scripted cinematic are going to be identical to those encountered during gameplay. The advantage to the use of the scripted cinematic is that there is no jarring change in graphical quality when the cinematic ends and the gameplay begins. The downside of the scripted cinematic is that a game's engine is not necessarily designed to create movies; it's intended as a game development tool. Therefore, the cinematics may not feature sophisticated camera controls, the character's movements may not appear convincing, and the level of detail and spectacle will pale in comparison to the prerendered cinematic.

In addition, while the prerendered cinematic is limited only by the imagination of the developers (and by the standard constraints of schedule and resources), the scripted cinematic may be defined by the assets that are available from the game.

Storytelling

During cinematic sequences, the developers can effectively create a short film that unmasks a villain, shows a hero's motivation, or creates a sense of dread and foreboding. Cinematics are a powerful storytelling tool, because while the player is experiencing them, there are no other in-game distractions. Gameplay ceases during the cinematic, and the player effectively becomes an audience member, focused on the events transpiring on-screen. Unlike a voice cue, which may not be audible over the din of a gunfight, the cinematic demands complete audience attention—at least in terms of the game experience. In terms of real-world distractions, the risk of the cinematic is that the player will push a button to skip the sequence because he just wants to get back to the action, or may get up to go to the kitchen, treating the cinematic the way that a television viewer might treat a commercial.

Setting aside the risk that the player will not view the cinematic, it is nonetheless one of the most effective ways to convey story elements, because there's no need to integrate action into the scene. The developers can focus on the evolution of the plot, the development of the main characters, and the establishment of mood. Games like the *Metal Gear Solid* and *Final Fantasy* series make heavy use of cinematics to accomplish all three of these functions.

Player Reward

The developers can use the cinematic as a marker indicating a certain level of achievement during gameplay. When the player completes a mission and views a cinematic that continues the storyline or shows the hero being praised for a job well done, the player is rewarded with a brief moment of congratulation, spectacle, or amusement. Even if the player elects to skip the cinematic, it's still an indication of progress made and helps the player define how far he's gotten.

Marketing

Owing to their expense, cinematic sequences are typically employed as marketing tools to defray the cost somewhat. Sometimes they are even passed off as gameplay footage in an attempt to deceive the customer into believing the game's graphics are better than they actually are. They're shown in television advertisements, on Web sites, and at trade shows in an attempt to build interest in and enthusiasm for an upcoming game.

The cinematic can make an effective marketing tool because the typical cinematic is only a few minutes long and can be edited into a 30- or 60-second clip far more effectively than captured footage from a game. For example, if edited footage from a first-person shooter is shown during a TV ad, the audience may not immediately recognize what they're looking at, and the context for the action may also elude them until enough elements have been shown on screen. However, if the intro cinematic is shown, depicting the hero character loading his weapon and squaring off against hostile aliens in a futuristic battlefield, the context has been clearly established, and any subsequent gameplay footage is likely to make more sense. As noted above, however, the developers may not show any gameplay footage, in the hopes that the audience will assume that the cinematic sequence is representative of the game's graphics. While this practice has been sharply criticized within the industry, it nonetheless persists.

Pacing

The use of cinematics can give the player time to breathe between action sequences. It's no secret that extended gameplay can result in sore thumbs or wrists, and players need time to catch their breath every so often. By including the cinematic between missions, the developers can give the player enough time to stretch.

This pacing can also be dramatic. Frequently, the last few moments of a gameplay are the most intense, either because the player is down to a few hit points and completely surrounded or because the other racecars are right behind him or because the timer on the bomb is counting down and there are only seconds left to get out of the building. After completing the mission or level, the player may feel a sense of exhilaration, which a victorious cinematic can help extend before segueing back into gameplay.

DIALOGUE

While playing the game, the player is exposed to dialogue that serves a number of different functions. It creates a connection between the player and the game world and establishes personalities for the characters. It also guides the player through the world, a process the game writer can facilitate through repetition, production, and connection.

Repetition

The dialogue in a game can convey crucial information to a player, such as the status of an enemy ("He's right behind you!"), the location of an ally ("I'm approaching your position."), and the next objective ("Enter the Citadel of Darkness and retrieve the Dragon's Heart."). If the player misunderstands or does not hear the voice cue, that information has not been delivered. In some cases, this means the game should eventually "realize" that the player hasn't understood the message, which must be repeated. For example, in *Call of Duty 2*, the player receives commands from other characters in the game. If the player fails to follow orders, they will be repeated. It's also possible that the player can try to obtain the information himself via conversation. For instance, in *The Elder Scrolls IV: Oblivion*, if the player forgets what he's supposed to be doing while on a quest, he can return to the person who assigned it to him and strike up a conversation about the quest, during which he'll be given the information once more.

Production

The writer's role is to ensure the highest level of production for the dialogue; this may encompass writing the text, directing the voice acting, and integrating the audio content with the gameplay. The important thing is that the production remain appropriate to the game vision. If the game is a grim-and-gritty triple-A shooter in which the player is a soldier storming the beach at Normandy, the dialogue's production should reflect the chaos and madness of war, while at the same time maintaining a high level of quality. This means the game should feature a rich palette of yells and cries amidst the gunfire and explosions, the voice acting should be frantic and nerve-wracking, and the death screams should be anguished. Despite the chaos, however, the player should be able to understand what's expected of him, and if he misses a voice cue, subsequent repetitions shouldn't be monotonous. The writer needs to understand the structure and mood of the game, but also the gameplay experience itself, in order to produce effective dialogue that matches the design team's vision.

Connection

In addition to its more utilitarian aspects, dialogue can give a game personality. Characters can take on believable attributes, and a virtual world can be made more immersive if the writer effectively imbues the characters with heart and soul. The techniques with which the writer can document the dialogue are covered in subsequent chapters.

Development

Various members of the development team will use the dialogue documentation in their day-to-day work, including voice actors, directors, scripters, and testers. By applying principles of technical writing when documenting the dialogue, the writer can ensure a smoother, more polished delivery and execution.

Voice actors and voice directors will be using the dialogue documentation to read and record the voice cues. The document should be legible and easily accessed by the actor, who is probably not a full-time member of the development team and thus has no understanding of the parameters under which the team is operating. There's no need to include extraneous information such as file names and mission numbers for the voice actor, since his or her primary concern is the content that's provided and the delivery that's expected. The writer needs to pare down the documentation for the voice actor but should give the director enough context so that he can guide the actors where appropriate. More information on this process is detailed in Chapter 9, Directing Voice Actors.

The scripter is going to use the dialogue documentation to script gameplay, placing the voice assets in the game through an editor of some kind. The document should clearly indicate the order and significance of each voice cue, so that the scripter knows where to put the recorded dialogue and in what context. Under a given set of circumstances, such as player victory, a specific voice cue may be played ("Good work, Officer!"). However, under a slightly different set of circumstances, another cue might be played instead ("Good work, Officer, but one of them got away!"). During the planning stage, the writer needs to consider how the assets will be integrated into the game. This is described in greater detail in Chapter 7, Organizing Dialogue.

Game testers will probably spend more of their time on gameplay, such as multiplayer features, than testing the story content. However, it will constitute a part of the testing process, so the writer must anticipate their needs during the planning stage. The easier it is for the testers to compare the voice cues in-game with the expected voice cues that are listed on the story documents, the more likely it is that they will locate bugs and inconsistencies, enabling the writer to remedy the problems. More information about this stage of development is provided in Chapter 12, Testing Story Content.

TEXT

Text can be furnished in menus, during load screens, and in artifacts that are located and examined by the player. Sometimes reading in-game text is vital to completion of the game. For instance, many tactical shooters communicate objectives to the player through text displayed on the screen. This helps the player prepare for what's about to happen and directs the player's actions. In other cases the text is provided merely to add flavor to the game or to create a mood. For example, in *Doom 3* the player finds and reads emails written by nonplayer characters. These emails contain observations, notes, first-hand accounts, and panicked journal entries, all of which are intended to establish tension and paranoia without communicating any information crucial to the game experience. If the player elects not to read these emails, the game and its story line are still enjoyable and meaningful; the emails only add a secondary level of emotion to the experience and can be safely ignored.

Text can also be used to communicate the player's status or his progress through the game world. In the *Elder Scrolls* games, the player has a journal that is automatically updated whenever new information is acquired or when the player's quest status changes in some way (because a new quest has been added or because a quest has been completed). The player can choose to read the journal at any time to get a feel for how much he's accomplished, to refresh his memory about the details of a recent quest, or to look up the name of a city whose location he can't quite recall. This journal rewards the player for his achievements and reinforces the illusion of a living world in which the player is engaging in real time.

During the planning stage the writer needs to know how much game text will be displayed on screen and what kinds of information will need to be conveyed. During the production stage it may be determined that only 80 characters can fit across the screen at any given time, forcing the writer to reconfigure his entire spreadsheet because this parameter was not sufficiently investigated prior to the production phase. To avoid this kind of extra work, the writer should find out whether the text on screen will be entered into a scripting tool or if it will consist of art assets (such as the notes and messages found in the *Resident Evil* games).

ART

The player's first impressions of a game are visual, and a great deal of story information is communicated without dialogue or cinematics. A game's artwork can inform the player's decision-making process and gameplay style within seconds of commencing gameplay. For example, consider the fictional game *Paintball Online*. This first-person shooter is a paintball simulator that features ordinary people in camouflage gear, wielding neon orange paintball guns. An opponent is running toward the player with a paintball gun, ducking and weaving through the bright green foliage. Since it's a first-person shooter, the player can strafe to the left and to the right and can return fire with his paintball gun.

Now, leave the gameplay intact, but alter the art assets. Transform the sunlit forest into a darkened alley strewn with garbage. Replace the player's orange paintball gun with a sawed-off shotgun. Replace the guy in camouflage with a demented, red-eyed homeless person wielding a bloody crowbar. Same game? No, it isn't. Without a single voice cue or cinematic, this game has been transformed into

Condemned: Criminal Origins™, and the game's context has been changed as well. The player will respond differently to events in the game and will say different things during combat. The play experience will be so altered by the change of textures and art assets that people will say the two experiences are two different games, even though the core gameplay and the game engine remain the same.

Artwork conveys context to the player and can dramatically influence mood and perception. By planning for this impact during the planning stage, the writer can ensure that the game's look and feel correspond to the story material. This is covered in more detail in Chapter 10, Knowing Technical Parameters.

TECHNICAL WRITING

When creating dialogue for a game, the writer should make an effort to develop content that's entertaining and well-written. The last thing he wants to do, after all, is to bore the audience by simply listing facts in a clumsy exposition sequence. However, when documenting the story content for a game, the reverse is often true. Of course, the writer still doesn't want to bore the audience (his fellow game developers). The best way to keep documentation from becoming tedious is to stifle creative urges and instead approach story documentation as a form of technical writing.

For the sake of discussion, let's define technical writing as nonfiction that explains or describes. The technical writer breaks down complex ideas and presents them in straightforward terms, with the intention of recording or communicating data. Technical writing doesn't entertain or impress or captivate; it merely presents information. In addition, it is written with a specific audience in mind. Technical writing is precise. It presents content briefly and accurately. It is impersonal, because the writer is communicating data, not observations or commentary. Technical writing is clear, employing a suitable organizational style and vocabulary. Since the audience may not be familiar with the content, the presentation is consistent, both in terms of content and format. Furthermore, in order to be trustworthy, the writer must be credible, presenting information that has been researched thoroughly. These concepts will be explored in more depth in the following section.

CHARACTERISTICS

The applications of technical writing are numerous. Technical writers document software packages, working closely with the programmers to learn the tools and terminology before writing user manuals, help files, and troubleshooting guides. Game design documentation meets all of the aforementioned criteria. The game writer breaks down complex ideas such as plot, character development, location, and game world and presents these ideas in straightforward terms. The audience is the development team, a specific audience requiring information. Let's examine the characteristics of technical writing and consider how they apply to the documentation of story and narrative in games.

Precision

It's important that all content be verified for accuracy, since any misunderstandings will result in additional work for the development team. For example, if one segment of the game features a scripted scene where one character climbs up a ladder, an animation artist may create a ladder-climbing sequence for that scene. Later, it may be discovered that the scene actually begins with the character crouching near the manhole. The ladder-climbing was supposed to take place off-camera, because there was no time to create a vertical shaft. In this instance a little more time dedicated to verifying the exact content of that cut scene would have saved time and effort.

Game writing should also be brief, omitting any extraneous content. It is sometimes difficult to resist the temptation to imbue story documents with drama or humor. The writer may think that if the game developers want to create a thrilling game, or a fun game, the documentation should match that sentiment. This is a mistake. While it is necessary to document the clever jokes and gut-wrenching drama, as well as the techniques for eliciting these emotions, it is not necessary for the presentation itself to be exciting or irreverent or dramatic. These extraneous elements can slow the reader down and create frustration. There's no need to write "well," either. Technical writing is straightforward and direct, not flowery or poetic. The audience isn't reading a game document in search of entertainment or diversion or spiritual edification; the audience is looking for specific content.

A final note about jokes. It has been said that humor makes it easier to read a document. Consider this: is the typical comedic film still funny the third or fourth time someone watches it? Bear in mind that the writers of funny movies are professionals; they get paid to write funny things. But even professionals can't always write dialogue that's humorous enough for a laugh the first time, let alone after 20 viewings. How will a game writer's design documents be any different? Generally, design documents are read more than once, particularly by those who work directly on content creation. Even if the jokes are funny the first time, they're going to be tedious by the third or fourth reading and unbearable after that.

Impersonality

Technical writing emphasizes facts and data. Game writing should be no different. When writing a character bio, a story synopsis, or a breakdown of the missions in a game, the writer should present content with the audience in mind. This means there is no room for intrusions, observations, or opinions in the document. For example, some writers must remind the reader of their presence: "As the humble writer, I propose that the main character should. . . ." The use of passive voice goes a long way toward removing author intrusion from technical documents, as does abstinence from the use of first-person pronouns. In addition, the writer should examine a technical document thoroughly for any inadvertent opinions that may have entered the document.

Clarity

Clarity is achieved through simple and concrete presentation. Through direct presentation of content, good sentence structure, and an appropriate choice of words, the game writer can create game documents whose meaning is understood immediately. Vocabulary is important. Words such as *ecdysis*, *meretricious*, and *ophidian* have no place in a game design document, unless they are in some way a part of the game experience. While they no doubt indicate the scope of the writer's vocabulary, they do nothing for the average reader except to extend the time and energy invested in reading a document. Reading these documents might be good for one's vocabulary, but most developers will just ask questions of the designer in person, rather than reading the documents. This wastes time and energy.

Clarity is also achieved through organization. Documents that are structured and legible are far more likely to be read by the developers on a team. Consider a game whose story and design docs were available as HTML files on an intranet. The documents were essentially raw text and, when viewed, appeared as a wall of text from one end of the monitor to the other. There were no margins, and nearly no formatting. For some reason the text was smaller than the default setting. Reading the text on a computer screen induced powerful headaches, so most developers would copy and paste the text into Word, format it, print it out, and then read it. Multiply this extra work across a couple of years, with a team of dozens of developers, and suddenly a great deal of effort could have been put to better use.

Organizing the content of a manuscript effectively will also improve the chances that the developers are actually going to read it. It is important to consider the elements that make a document easy to read: good use of white space, paragraph breaks, and accentuated headings.

Consistency

It's difficult, when writing dozens of story documents, across months and months of development time, to be consistent in one's documentation. Nonetheless, this consistency is the hallmark of technical writing and makes it easier to read and process the information being presented. Fonts, headings, and margins should be consistent throughout the document. MS Word features preloaded settings for headings, which can also be used to generate a table of contents at the beginning of a document. These settings can be changed to accommodate a specific font choice. Beware of multiple fonts, however. If the heading is a big bold Arial, the subheading is a small italicized Garamond, and the text is a mid-sized Times New Roman, the document will look haphazard and difficult to read. It's important to use features such as bolding, italics, and underlining as sparingly as possible.

Of course, no document should be presented to the team prior to spell-checking and proofreading. Proper nouns, such as the made-up names of characters, magic items, and locations will not be addressed properly by built-in spell-checking software unless added to the program's dictionary. The writer should be certain that the names are spelled consistently throughout the document and should refrain from abbreviation or nicknames, as this will only confuse the reader.

Credibility

When documenting story content, the writer should remember that the audience assumes his expertise from the beginning. Every mistake or misstatement will subtract some of that faith in the author and will begin to color their confidence in the veracity of the material itself.

It is good to support all assertions with factual data, particularly if they appear to be debatable. For example, the writer or story designer may indicate that a certain sequence will elicit specific feelings in the player: "When the monster attacks, the player will feel fear." There's no justification, no explanation, of why this is so. The assertion is made, and that's the end of it. "When the commander dies, the player will feel sad." How do we know? Are we sure the player's even going to like the commander?

Credibility is also established by familiarity with the content, including the gameplay, the subject matter, the game's themes, the genre, and the history of the series or license (where applicable). In order to develop the necessary connection with the material, the game writer will have to perform research, which may entail reading through design documents, game reviews, articles, postmortems, and technical manuals.

WRITING FOR THE AUDIENCE

The game writer may wind up writing much more than just storylines and dialogue. For example, he may be tasked with writing mission overviews, marketing copy, or technical documentation. In all cases the important thing to remember is that he's presenting core information to a specific audience. It's not important to share the minutiae of character development with marketing (unless they've specifically requested it or unless it's a core component of the game's sales pitch).

Marketing

When presenting content to game marketers, be sure to convey only the information they require. They may be interested in the core outline of the story and in the major characters. A 20-page document outlining the plot and characters in great detail may create additional work for them. One approach that works well is the inverted pyramid of journalism. If one reads the first couple of paragraphs in a newspaper article, the basic facts of the story are clearly presented. Subsequent paragraphs add more explanation and detail, but the first lines will convey what one needs to know. This format works well when presenting content to the marketing team. A terse, fact-driven synopsis followed by a longer document that explains the story content will deliver all appropriate content to the marketing team in a way that's easy to read and understand.

It's also important to separate types of information. For example, some information is necessary to contextualize the game's action. This data appears on the back of the box or in magazine articles. "Lead a team of fierce adventurers into the land of the Orcs." "Drive, fly, and shoot your way through a modern battlefield." But if there's privileged information, such as spoilers, it's imperative that they be labeled as such. If the design documents are haphazardly furnished to the marketing department, and they're left to pick and choose which elements to emphasize in the ad campaign, the developers might not be satisfied with the decisions that are made. For instance, a group of developers was furious to learn that the marketing team had spoiled the surprise ending of their game in the marketing copy on the back of the box, but why was the information presented to the marketing team? Was it labeled as a shock ending? Did the story synopsis simply present the identity of the game's villain as a fact, or was it presented as something that was better left for the player to discover while playing?

Production

When presenting story content to a game's producer, the writer should first determine the producer's needs. Is he writing a document that's intended to motivate the team and to contextualize the game's content for them, or is he putting together a list of characters and locations that will be used to determine the number of artists needed to create assets for the game? A story document intended to inform the team of a game's story line can help get everyone on the same page, but only if everyone reads the documents. The writer might print up a series of mission summaries for each of the levels, including the characters featured in the mission, the location, the major events, and the significance of the action in terms of the story line. Character artists, level designers, and other developers would be able to locate the specific information pertaining to their work, and the concise mission summaries would help keep the team in the loop about the core storyline.

If the writer's task is to furnish content whose focus is the determination of necessary budget and manpower, he may want to present the story documents as a series of spreadsheets indicating general locations (Swamp of Dread, Caverns of Despair) as well as specific mission areas (Lord Krygul's Palace, Lair of the Green Dragon). A similar document citing character models that will need to be created will also be useful.

SUMMARY

In this chapter we studied the methods of story delivery used by developers, as well as their implications for the development process. Then we examined the characteristics of technical writing, with an eye toward story design documentation. Future chapters will delve more thoroughly into each of the story delivery methods and will detail specific documents that the writer uses during production.

DEVELOPER INTERVIEW

Susan O'Connor, Freelance Writer, Susan O'Connor Writing Studio
Bioshock™, Gears of War™

STORY AND GAMES

When I write a story for a game, I know that I'm not in charge of the story—the player is! Player agency drives all of my creative decisions. My goal is to create a world where the player can tell his or her own story.

When I sit down to write a game, I start with the usual story elements—plot, setting, character, that kind of stuff. But when I'm developing stories for games, I focus on action and context. By action, I mean player action—literally, what the avatar is doing onscreen. Let's say it's a first-person shooter. So, right away,

I know that the story has to be visceral and action-packed. We won't have time for a cerebral, talky kind of story—the sort of thing you would find in, say, an RPG. I'm really interested in what the player is doing and where his attention is focused. If it's a real-time strategy game, then the player is thinking three steps ahead, trying to second-guess the AI. In that case, I can invest time creating a story for the world that is full of subterfuge and espionage. The player will probably respond well to that. And that's the context—what's happening around the player while he's playing the game.

THE CHANGING INDUSTRY

It's bigger in every way: bigger budgets, bigger teams, and bigger audiences. I love it.

Bigger budgets mean longer dev cycles, which means more time to craft a story and a script. I've worked on games with six-month dev cycles—ugh! It's rough. Longer schedules give the team time to iterate. And that makes all the difference. Look at Cliff Bleszinski's title for his GDC talk this year: "Designing for Gears of War: Iteration Wins." Yeah!

With bigger teams, every part of the project gets a higher degree of polish. People aren't being asked to do four jobs at once. They can focus on their part of the game, confident that somebody else (the lead designer) is keeping an eye on the big picture.

Bigger audiences are great, too, because that means higher expectations. Games are mass-market. They have to be just as entertaining as movies or television, because that's the competition. Yay! That's good news for every game writer.

WRITING GAMES

I like working in a new medium. Games are unlike films in the same way that films are unlike books—do you know what I mean? Filmmakers learned new ways to tell stories, using their medium. We're on the same learning curve now. I am always asking myself, How can I use this game to tell a better story?

Sometimes I wish that stories were more important in games. For now, gameplay still trumps everything. I may have a great idea for a character or scene or reversal, but if it gets in the way of gameplay, too bad: I have to cut it. As games evolve and change, stories and games may become more interdependent. I hope so. I work on my own projects, on the side, so that I have a place where I get to be in charge of my work.

$\rightarrow$

WORKING WITH DEVELOPERS

It's VERY collaborative. And I like that. Some writers are introverted: not me. I really look forward to onsite visits with clients. I want to interact with the team. And I have to; it's a key part of my job. A game writer can't just write a script, then hand it to the team and say "Here, put this in your game, will ya?" The story has to develop in tandem with the game. What films do in preproduction, in terms of story and character development, we do in production or even postproduction.

WORKING ON A PROJECT

As a freelancer, I work with several different studios every year. Everybody's a little different in their approach. The industry hasn't developed any standards around script development, the way the film industry has. But I can give you a rough idea of what to expect.

When a studio decides to make a new game, they are usually focused on two things: the technology and the gameplay. So by the time I come on board, those issues are usually sorted. "It's going to be a FPS, exclusive to the Xbox 360." And the game designer has probably already worked out some ideas about high-level story. So when I start a project, I usually work with the leads to flesh out the story into the different levels.

I also try to meet with the leads from each department to talk about their ideas for story. Some studios have a great audio department. In that case, I'll focus on creating a story that's going to rely heavily on audio for atmosphere and emotion. It's great to have that kind of awareness up front, so you know where to focus your energy.

Once the story is pretty solid, I start writing the script. I work closely with the level designers to tie story to gameplay. I literally sit next to them and walk through their levels, sorting out the pacing and timing. Level designers are the best. I love working with them.

At some point in development, the studio is ready to cast actors for the roles. On my early, cheapo projects, that meant finding someone in the studio who had a halfway-decent voice and putting them in front of the mike. Now you've got SAG actors, casting directors, voice coaches . . . the whole bit. Thank God.

Usually the team schedules multiple recording sessions. That gives the team time to take the VO from the first session and integrate it into the game. That's when you find out if you suck or not. Well, that's when you find out what works and what doesn't. Maybe you thought that actor would sound great, but he

$\rightarrow$

doesn't. Or maybe you thought that story point would come across, but it's not. So be sure to give yourself time to rework your script after each recording session, so that you can fix problems that come up.

It just becomes a long iteration cycle—write it, rewrite it, record it, rewrite it . . . and then next thing you know, it's over.

FINAL THOUGHTS

It's challenging, but if people want to write games, I say go for it. The more people get into this industry because they love writing, and they love stories, the better our products are going to be. There's definitely an audience out there that's hungry for games that tell great stories. The stories that games will ultimately tell are going to look so different from anything that we've seen in movies or books. That's really exciting.

4 Developing the Context

In This Chapter

- Story Design Process
- Planning Story Content
- Developer Collaboration

The development of a game's context during the planning stages requires that the writer understand the way the story is going to be designed. By considering the process of story design, the writer can plan for the production phase more effectively. In this chapter we'll look at story design methods, content planning methods, and developer collaborations that the writer may experience.

STORY DESIGN PROCESS

The process of designing a story depends on the core gameplay experience. Early in the development cycle, the development team will make key decisions about the game's design that will impact the story. Though there are myriad possibilities, many titles fall primarily into one of three categories: brick-and-mortar games, story-driven games, and open-ended games. Each has advantages and challenges that the writer must contend with while developing a game's context.

BRICK-AND-MORTAR DESIGN

When a game is designed via the brick-and-mortar method, the gameplay experience is created as a series of discrete levels, missions, or installments, and the story content is used as mortar to cement the game experience into a coherent narrative. The designers begin by designing a series of game levels, with little regard for the story implications of these areas. The locations are selected on the basis of other criteria, such as look and feel or spatial considerations. For example, if the first mission is set in a warehouse, the designers may set the second mission in a jungle, which has a radically different look and feel to it. Instead of bare walls and crates, the player is presented with lush greenery and tropical foliage. They might set the third mission in a series of alleys, replacing the lush spaces of a rainforest with the claustrophobic confines of a 10-foot-wide passage bordered by tall buildings. See Figure 4.1 for more details.

Brick-and-mortar	Story-driven
Story design is secondary to the gameplay design	Narrative sequence furnishes the structure of the entire game experience
Passive media is often employed between game levels	Passive and active media create complex narrative experience
Likelihood of dramatic narrative is low	Potential for strong, engaging narrative

FIGURE 4.1   Brick-and-mortar story design.

In these cases the story design is secondary to the gameplay design, and the user experience is thought of in terms of artistic and gameplay considerations. Context isn't a determining factor, so the challenge for the game writer is to create a meaningful and plausible context after the areas have been created (or after production has begun). Typically, this results in a series of short story arcs, each one lasting for a handful of levels or missions; in some cases each mission has its own story arc, unrelated to the other missions (as in the case of *Rainbow Six: Critical Hour*™).

The story isn't a driving force in this process. It's subordinate to gameplay and must be wedged into a fixed space. Dialogue is shoehorned to fit into the game world, and the events that transpire are primarily intended to create dramatic gameplay, not actual drama. As a result, passive media is often employed between game levels to create some kind of coherent narrative. In many first-person shooters, story is delivered to the player in a series of cinematic sequences and static briefings between missions. If the player skips these story elements, the gameplay is robbed of most of its significance.

When a game is designed via the brick-and-mortar method, the likelihood of dramatic narrative is low, because the story serves as a glue to give the action sequences some coherence. The situation is further complicated by two facts: game levels are often created out of order, and it is not uncommon for some levels to be switched around or cut from production during a game's development. Therefore, it's not inconceivable that of a game's 16 missions, the first mission will be created last and that it will be cut from production because the level artist is behind schedule. In this case the entire story will need to be rewritten during the final months of development, because the first mission is now going to take place somewhere else entirely.

STORY-DRIVEN DESIGN

When a game's design is driven by story, the narrative sequence furnishes the structure of the entire game experience. The story arc is significant, even epic, and can span the entirety of the game. Characters, locations, and events are all derived from the game's story line, which is typically communicated through sophisticated (and often lengthy) cinematic sequences. The *Metal Gear Solid* and *Final Fantasy* games are good examples of story-driven game design. In both cases lengthy prerendered and scripted cinematic sequences create a complex story line whose major events are played out by the player. Like an interactive movie, the story-driven game develops an elaborate narrative, complete with rising action, reversal, climax, and denoument. See Figure 4.2 for more information.

In a story-driven game the locations, characters, and events are culled from the narrative. The design team frequently begins by writing the story out from beginning to end and then selecting individual set pieces for use in a game. Conflicts and

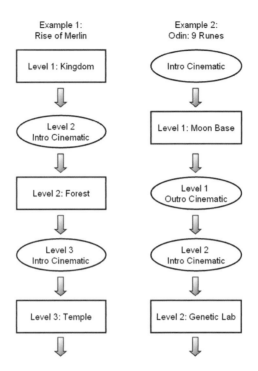

FIGURE 4.2 Story-driven game design structure.

action sequences, then, are not necessarily chosen for their significance as gameplay experiences, but are chosen because they will further the story line. The risk inherent in such design is twofold. First, there is the risk that the story will not deliver to the players' satisfaction, effectively neutralizing the game's appeal. Second, the interactive action elements may not receive sufficient attention, meaning that although the story line is effective and intriguing, the gameplay becomes monotonous and unenjoyable.

Story-driven game design can result in a strong narrative core but requires more than the usual amount of collaboration between writers, designers, and creative directors. Furthermore, to create the strong narrative that propels the player through the game, the story material must be prototyped and tested early on. If there are weaknesses or inconsistencies in the story line, these need to be discovered during the planning stage to prevent scheduling problems during the production phase.

Consider the following scenario: in an effort to create dramatic tragedy, one of the game's major characters is shot to death in a prerendered cinematic, but for various reasons is discovered to be the only character that can destroy the evil Dragon

King at the end of the game. The writer can elect to conveniently resurrect the character just before the final conflict, so that he can deliver the killing blow. This is a fairly cheap deus ex machina move, however, and may therefore be discarded. Alternatively, the writer can decide that the tragic death would work just as well if the character were seriously injured by gunfire, but not killed. Therefore, his appearance in the game's final moments is more plausible. To make this change to the story line will require additional resources, such as new voice cues or cinematic sequences. Making these changes while still in the planning phase would have minimal impact on a project's budget and schedule but during the production stage could cause significant delay and expenditure.

OPEN WORLD DESIGN

The open world, found in games such as *Gun*, *The Elder Scrolls IV: Oblivion*, *The Godfather™*, *True Crime™: Streets of New York™*, and the *Grand Theft Auto* series, allows the player to explore the world at his or her own pace. While the story may be linear in its progression, as in the *Grand Theft Auto* games, the game experience is nonetheless authored in great part by the player and is decidedly nonlinear. The narrative is generally communicated when the player has elected to complete a specific task. For example, while playing *Oblivion*, the player can only get new orders from the Mages Guild by completing a current assignment. This results in a game whose narrative develops at the player's pace, rather than the developer's.

In such a game the story line provides a context for the player's action, but it is not the focus of the game experience and can even be ignored while the player explores the environs. While such interaction might quickly grow tiresome in a more linear game, in an open-world game, there is a great deal of ancillary content that doesn't relate to the story line in any meaningful way. It's difficult to predict how a diagram of open-world design will look, but Figure 4.3 is one example.

On the one hand, this gives the gameplay experience an immersive quality; on the other, this can completely invalidate all of the time and energy spent developing the game's story line. Since the player is under no obligation to pursue the various quests and missions that constitute the core narrative, the player may never experience any of that content. It is also possible that the player will spend weeks (or even months) exploring the world before returning to headquarters for another mission and will therefore have little or no recollection of what was going on in the game's story line. In the *Grand Theft Auto* games, the developers begin every primary mission with a short cut scene to refresh the player's memory about the story line's major events and characters. *Oblivion* sidesteps the problem by providing the player with an in-game journal that is automatically updated every time the story line is advanced.

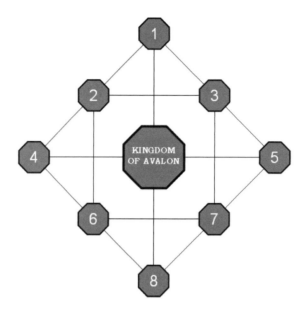

FIGURE 4.3   Open-world story design.

The open-world design allows a breathtaking freedom to explore and discover and guarantees that no two players will have the exact same experience. This freedom can be daunting, however, as many players will not be sure what is supposed to happen next. It's crucial that the developer of an open-world story line consider how the player is going to know what is expected of him or her. Maps, radars, pause menus, and friendly nonplayer characters (NPCs) can all be used to communicate story content to the player as needed. This is covered in more detail in Chapter 6, Structuring the Narrative.

PLANNING STORY CONTENT

Once the developers have established the game's structure, they can begin to plan the development of content. Through brainstorming and competitive analysis, the writer can begin to create a rough outline for the story design.

BRAINSTORMING

During the brainstorming phase the developers seek to answer questions not already determined by the project's parameters. If the game is a sequel or a movie tie-in, then much of the story content has probably been defined already, such as the name of the protagonist and the locations of the game's set pieces. However, some decisions remain, and these are made during the brainstorming phase.

While brainstorming, the developers discuss characters, settings, and scenarios, gathering as many ideas as possible without evaluation or censure. The group can include writers, designers, creative directors, and management, or the task can be undertaken by a single writer who presents his ideas to a lead designer or producer. Each project will approach the idea-generation process differently, but ultimately, a series of story ideas are developed, presented, and evaluated by members of the team.

In the case of a story-driven game, this process can last for weeks, or even months, after which development of a final story document will begin. After this document has been created and approved, the production of the actual game can commence. In the case of a brick-and-mortar game, the story creation may not even begin until production is underway and levels are being built.

COMPETITIVE ANALYSIS

While a development team is hard at work creating a game, other titles are being released. Some of these are direct competition and will need to be evaluated as they are released. This competitive analysis takes place on a number of different levels, including game design, programming, and art. However, it's also important for the writer to analyze the story design and presentation of competing games to see how other developers are creating narrative.

When analyzing a game, consider its story-delivery methods, such as dialogue, cut scenes, and text. How is the story being presented to the player? What kind of narrative structure is it? Is the story clear? Are the main characters easily identifiable? Are they likable? Do they stand out? What is being done to develop them? Why are the cinematics good or bad? What new storytelling techniques have been employed in this game? What technological advancements are the game's developers taking advantage of?

Consider the development of the characters in the game. Do they evolve? Is it something the player has control over? In *Jade Empire*™ the player can choose The Way of the Open Palm (the "light path"), or the more aggressive Way of the Closed Fist (the "dark path"). These choices have meaningful in-game consequences and further develop the player character in-game. Similar choices are found in games such as *Fable*® and *Star Wars: Knights of the Old Republic*. In *The Suffering*™ the protagonist is a convicted murderer who protests his innocence. If the player goes out of his way to help others while playing the game, flashbacks reveal that the man was, in fact, innocent, but if the player harms those around him, the flashbacks show that he committed the brutal murders in question. In many other games the characters may change and grow over time, but not at the behest of the player. All character development takes place during cinematic sequences while the player watches. For example, in *Panzer Dragoon Saga*, the protagonist, Edge, undergoes a transformation from idealistic young soldier to a cynical renegade bent on revenge. This is not something that the player has any control over.

While playing a game, it is not necessary to have an opinion about it. In fact, developing a feeling about a game one way or another may actually prove counter-productive; if a developer actively dislikes a certain game, for whatever reason, he may not notice a new feature introduced in that game that would also work well in his own. Therefore, it is important to remain objective while evaluating competing games, despite the temptation to succumb to one's own opinions.

The competitive analysis is presented to key members of the team and may even be made available to the entire company, depending on how such information is disseminated. If previous analyses are archived somewhere, it is always worthwhile to seek them out and read them, as they can provide distilled information about the way that the other company's games are created. After all, no developer has the free time to play the hundreds of games that are released each year.

DEVELOPER COLLABORATION

Whether the story elements are developed by a writer, a story designer, or a creative director, the work is always a group effort in some way. If nothing else, the story must be integrated into the rest of the game, which requires the writer to understand the working parameters. Three examples of this collaborative process include sound design, character design, and location design. The writer must at least consider these three elements of the narrative in light of the rest of the development team.

SOUND DESIGN

The developers need to discuss the audio portion of the game's narrative design. Several questions about voice acting, special effects, and prototyping need to be addressed. A robust narrative presentation requires a more thorough discussion and documentation of the sound design. People involved in these meetings can include writers, designers, creative directors, sound designers, audio programmers, and voice directors.

Voice Acting

Once the core concept for a game has been established, the sound design team needs to estimate the scope of the dialogue. Though final figures will not be available until later in the project, it's nonetheless important to estimate the number of characters that will be involved and the number of lines of dialogue that will be spoken in the game. It's easier when working on a sequel, in that the team can guesstimate the content based on line counts for prior iterations in the series, but the typical AAA game includes somewhere between 5,000 and 20,000 lines of spoken dialogue. For example, *Rainbow Six: Lockdown* featured 7,000 lines, *Star Wars: Knights of the Old Republic* boasted 14,000, and *Halo 2* offered an astonishing 20,000 lines of spoken dialogue.

Estimating the scope of dialogue is one thing, but getting approval for it is another. Typically, each voice recording is scheduled in four-hour sessions, during which a voice actor can probably record 200 lines of dialogue for up to three characters at a time. Mileage and methods will vary, but these numbers will serve as a decent starting point for the discussion. It is worth noting that after two or three hours of speaking in a normal tone of voice, the quality of delivery changes. Since many games, particularly action-driven titles, feature raised voices (orders yelled on the battlefield, maniacal laughter, death screams), a voice actor will not be able to deliver top-quality work for an entire four-hour session. This must be factored into the calculations.

Consider, based on the above information, a game that features 10,000 lines of dialogue. This will require at least 50 four-hour sessions. If the majority of the game's voice-over is furnished by a small cast of characters (the hero and his teammates, commanding officers, or a trusty sidekick), scheduling the voice-acting sessions well in advance is a very good idea. After all, if the developers wait to contact the voice actors during production, a few weeks prior to the voice shoot, the actors may have already been contracted to do voice work for another game, which can complicate the scheduling process, adding to the budget. If the developers are interested in working with film or television actors, which is often the case, they may find that the voice actor they're interested in is simply not available until the movie shoot has concluded. In such a case the developers may find that the actor who would have been perfect for a role is not going to be in the game after all, and an alternate must be selected.

It's also important to discuss the structure of the narrative with the sound design team. How will dialogue be handled in-game? Will it be a fairly linear experience and therefore fairly easy to organize? For example, *Call of Duty* featured a linear campaign and relied heavily on scripted events. As a result, when playing a single mission more than once, the player generally had a similar experience each time, hearing the same voice cues in roughly the same places. *Call of Duty 2* featured more open-ended environments, and the soldiers in the game responded to their environment dynamically. Consequently, a player would hear different dialogue and chatter each time the game was played. It's considerably easier to organize and record dialogue for a linear and scripted game than a title whose missions can be played in a different way each time; the nonlinearity of the latter requires a more robust planning stage and more precise collaboration between the members of the sound design team.

Special Effects

The use of special effects will add a great deal to the sound design of a game, but it is important to document their application while still in the planning stage. For example, in a game featuring a mission set in a cavern, the echo effect will need to be applied to spoken dialogue in that area. If the game's protagonist is a police officer who receives orders from dispatch, the orders will need the radio squelch effect. By anticipating these effects, the writer can add the requisite notations to the dialogue, so that the voice actors will know that they're not just communicating with another character in earshot. They're yelling into a walkie-talkie or whispering orders into a headset. Some dialogue, such as conversations heard through a closed door, are muffled in postproduction by the sound team. It's also common in many fantasy and horror games for voice actors to portray monsters or demons, and this dialogue is often further distorted to give it an otherworldly quality.

Prototyping

The writer and the sound team need to determine how the integration of audio assets will take place. If the schedule permits it, prototyping invariably saves time and money later on and improves the quality of a game's audio component. By recording placeholder dialogue and plugging the content into the game, the developers can more accurately judge how the voice cues will sound in-game. If a voice cue is too lengthy and overlaps with a swordfight, if the dialogue doesn't fit the mood of the game properly, or if the player requires additional voice cues to help make sense of a complicated puzzle or situation, it's best to find out during the early stages of development, before money has been spent on professional actors.

By employing members of the development team, the sound team can record placeholder voice cues that are then dropped into the game. To best approximate the final sound design of the game, these cues should be modified with whatever effects are appropriate, but the effects don't need to be precise. In other words, though a sound designer might wind up spending hours working to perfect the radio squelch for the final recorded dialogue, a generic squelch effect will work fine for placeholder voice-over.

If the placeholder cast is directed, however casually, then the end result will be superior to a group of people reading dialogue into a microphone without any context. By providing them with a setting, a motivation, and a sense of what else is transpiring during the scene, it is possible to get a higher-quality voice recording.

Quality is an issue that must be addressed during the placeholder casting process. While the temporary content is going to be discarded in favor of professional voice work, it is nonetheless important that the placeholder content captures the mood and feel of the game, despite its amateur nature. If the dialogue and story matter, it's worth holding auditions to make sure the placeholder cast are going to sound halfway decent. If your game takes place in England, but no one on your team can perform a believable British accent, either look elsewhere for temporary voice talent (such as a local theater group) or just have the development team perform with American accents. No accent is preferable to a painfully bad accent.

CHARACTER DESIGN

The design of a game's characters encompasses personality, appearance, and utility. Writers, designers, creative directors, character artists, and concept artists will all contribute to this phase of development.

Evolution

If the game is based on an existing body of work, including previous iterations in a series or a movie tie-in, the basic character design may have already been determined. However, with each new iteration of a character, changes are made, however subtle. For example, the character of Leon Kennedy appears in both *Resident Evil 2* (1998) and *Resident Evil 4* (2005). During the seven years in between the two games, Kennedy quit his job as a police officer (understandable, given that zombies annihilated the city on his first day as a rookie cop) and became a secret agent for the U.S. government. No longer clad in his blue police officer's uniform, Kennedy now wears a brown leather jacket (trimmed with fur) and fingerless gloves and his hair is noticeably longer.

These changes were internal decisions made by the development team, but in other cases, the evolution of a character's appearance may be related to changes in the source material. For example, the character of James Bond has resembled Pierce Brosnan in games such as *GoldenEye* ™ and *Everything or Nothing*. However, it is likely that future 007 games will not use Brosnan's likeness, as Daniel Craig is now playing the role.

Personality

A game's story is driven by the decisions made by its primary characters, regardless of whether these decisions are made on- or off-screen. The character's personality needs to be firmly established prior to the generation of dialogue, to make sure the voice work reflects the personality. During meetings and discussions the developers must answer key questions about each main character. Does he have a sense of humor? Is he menacing or comical? Is he brave? How does he react to stress or pressure? What is his greatest strength? What is his greatest weakness? How would the character react to a crisis?

Once the developers have established core elements of each character's personality, there must be an examination of the other main characters in the setting. If there is one central character (typically the player character), how do the others see him or her? For example, consider Marcus Fenix, the protagonist of *Gears of War*. Owing to his actions on the battlefield, he was considered a coward and imprisoned for dereliction of duty. This comes up early in the game, when his people are threatened by imminent danger, and Fenix's bravery is called into question. However, Fenix's persona is tough and grim, leading the audience to conclude that he was falsely accused.

The personality of the other characters must also display some kind of variegation; if there's no contrast between the characters in the game, it will be difficult for the player to differentiate them. This subject is covered in more depth in Chapter 5, Creating the Characters.

Appearance

During the planning stage, the concept artist will develop various proposals for the main character's appearance. At this point, it's necessary to answer several questions about the character. The more complex the story line and narrative presentation, the more important it is to be certain that the development team has considered several questions, detailed below.

What is the look and feel for the main character? What does he project? Is it menace, absurdity, or strength? What are the character's primary statistics, such as height and weight? Is there a visual distinction that sets him apart from the rest of the cast? For instance, Master Chief Petty Officer SPARTAN-117 of the *Halo* series wears the distinctive MJOLNIR battle armor. In the *Splinter Cell* games, Sam Fisher's green glowing goggles and black bodysuit are immediately recognizable and unique.

What kind of posture does he have? Does his body language communicate discipline, rebellion, or nervousness? What does his appearance say about his origin or his personality? In the *Devil May Cry*® games, Dante's trash-talking machismo is matched by his long hair, red trench coat, oversized sword, and permanent slouch.

As the concept artist, writer, and other members of the development team collaborate on the appearance of the main character, several needs must be served. The concept artist's goal is to create a memorable and striking image. The writer probably wants a cast of well-developed characters whose appearances match their personalities. The marketing department is most likely hoping for an iconic main character that can be used on the cover of a magazine to sell more copies of the game. Through a series of meetings and discussions, all of this must be considered as the characters are created.

Utility

Many games employ nonplayer allies or sidekicks whose actions can assist the player. Generally, these characters are controlled by artificial intelligence (AI) and act independently of the player. AI characters provide color in games through dialogue and by aiding the player in his objectives, but they can also contribute to immersion in the game. The developers must consider the question of the other characters' utility during gameplay, because this will have a serious impact on the player's experience. A higher level of utility doesn't just help immerse the player in the game world; it also gives the player another reason to keep the AI characters alive.

If the AI characters are competent on a fundamental level, this can further develop player immersion in the game world. If the teammates or allies are inept or useless, this will break the immersion and remind the player that it's only a game. In *Star Wars: Republic Commando*™ the player controls Delta-RC-1138, the unit leader of a small group of Clone troopers. The other three troopers, nicknamed Scorch, Fixer, and Sev, accompany the player and follow his orders in the field. If the player gives no orders, the three Clone troopers will defend themselves against the enemy, but they will not complete objectives without being ordered to do so. Their utility is deliberately limited so that they are not utterly ineffectual (if fired upon, they try to take cover, and they return fire as needed), but nor are they going to steal the player's thunder (by taking control of the situation and completing an objective). The end result is that the player gets to order a group of soldiers through a *Star Wars* battlefield but doesn't have to baby-sit the AI-controlled Clones through every firefight; they're competent enough to maintain the illusion that is so vital to the immersive gameplay experience.

AI characters can also fulfill special tasks, which makes them more valuable to a player. In *Star Wars: Republic Commando*, Sev is the sniper, Fixer is the mechanic, and Scorch is the demolitions expert. During gameplay each of these three operatives plays to his strengths at key moments in the game, thereby increasing his utility to the player. In *Marvel*™: *Ultimate Alliance*, the player begins the game with four characters: Wolverine™, Captain America™, Spider-Man, and Thor. The player controls one of these, and the rest are AI teammates, each with special abilities. Certain obstacles can only be overcome by characters with certain attributes (such as heavy objects that must be moved by super-strong characters). In addition, ranged weapons (like Captain America's shield) prove particularly useful against large numbers of enemies.

LOCATION DESIGN

The locations in a game are typically determined by the setting (science fiction, western, medieval fantasy). For example, the primary location design for *Gun* would be the Old West (as determined by its setting, which might be described as realistic western). Stagecoaches and revolvers abound, and the key locations in each area (mine, ranch, saloon) all correspond to commonly held perceptions about the Old West. The description for the setting for *Darkwatch®*, on the other hand, might be something like horror western, given the presence of vampires in the game. *Darkwatch*'s visuals are more sinister than *Gun*'s: there are still stagecoaches and revolvers, but the look and feel have been changed, with an emphasis on dark, evil-looking weapons and equipment. Correspondingly, the locations are also decidedly darker. For example, there's the Boneyard, an unconsecrated graveyard for criminals, and Hangtown, a literal ghost town inhabited by the undead.

Other factors in the process of location design include sequel restrictions, story design, art direction, and gameplay.

Sequel Restrictions

If the game is a sequel, there may be parameters governing how many times you can use a given location. Some developers of games with realistic settings believe that setting a game in the same country twice would be perceived as repetitive and therefore will go to great lengths to find new locations for their games. Others, like the developers of the James Bond series, routinely set missions in France, Switzerland, Russia, the United States, and (of course) the United Kingdom.

Story Flow

In a story-driven game, the locations are likely to be derived from the story line itself. While this can result in a more coherent narrative for the game, it's also possible that the various locales will be chosen more for their significance than for their facilitation of gameplay or their artistic merit. It's important to consider whether a space allows for the kind of game experience that you're interested in. For instance, if you are developing a third-person fighting game whose major selling point is large-scale martial arts battles in wide-open spaces, then having a mission take place in a post office is unlikely to contribute to the game experience in a positive way. After all, how many places in a post office actually permit that kind of multi-combatant fight? To create an appropriate space, the level designers may have to create an unrealistically large office and warehouse to facilitate the game experience, which will erode the player's ability to suspend disbelief. Another issue can be encountered if the area is supposed to constitute a single mission, even though the area isn't really long or large enough to do so. For example, consider a first-person shooter in which a mission takes place in a police station. If the entire 15- to 20-minute experience takes place in a single police station, and the player's characters are moving at a good pace, the police station will need to be unrealistically massive fill up 20 minutes of gameplay. This detracts from immersion and results in monotonous visuals.

Art Direction

A key factor when selecting locations for a game is often the art direction. Since a great deal of the game experience is delivered through the graphics, it's not surprising that many development teams evaluate locations based on how they look and how well they can be juxtaposed against one another. For example, *Half-Life 2* features a number of distinctive settings, including City 17, with its Eastern European style, the subterranean canals, and the high-tech interior of the Combine Citadel. In *Silent Hill* Harry Mason explores a foggy New England town that suddenly transforms into a hellish world of decaying bodies, glaring red lights, and endless chain-link fences. As the player progresses through the game, the world slips back and forth between the "real" and the "infernal," so that each area the player visits (city streets, hospital, school) is actually two areas in one.

Gameplay

The choice of locations can have an impact on gameplay. The effect can be negative, as described in the Story Flow section, or it can be positive. If a game's protagonist has access to a sniper rifle and the locations all offer areas with long line of sight and targets of opportunity, then the gameplay experience will be more enjoyable for the player. If, on the other hand, the entire game consists of close-quarter firefights, because all of the spaces are indoor areas with limited line of sight, then the game will be less satisfying for the player.

SUMMARY

A great deal of a game's story content is determined before a single word of dialogue is written. By understanding a project's parameters, a writer can create a story line that fits most appropriately with his project. In this chapter we examined the story design process, planning methods, and developer collaboration.

Mac Walters, Writer, BioWare
Jade Empire, Mass Effect™

CHALLENGES FOR GAME WRITERS

At BioWare, the people that we've seen struggle the most with game writing are mostly transitioning from other fields and not necessarily new writers that are just starting off. The new writers often have an edge, in that they haven't developed a set way of doing things. They're not stuck thinking, "This is the way you write a novel," or "This is the way you write a screenplay." We often find we can get them trained up quite quickly. On the other hand, some really talented writers from literature, or other fields, have struggled with the nonlinearity and the choices presented by our games. The player is driving the experience, which is so different from the structure of a novel, where the author is really dictating what's going to happen all the time. It's about giving up control. You want the story to move in a certain direction, but you have to leave it open for the player.

If you look at *Neverwinter Nights*, a lot of what we did was accomplished through dialogue. You couldn't see the NPCs faces up close. You couldn't see what they were emoting, so a lot of the story would be revealed through choice of words. You couldn't just have a character come up to the player and say, "Where were you?" It would need to be qualified with something like, "I've been waiting forever," to convey anger or impatience. Now, with voice-over, and facial animations, you can just write a short line of dialogue, accompanied by a lot of description for that line, and the artists and voice-over people can fill in the rest of the nuances.

THE ROLE OF THE WRITER

As I noted at the Game Writers Conference, writers at BioWare are moving from pure writing to direction as well. You write a few lines of dialogue, but then you give a great deal of direction as well. People with experience in television or film are actually going to have more of an advantage than they did in the past.

The role of the writer has changed because we don't write as much in a vacuum anymore. In the past, we were given a toolset and we'd just start typing. Now, we have to take into account the fact that the NPC who's going to be speaking will also have gestures that will play during the conversation, and he's going to look a certain way, and there's also the question of how he's going to sound. As a writer, you have to be ready to collaborate. You have to be clear

→

from the get-go about your goals. What is the story that you want to tell? What are the scenes that you want to show? How will the dialogue support your narrative? Once you've answered these questions, you want to stick to your plan as much as you can. Even slight changes made to story content can have a huge impact on other people's workloads. On *Mass Effect*, we're seeing small changes that affect a large number of people. Writers need to think like directors in the sense that they own the story, and that they're maintaining the vision for the narrative. Obviously, everyone else has something that they're going to contribute, but you want it to all mesh in the end, and you want it to work together seamlessly.

PLAYER CHOICE

Our games tend to feature branching story lines and choices for the player. In *Knights of the Old Republic*, it was the choice between light and dark. In *Jade Empire*, it was the Way of the Open Palm or the Closed Fist. Our tools are designed to support that structure. We often get asked what kind of spreadsheets we use to document our text. There was a time, way back in the day, when that's what we used, but now we employ in-house tools, much like the *Neverwinter Nights* toolset. It's a bit of an adjustment if you're coming from a different medium and you're accustomed to writing story content in a purely linear fashion, but without those tools our job would be a nightmare.

EVALUATING THE NARRATIVE

One of the things we do as writers is to test our own stories and plots. That's key, because even though we have an excellent QA department, nobody's going to know that story or plot better than the writer. You need to get in there and play it and realize that you didn't leave an option open for this plot point. And it's not something that can be left until the end of the project; it's done throughout the development process.

INDUSTRY MATURATION

There are some great games out there, and our industry is booming, so people are starting to realize that expectations are being raised for storytelling. There are, however, games out there that are sent to market rather quickly, and the level of refinement and attention to detail just isn't there. I think that the industry is maturing. Writing and storytelling are becoming a major part of the game industry, and this will continue to attract more talent. When I started at

→

BioWare, it was one of the few places that would hire a writer to be a writer—and it still is. Other studios have writers who also bear other responsibilities, such as game designer. As we move forward, you're going to see more and more companies hiring dedicated writers who will champion the story. You're going to see deeper and more interesting stories, and the people buying the games are interested in that. They're expecting game stories on par with TV or movie quality.

ADVICE FOR ASPIRING WRITERS

If you want to write novels, read a lot. If you want to write video games, play a lot of games. Focus on games that have complex narrative and large amounts of dialogue. You might not be seeing the back end of the game, but you can imagine what's required while you're playing the game. You can also use tools like the *Neverwinter Nights* toolset to experiment. Ever since the game's release, we've required that candidates submit a module created in the toolset when applying for a writing job. It can't hurt aspiring writers to study the tools and learn how the work is done.

5 Creating the Characters

In This Chapter

- Process
- Voice Acting

During the planning stage the developers lay the groundwork for the development of the primary characters through the course of the game. The challenge is to integrate that evolution into the core narrative and into the greater scheme of the gameplay experience.

PROCESS

Several steps can be taken to ensure a higher caliber of character development in a game. Thorough preparation for the task of casting and directing voice talent will pay off later in the process. Identity is also communicated through other means, such as appearance and body language, both of which ought to be addressed prior to the production stage. Finally, the writer should consider various character-development techniques before commencing work on the dialogue.

VOICE ACTING

A series of voice notes should be assembled for all major characters. Depending on the scope of the game, the voice notes may consist of a few lines of information or a document with several sections. The voice notes should include the character's name, gender, age, accent, personality, background information, and voice description. The document may also contain some sample phrases that convey the character's attitude.

THE ACTORS

Typically, a cast will consist of a small group of major characters and a large group of minor characters. Some of the minor characters may have names, and some may be referenced via description, such as Doctor #3, Hostage #2, or Vampire #14.

During the recording process a voice actor will be able to record up to three roles at one time, for a period of up to four hours. However, to be realistic, it's unlikely that a voice actor will be able to deliver four hours of content at one sitting. After two or three hours, an actor's voice will probably become hoarse, particularly if recording high-volume dialogue. Many action games feature screams and yells that can take their toll quickly. By anticipating this eventuality, a developer can begin to organize the voice shoot schedule, setting aside a small number of high-volume lines for the end of each shoot, thereby improving the overall quality of the recording session.

The primary consideration at this stage of game development should be the budget, as it will determine the scope of the sound design. By gathering as much information as possible about the amount of voice acting that will be required, the developer can figure out how best to maximize the time and resources available. For example, if one actor will be playing a single role, that of the main character, then at the end of a two-hour recording session, that actor may still have the time and energy to record an additional (minor) role, such as that of an NPC civilian.

The power of current-generation console systems has allowed developers to raise the bar in terms of voice acting. At its best, it is abundant and varied, further immersing the player in the game world, but this has also raised expectations; while playing a game, the average gamer is likely to notice repetition and to be disappointed by it. If the player hears the same line of dialogue over and over again, or hears the same voice uttering all of the lines in a group of NPCs, then the spell will be broken and the player will be reminded that it's just a game. The developer must rely on breadth to maintain the illusion. Breadth is achieved through the use of multiple voice actors uttering varied lines of dialogue. The player hears different voices uttering multiple lines, and even conversing amongst themselves, and this is enough to keep him immersed.

Once the rough estimates for lines of dialogue have been calculated, the developers can begin to determine how many speaking roles there will be and how many voice actors can be brought in to read those lines. By careful assignment of roles, it is possible to create breadth, resulting in a more robust soundscape.

A prominent first-person shooter was released on the Xbox 360 shortly after launch, and many commented on the fact that in the very first mission, a single line of dialogue (an order to the player from a superior officer) was repeated over and over again until the objective was completed. This was disappointing, given the opportunities that this console afforded, and it could have been avoided in two ways. First, the order could have been given by more than one person. Second, the order could have been phrased differently each time. Either method would have reduced the monotony and improved the game experience for the player.

Variegation of Actors

By varying the number of actors who utter certain lines, the developer can keep the experience from becoming repetitive. For example, if the player is a criminal, on the run from numerous police officers, the shouts of "Halt! Police!" and "Freeze!" should come from several different voices.

Execution of this kind of variety results from carefully planning the number of additional voice cues that will be needed, and this requires familiarity with the game experience. Unless the writer knows what kinds of situations the player will get into, it will not be possible to predict what kind of cues will be needed to create this kind of breadth. Therefore, the writer must play the game, regardless of what state the build is in, and read the design documentation and sit down with the game's design team or creative director in order to fully understand what's going to be happening in the game.

One method for increasing the variety of actors is to categorize all minor roles into broadly defined groups and then assign a small number of randomly selected lines of dialogue to each one. For example, consider the following roles from our fictional game, *Rise of Merlin*:

■ Merlin, 800 lines
■ Archlord Schvyzen, 100 lines
■ Magister Deming, 100 lines
■ Lord Adam Pytman, 100 lines
■ Lady Meredyth Pytman, 100 lines
■ Vivienne, 100 lines
■ Knights, 600 lines
■ Peasants, 500 lines
■ Nobles, 100 lines
■ Brigands, 300 lines

If the player, as Merlin, encounters a number of NPCs in the castle of Lady Meredyth, it is likely that the player will notice if a single actor is voicing all of the content. Assuming that the developers have hired a total of six voice actors (one for each of the six major characters), it would be best to divide the remaining four roles (knights, peasants, courtiers, brigands) as evenly as possible between the six actors. The actor playing the role of Merlin bears the brunt of this game's recording, and thus will probably wind up reading for several sessions (at least four, judging from the line count of 800). Thus, it's unlikely that Merlin's voice actor will be employed for any of the minor speaking parts. This leaves the developers with five actors; three are male and two are female. The knights, with 600 lines, will all be male, so the developers can split those into three speaking roles of 200 lines apiece. The dialogue spoken by the peasants can be split into fifths, as there are male and female peasants (100 lines each). The courtiers are also split into fifths (20 lines each), but the brigands are all male, and thus are divided into three roles of 100 lines each. In the end, the following line counts are calculated:

ACTOR 1: MALE (800 lines)
■ Merlin, 800 lines

ACTOR 2: MALE (420 lines)
■ Archlord Schvyzen, 100 lines
■ Knight #1, 200 lines
■ Peasant #1M, 100 lines
■ Courtier #1M, 20 lines
■ Brigand #1, 100 lines

ACTOR 3: MALE (420 lines)
- Magister Deming, 100 lines
- Knight #2, 200 lines
- Peasant #2M, 100 lines
- Courtier #2M, 50 lines
- Brigand #2, 100 lines

ACTOR 4: MALE (420 lines)
- Lord Adam Pytman, 100 lines
- Knight #3, 200 lines
- Peasant #3M, 100 lines
- Courtier #3M, 20 lines
- Brigand #3, 100 lines

ACTOR 5: FEMALE (220 lines)
- Lady Meredyth Pytman, 100 lines
- Peasant #4F, 100 lines
- Courtier #4F, 20 lines

ACTOR 6: FEMALE (220 lines)
- Vivienne, 100 lines
- Peasant #5F, 100 lines
- Courtier #5F, 20 lines

This means that if a player talks to a random male peasant, there are three different voices that might respond. If a player talks to a random female peasant, there are two voices. Of course, the example above is atypically brief. In a full-length AAA title, many more voice actors may be required. *Halo 2* and *Gun* both featured a cast of 30 actors, for example.

The more voice actors are involved in the recording process, the less likely it is that during gameplay a character will talk to one character (say, a police officer) whose voice is performed by the same actor who voiced another (such as a gang member from the previous scene).

Variegation of Dialogue

To continue with *Rise of Merlin*, let's consider the following scenario. The player, as Merlin, is entering the castle of Lady Meredyth Pytman. As he walks across the bridge, one of the knights tells him that Lady Meredyth is expecting him in her throne room. Inside the castle walls, there are knights practicing combat, a black-smith working at his forge, and peasants carrying grain into the citadel. The player is free to explore the area and engages several NPCs in dialogue. However, the player eventually remembers that someone is looking for him. He finds a knight, who tells him that Lady Meredyth is expecting him in her throne room. The line of dialogue is exactly the same as the one that was delivered just a minute ago. As the player walks along, encountering a knight, he hears the exact same voice cue a third time. This gaffe could easily be avoided through the use of alternates.

Variegation of game dialogue requires the writer to consider which lines of dialogue will only be uttered once and which lines might be repeated. The circumstances of gameplay will generally dictate which lines are which. For example, if the player is the pilot of a spacecraft, escorting an unarmed freighter vessel to a way station, and hostile aliens destroy the freighter, then the player's NPC wingman will probably only need to inform the player of this development once. A simple "They took out the freighter!" will suffice. Even if the player doesn't hear the line of dialogue because he's too busy returning fire, he's going to notice the absence of the freighter on his radar, and he's going to see the ball of fire in front of him. Variegation will not serve any practical purpose in this scenario, but after the freighter has been destroyed, and the player is engaged in combat with the enemy ships, the wingman may have critical information that needs to be delivered on a regular basis. For example, the player may order the NPC wingman to return fire or to hold fire and power up his shields before returning to combat. In either case the wingman will reply in the affirmative. If the wingman responds with "Yes, sir!" after each order, this will quickly become tedious. By recording multiple responses ("Affirmative!" "Understood!"), the developer can create sufficient variegation to ensure that the player does not hear the same response over and over again. See Figure 5.1 for an example.

Town Guard	What seems to the problem, citizen?
Town Guard	Is there a problem?
Town Guard	Why have you summoned the Guard?
Town Guard	What's going on here?
Town Guard	Does someone require our help?

FIGURE 5.1   An example of dialogue variegation.

It is also possible to vary a single response, so that the player may hear "Affirmative!" more than once without hearing the exact same line. During the recording session, the voice actor will typically give multiple readings of a line, after which the best reading will be selected. If more than one reading of a line is suitable for the game, they should all be included. That way, the character will have two deliveries of the line "Affirmative!" In one, perhaps he sounds a little more aggressive, or accents the second syllable just a little bit more. The end result is that the character now has a little more depth and breadth to his dialogue, resulting in the reinforcement of the illusion and a more robust immersive experience for the player.

Variegation is limited by a game's budget and by its technical parameters. Setting aside these two constraints, which determine most of the game's scope of development, a developer can never have too much variegation of dialogue. It can only enhance a game.

IDENTITY

The identity of each major character in a game must be determined and communicated to the player through the means that are available: voice acting, text, visuals, and behavior. During preproduction the developers must decide the nature and extent of each character's identity on the screen.

Persona

Is the main character defined, like Joanna Dark, the heroine of *Perfect Dark* and *Perfect Dark Zero*™? She is depicted in the game as pragmatic, reasonable, yet suspicious of others. Or is the main character a cipher, like the protagonist of *Grand Theft Auto 3*? Though the character clearly has goals, such as seeking revenge for the double-cross that sent him to prison, he has no name and never speaks. Or is the main character a blank slate, as in *Oblivion*? The character-creation process at the beginning of the game allows the player to create an avatar whose gender, race (human or otherwise), and appearance are all customizable. Nonetheless, the main character is an integral part of the story line and will be a force for positive change if the primary missions are completed (regardless of whatever else the player might do during gameplay).

Communication

Once the persona has been established, the developers must decide how this information will be conveyed. Will the character's personality be reflected in his appearance? For example, the appearance of Marcus Fenix (*Gears of War*) accurately reflects his grim, tough personality. His face is weathered and scarred, and his features are broad and vaguely Neanderthal. His bulky, dented armor is decorated with a stylized skull, and his head is covered with a black do-rag. Overall, Fenix looks obdurate and menacing. Heather, the protagonist of *Silent Hill 3*, is a moody introvert with few friends. Though not unattractive, she wears her hair in a ragged mop that covers her face and dresses in a puffy vest that conceals her figure and ill-fitting orange galoshes. Her overall appearance is ragged and homely, matching her troubled persona.

Verbal communication of identity is commonly used in games, as it only takes a moment to establish a character's personality through voice or through text on screen. The choice of voice actors can determine a great deal of personality, as in the case of *Metal Gear Solid*'s Snake. The acting of David Hayter lent Snake a tough, macho voice that has continued to develop through numerous sequels. It is also possible to convey a great deal of information through word choice. The writer can make a character petulant, forgiving, confident, sarcastic, brave, or malicious with a single sentence. It is important that the dialogue effectively communicate the personality of a character early on, as first impressions will color the perception of the character for the rest of the game.

Body language will tell the player a great deal about a character. How does the hero stand? Does he lean? Does he hook his thumbs into his pockets, or do his fists hang at his sides? Does she walk gingerly, or does she stride into a room and cross her arms? The way a character moves can tell the player what to expect when a new character is introduced, and given the capabilities of modern motion-capture systems, it's possible to convey a great deal without the utterance of a single word.

The audience is constantly taking in and evaluating stimuli, whether seen or heard, and the presentation of a character's identity must be consistent.

Decisions

Ultimately, a character's nature is revealed through choices. If these are incongruous with a character's presentation, then there are two possible outcomes: either the player will be intrigued by the character's decision or the player will be confused. For example, in *Dino Crisis*™ a character named Gail is supposed to be searching for a missing doctor. However, when the doctor is found, Gail insists that he has unfinished business elsewhere and leaves the player to escort the injured doctor to safety. Later it is revealed that the doctor was not part of the actual mission and that Gail deliberately misled his teammates. The other characters are initially confused by Gail's decision but become angry when they find that they've been duped. In this way we learn more about Gail (he's willing to use his own team as pawns or human shields), and we learn about the player character (she resents being used and she values human life). If Gail had instead been shown to retreat from the doctor because he was nauseated by all of the blood, this would have caused some confusion, because the player has by this time already seen Gail's stoic response to mangled bodies elsewhere in the game.

Other decision-making processes can allow the player to mold the character and persona of the protagonist. In games like *Jade Empire*, *Fable*, and *Oblivion*, the player can choose how to respond to key situations, and this can allow the player to take ownership of a character's personality and attitudes.

CHARACTER DEVELOPMENT TECHNIQUES

These techniques are a means to an end and can be used by the writer or designer who is responsible for the storytelling elements. In and of themselves, these techniques aren't going to create strong characters, but they can help the writer create more believable, three-dimensional characters. These exercises can be used during the planning stage as part of the process of creating the characters. Using these techniques will open doors and start conversations, like brainstorming. The methods described here include the tarot deck, the quandary, the conversation, and the character web.

Tarot Deck

The tarot is a card deck imprinted with symbolic images. There are numerous variants on the deck, some of which date back to the 15th century. Traditionally, the cards are used by fortune-tellers to divine the future by laying cards out in different patterns. Some believe the cards allow psychics to exercise precognitive abilities, while others hold that the cards' symbols merely jog subconscious beliefs, or that meaning arises from the random juxtaposition of images, triggering sudden epiphanies. Some people think it's all nonsense.

If used during preproduction, the tarot deck can help the developers create more fully realized characters. The tarot deck is a free-association tool. Think of it as a starting point—a Rorschach blot that the development team can draw inspiration from. The writer will need a deck of cards, which he can buy or make. Tarot decks are sold at game and hobby stores. Numerous breakdowns of the deck can be found online.

Before shuffling the deck and dealing the cards, it is important to become familiar with the symbols and their meanings. For example, according to some, the Tower symbolizes the fall of pride, or impending doom. The Magician indicates a divine motive of some kind, and the Star suggests hope or immortality, and so forth.

After preparing a list of symbols and their meanings, deal two or three of the cards for each of the major characters in the game. Consider the symbols and the order in which they appear. For example, let's say the writer is working on a science fiction game. One of the characters is a scientist named Lennix. We deal three cards for him and come up with Star (hope/immortality), Magician (divine motive), and Tower (fall of pride/doom). If we consider the symbolic meaning for these cards, we could come up with hope, divine motive, and a fall of pride.

Perhaps Lennix sees technology as humanity's last hope, a way for humans to transcend their pettiness and bigotry. Through science, he hopes to accelerate the evolution of humans, advancing us to a stage of elevated consciousness. This quest ends in failure, resulting in a fall of grace because of his pride. Possibly his experiments result in death (or worse), or possibly he is discovered and expelled, so

Lennix is driven by guilt. He knows what he wanted to achieve, and he may feel that he was wrong and that he has learned a lesson. Or he may feel that he was thwarted, and he may be continuing his experiments in secret.

Reading the cards in another order produces different results. Let's say we've dealt Tower, Magician, and Star. In this light, perhaps Lennix underwent some personal tragedy, a catastrophe that caused him great pain. He lost his faith in science but has recently found a different kind of faith—religion, magic, communion with nature, or whatever—and now he believes that there is hope after all.

What do the cards stand for? Does that interpretation really fit with the kind of game that's being developed? As patterns emerge, the writer should think about the personalities of the characters and ask whether they really fit. If the icons seem to work, but aren't necessarily in the "right" order, they can be rearranged.

The alternative method is to create a tarot deck (Figure 5.2), based loosely on the iconography of the deck. This is not uncommon; T. S. Eliot played fast and loose with the tarot in his poem "The Waste Land," as did Stephen King in his *Dark Tower* novels. It may be easiest to create a custom tarot deck of archetypes, each with its own set of symbolic significance.

The Magician	Divine motive, determination
The Empress	Prosperity, beauty
The Chariot	Honor, pride
The Hermit	Silence, isolation
The Wheel	Destiny, surprises
The Tower	Fall of pride, doom
The Star	Hope, immortality

FIGURE 5.2   A sample Tarot deck.

Conversation

The conversation is used to establish the vocabulary and speech patterns of the major characters in the game. One of the things that can help differentiate major characters from one another is the choice of words—the way that they talk. The choice of words can help establish a character's identity. Key words or phrases, diction, accent, slang, code phrases, sentence structure, profanity, even the amount of dialogue—all of these can tell the audience a great deal about the character's persona.

In order to develop these voices, the writer can create fictional conversations between major characters. This process is an exploration of the way the characters talk in a hypothetical conversation that takes place in the game world. However, the conversation isn't going to be featured in the game. It's an asset that is created as part of the game's design, but it's not intended for inclusion in the game's dialogue. It's a writing exercise, nothing more.

There's no need to set the scene with text. The writer just needs to pretend that the two characters are talking to each other about a topic of significance in the game world. Gradually, as they talk, the writer should hear differences begin to emerge. For starters, select characters who have opposing philosophies, so there will be disagreement of some kind. As the conversation progresses, voices will emerge. The writer should focus on one character through various conversations until he or she begins to develop a specific speech pattern or vocabulary. These conversations don't have to be very long. After a few pages, the writer should really begin to have a feel for the way the characters talk. If it helps, instead of writing the conversations down, the writer may want to role-play them. Using a pocket tape recorder, he may try talking aloud in the voices of two of the major characters. Afterwards, the writer should listen to the recording or read what's been written. What phrases reappear—what diction, style, vocabulary, accent? It's good to free-associate. It's not necessary to worry about grammar or spelling when writing by hand. It's important to keep writing, even when the writer doesn't know exactly where the conversation is going. Yes, most of what's being created is going to get scrapped, but the process will be a beneficial one.

It may help to sit down with a highlighter and mark key phrases that made an impression in some way. If the writer sees something interesting or noteworthy, he should ask where it came from. What in that character's nature inspired that particular turn of phrase? Does it fit with where that character grew up or received an education? If ideas occur to the writer during this part of the process, it's crucial to take copious notes. When it's all over, there should be a clear idea of where the characters are coming from, and this may later inspire scenes in-game or in cinematic sequences. This may also provide an idea of where the characters stand philosophically, which can help establish what some of the major conflicts will be in the game.

It's not always necessary to pair up two heroic characters for a conversation. Some of the more interesting conversations take place between heroes and villains. For instance, DeNiro and Pacino had a fascinating talk in a diner in the movie *Heat*. They talked about dreams, death, and each other. This conversation, a calm discussion between a criminal and a police detective over coffee, foreshadowed the film's final scene.

Conversations between heroic characters don't have to be smooth or friendly. Toward the end of *Rainbow Six: Lockdown*, two of the counter-terrorism operatives engage in a heated discussion about how to handle the terrorist group they're fighting. Both operatives have the same goal in mind, but they disagree on how to handle a critical, life-or-death situation, and long-simmering disagreements between the two culminate in a vicious argument about who gets to make the call. This scene emerged from various conversations between the two characters that were written during preproduction and later discarded.

The Quandary

The quandary is used to describe the various ways in which characters react to stressful situations. It's an insoluble dilemma of some kind, a hypothetical situation set in the world of the game. It is a problem with no best option—no clear best choice to make. It presents each character with a crisis requiring a solution but affording no easy way out.

For each of the major characters in the game, the writer should create a description of how the character resolves the quandary and how the situation plays out. One quandary should be written for each of the major characters in the game, whether heroes or villains. It's not necessary to consider how the character ought to behave. Many of the most interesting moments in games occur when ostensibly heroic characters are shown to be petty or self-absorbed (like Wesker in the original *Resident Evil*) or when presumably villainous characters display humanity or mercy (such as the brutal zealot Craymen in *Panzer Dragoon Saga*).

It's not necessary to end on a happy note for all of these scenarios. The writer may want many of these quandaries to end in victory or tragedy; it depends on the feel of the game. If the game is dark and serious, an unhappy ending is obviously more appropriate. The important thing is that the writer understand why the characters are making those particular decisions. What's motivating the characters to behave the way they do? Is the character capable of making serious mistakes in judgment? Figure 5.3 shows an example of the quandary.

Crisis: A building is aflame, and children are trapped inside. The Red Dragon has seized the Sword of Legend, and is preparing to fly away, to deliver it to the Horned King. If the dragon escapes, then the Horned King will use the sword to lead his undead army to battle, and the kingdom will be destroyed in the ensuing war. If the children are not saved, they will die in the fire. There isn't enough time to do both.	
Merlin	Merlin summons a wall of water that smashes into the dragon, halting its flight. The wall of water cascades over the building, extinguishing the flames.
Talerios	As Talerios sprints towards the building, he slashes the dragon with his dagger to get its attention, then rams the door down with his shoulder. Inside, he grabs the children and hauls them to safety. As he emerges, the dragon seizes him in its jaws, crushing him to death. The children escape, and Merlin attacks the dragon.
Vexalyss	Ignoring the children, Vexalyss transforms into his dragon form and attacks the Red Dragon. After a grueling battle that destroys the village, Vexalyss kills the other dragon and retrieves the Sword of Legend.

FIGURE 5.3 The quandary puts characters in a critical situation.

One of the big shortcomings of many games that feature heroic characters is that the protagonists are superlative in every way, eliminating many opportunities for depth or drama. If the heroes can't be fooled or betrayed or outdone, the drama becomes extremely thin and boring. There's no threat, no chance that the hero will be undone. If the characters are human, and therefore fallible, they become more interesting.

The writer should establish the reactions of the major characters to problems or crises and see how they respond to situations of loss. Do they adapt? He should be aware that it's acceptable for some of the characters behave similarly, but they shouldn't all react in exactly the same way. For example, in the fictional superhero game *Justice Unit*, one of the heroes (Ice Queen) is getting ready to fire a plasma beam at a group of bank robbers and isn't aware that there's a bus headed straight for her. The bus driver has just slammed on the brakes but isn't going to be able to stop in time, and Ice Queen will be killed when the bus hits her. On the other side of the street, a group of bank robbers has just emerged from the bank with the stolen money, and one of them is about to shoot an innocent bystander cowering next to his car.

The protagonist, super-powered marketing executive Bulletpoint, has a choice: rescue the bystander or save his partner. It's impossible to save both. His choice depends on what the character values. If Bulletpoint believes the hostage must be rescued above all else, then Ice Queen dies, but he may believe that electing to don the costume means placing one's life in danger again and again, with the under-standing that one day your luck will run out. Therefore, the innocent bystander is the person who deserves to live the most. Or Bulletpoint might feel a strong bond of loyalty and save Ice Queen's life, even though it might result in the death of a hostage. Or he might save her because he believes that keeping Ice Queen alive will result in saving hundreds (even thousands) of lives down the line. Thus, rescuing his partner is for the greater good, and the death of that innocent person is a nec-essary evil. Or he might choose to save Ice Queen's life because he's got feelings for her.

This process reveals how Bulletpoint feels about his work, about the people whose lives he saves, and about his teammates. It shows how he sees the world. The scenario might continue after the quandary has been resolved. For instance, after saving the hostage, and thereby losing his friend, Bulletpoint might then kill the bank robbers in a fit of rage. Or after saving Ice Queen, but letting an innocent per-son die in the process, he might decide to give up crime-fighting out of guilt.

The Character Web

This technique is used to develop major relationships between the characters in the game and explores how they feel about one another. The character web is used to define interpersonal relationships in the game. The idea is that the writer creates a web, a flowchart that diagrams all of the major characters in the game and all of the relationships between them. It defines how the characters feel about each other and relate to one another and the kind of affections or animosities they hold for one another. It's more complicated than mere like or dislike. A fully developed character web will delineate allegiances, factions, attitudes, and hierarchies. It's more complicated than love or hate.

The important thing to remember is that two characters aren't necessarily going to feel reciprocal feelings for one another. There will be unrequited love and concealed animosity or grudges, and there will be a number of dissociative elements. For example, between a mentor and a student, one may see the mentor's pride in his student's achievement and the student's resentment for being held back by someone whose time has passed. Not all of the emotions will be shared by the two characters, but there will be some common feelings. For example, they may share the love of a father and son.

Different layers of emotion and relationships can exist between the characters in the game, which brings us to the idea of multiple character webs. There may be different character webs for the different characters. For example, the writer may create a character web for the heroes and one for the villains, or one for the major characters and one for the minor players. Certain characters in the game may only appear in cut-scenes, or in certain missions, and this will require specific webs that only deal with these characters and their attitudes toward one another.

The writer may also create character webs devoted to specific types of relationships (Figure 5.4). For example, if working on a military shooter, the writer might create a character web that pertains to hierarchy and rank and the way soldiers relate to one another and their superiors in that context. One of the characters, a macho private who does things his own way, may resent one of his superior officers. The officer might not even be aware of the private's resentment and may believe the private is a loyal and reliable soldier. Another web for the same group, focusing on interpersonal relationships outside of rank, could delineate mutual respect between the two dating back to an incident that transpired years ago. Conflicts arising in the game could bring the resentment to the fore or could strengthen the bond between the two characters. This series of character webs can deepen the relationships between the characters in the game.

The other thing to think about when creating a character web is the idea that different-sized webs require different levels of detail. For a large web with multiple characters, it's good to keep it as simple as possible. If the web features a dozen characters, the writer will probably want to keep the interpersonal descriptors down to a single-word relationship.

If there are only three characters, the web can feature more complex relationships and attitudes between them. For example, the writer may connect the char-

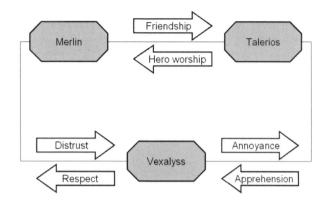

FIGURE 5.4   The character web establishes relationships between characters.

acters with two lines, instead of one. One of the lines can indicate connections between a king and a warrior, such as their attitudes toward each other. The warrior envies the king's wealth and power yet admires his inner strength. The king envies the warrior's youth and admires his loyalty to the crown. The writer could indicate their working relationship, which is straightforward: the warrior is completely loyal to the king, and the king is ready to send the warrior out to do battle. The web can feature multiple threads connecting characters in a tightly focused relationship map. On a map with more characters the writer may simply feature a single word or concept, such as obedience. The king issues orders, and the warrior obeys.

It's also important to consider the web's structure. There are a number of different possibilities. With a single major character, the writer might consider a radial web, where the major character is in the middle and all other characters emanate from her (because they're defined in relationship to her).

A few characters will have feelings for one another in this web, so the writer will want to think about where to place them in relationship to one another. Ideally, characters should appear next to characters they interact with routinely, so that these attitudes can be defined on the primary map. Another map will probably be required to define the minor characters outside of their relationship to the player character. Ultimately, the central character web deals with the major character and how she relates to all these people, because when writing the dialogue, or when developing cut-scenes or storytelling elements, the writer will want to know how the player character relates to the other characters and how they feel about her. Is she admired? Is she loved? Is she feared? Is she underestimated?

When working with an ensemble cast, if the player controls several characters at once, a number of them will still shine through as principals. Watch an ensemble movie like *X-Men*, and see how a small group of characters seizes the attention of the audience. The writer should build a web that focuses on that small cast of central characters and focus on them.

The last thing to consider when creating character webs is the idea that characters can evolve. The character web can change over time depending on the events that transpire in the game, because relationships between these characters, their emotions and attitudes, can evolve as things change. Characters attitudes do change as characters interact with one another, so, depending on the storyline, the writer may want to create multiple character webs to support major evolutions in the storyline.

If the protagonist's closest friend is murdered after the fourth mission, and then it's revealed after the seventh mission that the murderer is an ally of the player (who was a double agent all along), then the developers will need three maps—one for each of those stages. After the murder, the major characters may feel grief and anger, which may alter the way they relate to each other. Some may swear vengeance, while others could advise forgiveness. They may split along those lines. After the revelation of betrayal, suspicion may cloud friendships, or it may draw the player's allies closer together as they band together for a final stand against the enemy. Either way, the writer should define these emotional ties between characters in the context of the major events of the game.

In Figure 5.5 we have the Justice Unit, from the fictional game of the same name. The player controls Bulletpoint. There are four other characters in the unit. Sensei is the leader of the unit, an old, wise karate master. He trained Bulletpoint and taught him to fight for justice. Their relationship is garden-variety mentor—pupil relationship. Ice Queen is beautiful but aloof, and Bulletpoint carries a torch for her, but she gives him the cold shoulder. Major Malfunction, the old army veteran who breaks everything he touches, likes to drink a few cold beers with the kid every once in a while, and the feeling's mutual. They hang out; they get along. By contrast, the demented Canadian ninja, Caribou, really intimidates Bulletpoint. Mainly, it's the antlered warrior's enigmatic nature and his tendency to fly into the terrifying Caribou Rage. Bulletpoint is also a little jealous of Caribou, because enigmatic warrior guys who fly into a rage but also have a code of honor are just a lot cooler than normal guys with superpowers.

After the battle with Overcharge (a former credit card industry CEO who laid siege to Wall Street in an armored exoskeleton), Bulletpoint demonstrated astonishing powers that the Justice Unit didn't even know he possessed. In the aftermath of this battle, during which Bulletpoint pretty much saved the day, the relationships have shifted somewhat (as shown in Figure 5.6). Major Malfunction sees the kid pretty much the same way, but Caribou has gained a little respect for the guy—he earned his chops in the field. Ice Queen has thawed just a tad, and Bulletpoint has enough confidence now to be honest with her about his feelings. Not that it matters. She's still frosty toward him. Sensei is now intimidated by Bulletpoint, who may well be the Golden Warrior promised in the ancient prophecies.

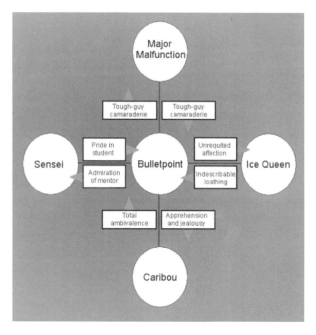

FIGURE 5.5   The *Justice Unit* character web.

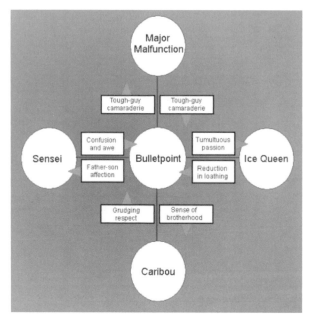

FIGURE 5.6   Various relationships have shifted in this character web.

SUMMARY

Each technological advancement increases the expectations for character development in games. As writers continue to explore the possibilities, it's important to consider the process of character creation, as well as different methods that can be used to imbue game protagonists with personality. In this chapter we examined the process of character creation, and then we looked at some ways developers can add more depth and complexity to their protagonists.

DEVELOPER INTERVIEW

Randall Jahnson, Freelance Screenwriter and Game Writer
Games: Gun
Movies: The Doors, The Mask of Zorro

ENTERING THE FIELD

When I started working on *Gun*, I was completely new to game writing. I had no previous experience. I was interested in the medium, conceptually. I got the call from my agent, who said that there was a company that wanted to hire me to write a video game, and it only took me a few seconds to say yes, definitely. I had no idea what I was getting into. It was a very involved and lengthy process, but I learned a lot.

    I was very concerned at first. I told the guys at Neversoft, "You know I have no previous experience, right?" They said that they'd teach me everything I needed to know. Their bottom line was that they wanted a kick-ass story, but something that didn't necessarily unfold like a typical game. They wanted a sweeping epic, a game that people would really get into.

WORKING ON *GUN*

The game was a western set in Dodge City and a small town in the New Mexico territory, and they wanted to start it in Dodge, then move into the other area. Other than that, they had no story, no character concepts, nothing. They wanted to bring in as many western archetypes as possible, including bandits and lawmen and bounty hunters and Indians and buffalo hunting—everything that you could imagine. However, other than the major set pieces, they wanted to make sure that the game was completely original and didn't bear too much resemblance to other western games like *Red Dead Revolver*™.

$\rightarrow$

The head of Neversoft put a controller in my hand and pointed to the skip-ahead button, and he said, "You see that?" I said, "Yeah." He said, "That's the enemy. As you're writing the story, imagine that there's a player sitting there with his finger on the button like a gunslinger with his finger on the trigger, looking for an excuse to skip ahead. Your cut-scenes have to be quick, creative, interesting, and driven by great dialogue and characters. It has to be accomplished in under two minutes."

I thought, two minutes? In movies, a single scene could last three to five minutes, sometimes longer. So I wasn't sure that it could be done. He assured me that it could, and that I would do it.

DEVELOPMENT

Once I got into the rhythm of it and began to see some of the early artwork and animation, I could see it coming to life. I would give them a few scenes, and they'd say, "Great, let's cut it in half." These are rules that I've learned in screenwriting as well, because in film, it's all about economy of image and language. You want to get as much information across as quickly as possible, but with artistry. This was that principle on steroids.

I wrote the scenes fast, and they had the animation and temporary voice acting up and running very soon, so I was able to see how the scene was going to work.

In a traditional feature film screenplay, you're talking about 100 to 120 pages of script. The cut-scene script for *Gun* was 60 pages. At the outset, once we had the story nailed down, and we were committed to writing a cut-scene script, I was thinking that it was going to be easy. But I hadn't factored in the side missions and the interactive dialogue. Once I finished the cut-scene script, they said that they'd get back to me when the next phase began.

They would send me modular charts for each character, along with each character's respective moment of gameplay, in which I'd write a half-dozen to a dozen lines for each situation. For example, for Colton, the main character in *Gun*, I wrote dialogue for when he'd been struck by a bullet. I had to write six reaction lines. "I'm shot!" "Damn, I'm gutshot!" And so on. Then another six lines for when he's been hit in a fistfight, or for when he's attacking a villain, or riding his horse and trampling a bad guy. There were maybe 20 different categories for at least 20 characters and their respective factions, so it quickly added up to thousands of lines of in-game dialogue. Neversoft said that the important thing at this point was sheer quantity, giving their voice actions plenty of options, as opposed to quality. In movies, you would call these "wild lines." It's just stuff

$\rightarrow$

that gets recorded off-the-cuff, and it's thrown out in the heat of battle, so to speak. The important thing was to keep it short, because they indicated that shorter lines cut through the action best, rising above the on-screen din.

GAME WRITING

I've been a screenwriter for 20-plus years, and in Hollywood, they always talk about the collaborative process. Usually, the writer reports to a producer or executive, and once the script is in good shape, they give you your walking papers. The director usually has his own personal rewriters come in and take a stab at it. I've been hired and fired from many projects, and all supposedly were collaborative, but I have to say that my experience on *Gun* was the best experience I've ever had as a writer. We had frequent roundtable meetings where we'd talk about story elements or scenario ideas. The art department would come in with renders of set pieces or characters. As a writer, this is very exciting and stimulating. You're actually collaborating with the artists and programmers, and all of the people who are making the game come to life. And that's fun.

VOICE ACTING

I attended most of the voice recording sessions. One of the delights of the writing process was watching Lance Henriksen and Tom Jane in the studio together, working off of each other as they recorded the final encounter against each other. It was tremendous. However, as a writer, you will find that what looks good on paper doesn't actually sound as good as you had hoped. You have to be ready to do some rewriting right there on the spot. This is oftentimes exciting, and it can involve the actors who are working with you as well, and so they're throwing out lines spontaneously.

NONLINEARITY

As a screenwriter, I've always found myself struggling somewhat against the traditional linear form. I've aspired to bring a kind of dimensional quality to whatever it is that I'm writing about. For example, *The Doors* deliberately became very surreal and nonlinear at times, mostly due to the fact that the subject material warranted it. I don't necessarily start with page 1. I might start with an image or character that might be in act two of the script, but it's a starting point for me. It's my entrée into the world and the story, and I work out from there. Frequently my work-in-progress scripts are a real patchwork. The beginning might be written, and the ending might be written, but there are holes in

$\rightarrow$

between. I see the game writing process as very suitable for that kind of approach. Gun didn't necessarily follow that, because there was a linear narrative, but there were some dimensional elements involved. For example, the side missions can interrupt or disrupt the main thrust of the story.

Video games as a form are much more dimensional than a typical screenplay because of the open world that is present in so many games. You can proceed at your own pace, explore the world, and create your own time line and sense of urgency. You never have that option in a screenplay, because it's all about advancing the plot or revealing a character through dialogue. In film, there's no way to sit and watch the sun set, or turn left instead of right, or to explore a dark alley—unless the director wants you to. Because of the dimensional nature of games, I'm much more attracted to writing them because it suits me better.

LESSONS LEARNED

If I had a chance to do it over, I'd say that communication is very important. No one wants to have something dropped on them at the last second or to learn that an entire section of the game has been cut. There was another part of *Gun* that was originally scheduled in Mexico, featuring a very Sergio Leone kind of setting and some cool gunfights. But this area was cut from the game, and I didn't find out that the story line had changed until some work had been done, so I had to go back to the drawing board.

Still, I'd do it again in a heartbeat. I can't imagine another medium in which a writer is allowed to get into this kind of detail. For example, I got to create the text of a wanted poster. There were 10 posters in the various side missions. In a film that kind of content would be created by the props department, and the writer wouldn't work on it. But I actually got to create the text, and that, for me, was a lot of fun.

6 Structuring the Narrative

In This Chapter

- Logocentric Narrative Design
- Mythocentric Narrative Design

During gameplay the player will experience a broad spectrum of interactive stimuli, which he can respond to in different ways. In some cases the player will assess a situation and make a decision, thereby initiating the action and encountering a response of some kind. In other cases the player will be acted upon and will be forced to respond to a stimulus that has been engineered by the developer. It is tempting to say that a game falls into one of these two categories, but the truth is that most games occupy a place on a spectrum between these two scenarios. Even the most linear game offers some player choice, and even the most open-ended game does corral the player at one time or another into a specific scene or action sequence.

Plato defined two ways to reach truth: mythos and logos. Logos refers to reason and science and is precise and exact. It can be demonstrated, and it can be proven independently through empirical means. Logos corresponds to our reality and is irrefutable. Mythos, on the other hand, is elusive and spiritual, the domain of dreams and myths. Mythos explains that which science cannot, such as the reason for suffering in the world.

We will use the terms *logocentric* and *mythocentric* to describe the two points on the spectrum of narrative structure (Figure 6.1). Logocentric design is specific and precise and is primarily authored by the developer. Mythocentric design is wide-open and subject to interpretation, and is therefore player-authored.

Logocentric	Mythocentric
Specific moments that are determined in advance	Player has the opportunity to create specific moments
Linear and controlled	Wide-open and free-ranging
Plotted out and documented by the designer	Player is the author of the core experience

FIGURE 6.1 Mythocentric versus logocentric narrative design.

LOGOCENTRIC NARRATIVE DESIGN

A logocentric game's core experience consists of a series of specific moments that are determined in advance.

AUTHORITY

Logocentric design is linear and controlled and has been plotted out and documented by the designer. The developers want to evoke a specific emotion or divulge a certain amount of information for the benefit of the player, so they carefully measure and control the elements of gameplay in order to achieve these goals.

The design documentation clearly identifies these goals and describes the steps required to effectively produce the desired end result. Because of the specific requirements, no divergence from these parameters is permitted. For example, in a World War II shooter, the developers may want to startle the player by having an enemy soldier suddenly appear at the top of a flight of stairs, yelling in German as he tosses a grenade towards the player. If there are two sets of stairs accessible from the ground floor, and the player chooses to climb up the other stairs, then this sequence will not play out, and the grenade won't come bouncing down toward the player. The developers may therefore choose to block the second stairway with debris or to remove it from the map entirely, or they may block it with a door that can be unlocked later. Whatever the case, to ensure that the player is appropriately startled by the grenade, the developers will remove any variables from the equation to prevent divergence from the script (see Figure 6.2).

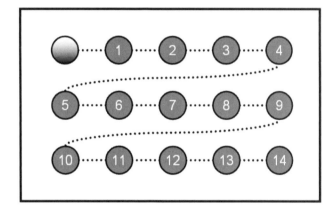

FIGURE 6.2   An example of logocentric narrative structure.

EXPERIENCE

The result of this planning is a tightly controlled construct that delivers a specific experience to the player in what is often described as *cinematic gameplay*. There are positive and negative side-effects of this construct.

Owing to the linear nature of the logocentric structure, the player's options are limited. Although the game world may resemble our own, there are differences that have been engineered to restrict player freedom in specific ways. While these restrictions are designed to prevent deviation from the game plan created by the developer, the end result can result in an erosion of player immersion if not handled carefully. For example, if the player is moving through an apartment building, looking for an exit, and some of the doors can be opened, while others cannot, this may frustrate a player. After all, many other game elements correspond to reality, so why can't doors? Worse, if the player has access to a firearm and can shoot some doors down, but not others, the problem is compounded. One can explain a door that can't be opened by pointing out that it's locked. The *Resident Evil* games often note that a door has been locked or that it is blocked from opening by something in the other room, for example. But a bulletproof bathroom door in an elementary school? It's difficult for the player to maintain the suspension of belief when a game's core mechanics aren't consistent with our reality, or even consistent internally. It's also frustrating if the player's character is supposed to be heroic and athletic but can't climb over a two-foot-high wooden crate blocking a doorway (a tactic employed by far too many "realistic" first-person shooters to list here).

The logocentric structure also limits the replayability of the game, because every time the player accesses a mission or level, the experience will be exactly the same. This can cause frustration when a player must repeat portions of a scenario, such as when the player dies and then must reload the game from a save point earlier in the mission. Returning to previously played areas, the player is able to anticipate exactly where the enemy will appear and is able to pick off foes or sidestep obstacles with ease, because the shock of a sudden stimulus is no longer coloring the experience. The challenge is diminished considerably, and all that remains is the button-mashing that's required to get to "the new part," where the player will once again be presented with unfamiliar and challenging situations that require concentration.

Another problem is the pattern-repetition that sometimes afflicts the design of logocentric games. After playing through several missions, it may be possible for the player to anticipate coming events by paying attention to developments in the game. For example, if the player discovers a large cache of ammunition and then finds a save point, it is probably safe to conclude that the player will soon encounter a major enemy force of some kind. This can rob some encounters of the element of surprise.

If the player does not take the action that the developer has predicted, the game experience may prove unsatisfactory. Unless the player has been apprised of the expectations, it's possible that he is going to zig when the developer expects him to zag, and if the game is so tightly scripted that deviation fails to trigger the necessary sequence, the player may wind up "breaking" the game and finding himself in an unplayable situation. For example, imagine a first-person shooter in a horror setting. The developer has created the following situation: when the player reaches a dimly lit corridor, a door opens at the far end and a monster begins to run toward the player. There's a machine gun on the floor, and the door behind the player is locked. There's only one way to go, and that's forward, through the monster. However, as the monster approaches, the lights begin to flicker, and eventually go out altogether. When the player picks up the machine gun and fires, the muzzle flash illuminates just a little bit of the corridor, so that the player is able to find the monster in the flickering light. Since the player has no flashlight, and the corridor is now completely dark, the player must hold down the trigger of the machine gun in order to locate and kill the monster. After the monster is dead, the player can move forward into the next room, which is lit.

There are numerous problems with this scenario, but the most glaringly obvious is the expectation that that player will pick up the machine gun. There's no way to be sure that this will happen. After all, the player may be happy with his shotgun, or he may not see the machine gun on the floor, or he may pick up the machine gun and then switch back to the shotgun to conserve machine gun ammunition. There's no reason to expect that the player is going to understand that it's necessary to load the machine gun and use it on the monster. Though it may seem obvious to the developer, the player is by no means going to see it the same way and consequently may find himself in a darkened room, being attacked by a monster he can't see. This scenario is not as far-fetched as it might sound, unfortunately. One of the riskiest elements of the logocentric approach is that it exposes a heavily scripted scenario to the public, and players will invariably find and exploit (or complain about) every single mistake, loophole, or miscalculation.

The logocentric style has many disadvantages, but at its best, the structure affords developers the opportunity to create some of the most memorable moments in gaming. By carefully structuring the progression of events, and by guiding the player from encounter to encounter, the developer can arrange for specific moments that elicit awe, amusement, fear, or exhilaration. The attack of the Flood in *Halo*, the sudden pounce of the MA-39 Doberman in the original *Resident Evil*, the death of Aerith in *Final Fantasy VII*, James Sunderland's discovery of his wife's killer in *Silent Hill 2*, and the first glimpse of a Strider in *Half-Life 2* were all made possible because of the games' logocentric design.

DESIGN

The design of logocentric games requires the anticipation of all contingencies. Developers must consider the players' urge to break things during the planning stages and spend as much time as possible during production and postproduction testing the game and examining scripted sequences for mistakes. By polishing the game until all such issues have been addressed, developers can obviate many of the problems described in the preceding section.

Developers must resist the temptation to identify a player response until such has been verified through play-testing or focus groups. For example, it is not safe to indicate "Player will feel sad when Officer Davis dies," because the developer simply does not know if this is true. While it may be true that the game will be more difficult when Officer Davis dies, because Davis was able to return fire and help defend the player during firefights, it does not necessarily follow that the player will feel enough of an emotional attachment to the character to actually mourn his passing. It is also risky to insist that the player will feel fear or amusement without some kind of empirical evidence to suggest that this is actually the case. The designer must consider the reality of the player experience, and any story elements in the game must be tested as vigorously as art or code assets to ensure that the appropriate emotional response is elicited.

The documentation of a logocentric game is simplified by its linear nature, although the movie script format is still inappropriate (as discussed in more detail in Chapter 7, Organizing Dialogue). Since the events of the game follow an A-to-B-to-C continuum, where the player absolutely must experience the events of area B in order to reach area C, the developer can create story lines that follow the standard narrative model of rising action, climax, and denouement. This three-act-story approach is therefore most commonly seen in logocentric games, whose linear structure can accommodate that kind of fixed progression.

However, it is important to bear in mind that the player experience is not necessarily contiguous, or bound by the same parameters that govern the viewing of a film or reading or a book. When watching a film, the audience is generally expected to view the work all at once, although video and DVD have made it possible to watch films at the viewer's pace. Even weekly television programs feature a "Previously on. . ." segment at the beginning of the episode to refresh the memories of the audience. While books can be read, then set down, then picked up again much later, their structure (text on paper) makes it easy enough to flip through the pages and glean the crux of the narrative so that the reader may resume the experience. Games, however, are generally easy enough to pick up, even after several years. However, though the control configuration will doubtless be accessible to the gamer, the story line will probably be a distant memory. Thus, it is not realistic to hope that the player will be emotionally affected by a climactic scene that references events from the beginning of the game. After all, the player may play one mission per night and still not remember that first scene when he's reached the end of the game.

Conveying your expectations to the player is a tricky business. While the developer may be convinced that it's easy to see what's next in a game, the player may not be so sure. During the chaos and tumult of combat, or while solving puzzles, the player may forget which way he's supposed to go next. The player may also forget what he's supposed to be doing, because he's picking up the game after several weeks of playing something else. If there are elements that remain as current objectives or goals, the player needs to be able to identify these. Euphemisms typically muddy the waters, regardless of how common-sense they may seem to the designers. For example, directing the player to "clear the area" may seem relatively straightforward, but not every player is going to understand that this means "Kill everything you see until you run out of adversaries." If this information isn't conveyed properly, the player may be frustrated because he doesn't understand what he needs to be doing in order to move forward.

In brief, if the player must jump through hoops, the designer must ensure that the hoops are clearly visible, so that challenge does not become frustration.

RAMIFICATIONS

The logocentric narrative facilitates the Hollywood experience that so many developers seek to create, which is why movie tie-ins like *The Chronicles of Riddick: Escape from Butcher Bay*, *Star Wars Episode III: Revenge of the Sith*, and *Peter Jackson's King Kong: The Official Game of the Movie* all feature logocentric design. By employing the linear design and tightly controlled game experience, the designers can pretty much guarantee that the player will be at a certain location at a given time, enabling the developer to furnish the player with a necessary resource or an escalating threat. In *Quake 4*, when the player is directed to head back to the front lines and locate a medic (encountered earlier in the game), the player must retrace his steps, which are now blocked by Strogg aliens who open fire. Without the linear corridors and locked doors, there wouldn't be the specific kind of tension that the developers hope to create as the player fights through the enemy, toward the medic waiting outside. If the player could duck into other corridors or open doors that led into other rooms, a different kind of tension might be present, but it would not be the effect the developers aimed for in their design documents.

This kind of design focuses on the metastory of a game, the events that transpire around or beside the player's actions. In such cases, the player's actions, however central, are part of a larger picture, and are often driven by these external events that appear in cut-scenes, or remotely (such as when the player can look out of a window and see an enemy starship landing, foreshadowing an imminent conflict). The result is that the player becomes the object of the action, and the external forces in the game, which initiate and guide the conflict, are the subject of the action. The player doesn't initiate conflict, but instead resolves it as required in order to proceed through the game world. The developers startle, ambush, and confront the player with pyrotechnics, shocks, and visuals, and the overall effect is akin to being the passenger on a theme park ride.

The sheer volume of control that must be exerted over the experience requires that the design be well though out in advance and that all screws be tightened prior to the game's release.

MYTHOCENTRIC NARRATIVE DESIGN

A mythocentric game's core experience consists of an open space whose numerous moving parts afford the player the opportunity to create specific moments.

AUTHORITY

Mythocentric design is wide-open and free-ranging and consists of arenas for player action that have been created by the developers (Figure 6.3). The player, as author of the core experience, gets to choose the goals and means of the game experience. Unlike logocentric design, the developers are facilitators, not creators, of the events that transpire.

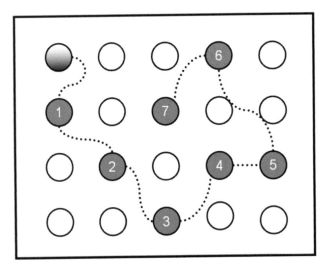

FIGURE 6.3   An example of mythocentric narrative structure.

For example, in *The Elder Scrolls III: Morrowind*, the player may choose to abandon all quests and assignments and spend time searching for a complete suit of green glass armor. This armor, made from volcanic glass, is rare and expensive and is not generally available in shops. Consequently, the player must go to great lengths to find the individual pieces (such as helmet, boots, and greaves). Once acquired, the armor is quite impressive and boasts a very high armor rating, but the player may have to risk a great deal to assemble the suit. For example, the player might attack and slay the Armigers in Vivec, since they both wear partial suits of green glass armor. True, this will help the player achieve his goal, but it may also result in a bounty being placed on the character's head. If the player is caught in the act of attacking the Armigers, others in the building may attack him, possibly killing him. The risk may or may not be outweighed by the benefit of a powerful and lightweight suit of armor; the decision is the player's to make.

The player may instead decide to become a great potion-maker and may spend all of his time creating magical elixirs in his workshop. To do so will require rare and exotic herbs and components, which means the player will have to travel far and wide to acquire these items. This enterprise is not without risk, as many powerful components must be gathered from the bodies of dangerous demons (such as the frost salts culled from the corpse of a Frost Astronach). However, if the player is willing to invest time in such a pursuit, he can develop a character whose arsenal of potions makes him a lethal combatant and a capable adventurer.

In *Grand Theft Auto 3* (*GTA3*) the player may decide that he wants a firearm. By completing missions and earning money, the player can purchase a weapon at Ammu-Nation, or the player can simply mug people and take their money once they're incapacitated. By attacking and subduing a police officer, the player can take his weapon. The player can also make money by driving injured people to the hospital in an ambulance. There are many ways for the player to achieve this goal (whose outcome is not crucial to the game's story or completion, although it's always helpful to have a gun when playing *GTA3*).

In each of the above cases the player has evaluated the game world, considered the state of his character, and elected to pursue a course of action with a specific outcome in mind. The goal is determined by the player and unrelated to the game's primary story line. It is not derived from any assignment or mission, and it has no direct bearing on the player's completion of the game. However, the goal is only worth pursuing because the game world is sufficiently open-ended that the player can choose (and achieve) meaningful objectives. In a logocentric game, the player might choose any of the above but would have no chance of achieving the goal, because the game is so tightly scripted that there is only one solution for a given problem or scenario. The player's ability to create and resolve meaningful goals requires a nonlinear game world, freedom to explore, and a series of believable consequences for player action.

Even if the player does not elect to pursue any goals other than those assigned in-game, the mythocentric structure allows the player to choose which goals are pursued and in what order. For instance, while playing *Gun*, the player can choose to pursue a story mission or can play one of the side missions, such as tracking bandits or mining for gold.

EXPERIENCE

The mythocentric design results in a game experience whose individual moments are created by the player, not the developer. Because of the open-ended nature of the mythocentric game, the player's options may be numerous. For players new to the game, this may even be daunting.

In some cases the mythocentric design consists of a series of linear objectives that must be completed one at a time before new areas of a game world will open up. Such is the case with the *Grand Theft Auto* series and the *True Crime* series. In other cases the entire world is more or less available, and the player can explore to his heart's content, as in *Morrowind* and *Oblivion*. In *Saints Row* the player must earn Respect to open up new missions. Respect is earned by completing story missions and various side missions, and extra points are given for the amount of damage done during the completion of the mission. The player can still choose what to do, and how to do it, but the developers have created a framework that more or less requires the player to go forth and explore, so that the player doesn't just zip through all of the story missions and complete the game without taking on some of the side missions.

In most of the above cases the level of narrative coherence is directly tied to the player's actions. If the player plays one story mission and then delves into exploration and side missions for the next few hours, the narrative impact may be completely dissipated by the time the player opts to pursue another story mission. This permits the player to control the pace of the game, but can pose an obstacle for the developer who wants to tell a story. Since the player can spend hours with some mythocentric games without completing a single story mission, the developer may find that the mythocentric structure simply does not allow for a story-driven game experience.

Because of the game's "sandbox" structure, the player controls the pace of the gameplay, which also means that the player can (to some degree) control the level of the challenge. If the player is in a logocentric game and is under fire, the door behind him may be locked, and since he has already progressed through the linear space, he's probably located all of the ammunition that he's likely to find. However, in a mythocentric game, if the player is running from assassins and is low on ammunition, it is likely that he can outrun them in the streets of the city (or the jungles or the hills) and come back when he's found some new weapons and ammo. In this way, the level of escalating threat and difficulty that the developers work so hard to create in a logocentric game will not work for a mythocentric title.

The story missions in a mythocentric game can vary in linearity. For example, in *GTA3*, if the player must steal five cars in four minutes, then that's what the player must do to progress through the story missions. There's no way around it. If the player steals five cars but takes longer than four minutes, the mission is a failure and must be replayed. In *Oblivion*, if the player must help a group of fighters clear out a cave full of goblins, this can be achieved in numerous ways. For example, the player may race ahead of the fighters and kill all the goblins himself, racking up gold and experience points, or the player may hang back and let the other fighters do all the dirty work and then collect the gold afterwards. If the player completes the mission, and the other fighters all survive, the mission is complete. If the player completes the mission, but the goblins manage to kill all of the other fighters, the mission is still complete. As long as the core instruction is followed, the details can be left to the player's discretion.

DESIGN

The design of mythocentric gameplay requires the developer to anticipate the player's actions in the wide-open worldspace. It may be that the player can, from starting the game, begin to wander in a random direction until encountering challenges too great for a novice to handle. For example, in *Morrowind* the player can simply head in one direction, fighting minor adversaries such as rats, until suddenly coming face-to-face with a demon that kills the player instantly. Because there are few imaginary boundaries to hold the player back, it's possible to keep going until an adversary terminates the player's progress with a lethal burst of flame. This can be discouraging or exhilarating, depending on the player, but it can also be avoided. In *Oblivion* harder enemies only appear when the player has progressed past a certain level. If the player enters a cave while at first level, he might find a lone goblin. If he returns to the cave while at a higher level, he might find trolls or necromancers. In this way, the challenge is always appropriate to the player's ability. In *GTA3* parts of the city are blocked off by construction; the player can explore a great deal, but his progress is limited until he's become more familiar with the game world, at which point the rest of Liberty City opens up to him.

Designing the narrative of a mythocentric game can pose a major challenge, given the amount of player freedom that the structure permits. Often, mythocentric games are designed as linear stories whose major plot points are doled out in short installments. The player is given a single major plot revelation with each new task, and if the player does not complete the task, then nothing happens in the game world until the quest has been completed. Each task is preceded by a quick summary of what's going on in the game world, so that the player is reminded of the situation just before embarking on a new quest. This way, the player doesn't lose the narrative thread while playing the game.

The narrative context will not be as robust as that of a logocentric game, because the tools are simply not available. The player isn't being corralled into a scenario calculated to surprise or amuse; instead, the player is free to choose whether to even undertake the scenario in the first place. It's difficult, therefore, to weave dramatic or compelling narrative into the freeform experience. Games such as *Gun* are able to create drama through the use of cut-scenes that advance the story line. However, during the freeform portion of gameplay, most of the dialogue consists of AI chatter that reflects the player's actions at the time.

DEGREE

Neither logocentricity nor mythocentricity is an absolute. As noted at the beginning of this chapter, both terms describe points on a spectrum, and a game might contain elements from different parts of that range.

Ghost Recon, for example, featured several mythocentric elements. The game took place on a series of large maps, most of which were large squares full of variegated terrain such as mountains and buildings. The enemy consisted of a few dozen hostile soldiers, and the player's goals were a small number of objectives that could be fulfilled in any order (some of which were entirely optional). The player controlled up to three small teams of soldiers and could switch between them at will. As a consequence, the player could address the objectives in a number of different ways. He could set up ambushes and lure the enemy into a crossfire or use long-range weapons to pick them off one at a time. Using his three teams to scout ahead, he could locate enemy forces on the map through reconnaissance and change his plans on the fly. Because of the many variables, the game offered a great deal of replayability. The mission structure was logocentric, in that each mission had to be completed in order when playing through the campaign, and the player could not leave the square map he was on; in some cases the boundaries were invisible, representing the fact that the player characters were soldiers who would never voluntarily retreat from battle.

Medal of Honor, on the other hand, was more logocentric, featuring linear maps that directed the player from one attack to the next. Rather than searching the area and forming an attack, the player would react to stimuli. The end result was a more tightly scripted experience that provided for developer-controlled moments of spectacle or surprise.

RAMIFICATIONS

The mythocentric narrative allows the player to take control of the gameplay and narrative experience, effectively creating the kind of gameplay in which he wants to engage. By employing the nonlinear design and freeform structure, the developers allow the player to decide what to do and where, resulting in a game experience that is unique for every player. In *Grand Theft Auto: Vice City Stories*™ the player is ordered to take out a rival mob boss. If the player ignores the order and spends the next few hours stealing cars, robbing people, and getting into shootouts, the game remains fun and meaningful, and actual consequences ensue. There are risks and rewards for the player, even though the story-based campaign does not progress. In nonviolent games, such as *Animal Crossing®: Wild World*, the player has the ability to decide how to play the game. While he can accept the various missions (usually phrased as "favors" or "tasks" in the game), he can also elect to spend his time gathering apples to eat or seashells to sell and enjoy a game experience that proceeds at his own pace.

This kind of design means that the player may completely ignore the metastory and that all of the time and energy spent on creating a story line for the primary campaign will result in wasted time (from that player's perspective). The result is that the player becomes the subject of the action, frequently deciding when and where the action takes place. Rather than merely responding to threats and surviving attacks, the player can decide how to engage the world.

The amount of planning that must go into a mythocentric design requires that the designers spend a great deal of time testing and polishing the content to ensure that everything works properly.

SUMMARY

Story and gameplay are inextricably linked, and the writer must understand the kind of game that's being developed before commencing the design of the story line and dialogue. By considering the author of the game's experience, as well as the structure of the game world, the player can create a story that most closely matches the gameplay experience. In this chapter we studied the logocentric and mythocentric narrative structures and considered their ramifications for the working game writer.

DEVELOPER INTERVIEW

Rob Brown, Senior Lead Designer, Edge of Reality
Over the Hedge, Microsoft Combat Flight Simulator 3

WRITING A GAME

It helps a lot if the writer on a project is also a gamer. I've worked with several writers that aren't really gamers, and some of their work doesn't translate well into gameplay.

Gameplay usually trumps narrative, but there's definitely a way that these two elements can work together. The two can coexist, so you want to tell a good story. For example, when you're working with an existing IP, like a movie, it's a given that you need to tell a good story. The designer and writer need to work together to figure out how they're going to pull off the key moments from the movie in the gameplay. There's a synergy there, and you see more and more games doing a better job of telling stories because game designers are getting better at incorporating narrative into their games.

WORKING WITH WRITERS

The best working relationships that I've had were with game writers that understood the basic principles of design. When writing dialogue or creating characters or designing scenarios, they understood how those elements would translate into fun gameplay. At that point, the game designer now has a lot to work with, and the two can bounce ideas off each other, resulting in a design that's stronger than what either would have come up with on his own.

I think that the game that had the biggest impact on me was the first *Halo*. It had a well-written story that fit in really well with the gameplay. *Half-Life* and *Half-Life 2* also featured really compelling storylines. They both had high-quality presentation, and I really liked the way that the story was conveyed to the player. You felt that you were discovering the story as you went along, rather than just having it spoon-fed to you. I think you're seeing writers and designers getting better at integrating the story into gameplay.

INTERACTIVITY

If you look at movies or novels, the key that separates them from games is interactivity. When playing a game, I feel like I'm actually engaging part of the

→

story, and that's something that only our medium can provide. You're part of the story line or you're creating it as you play. There are so many people entering the game industry from film, or from other writing backgrounds, that you're going to see game story lines change and mature until they're on par with what's being done in film or literature.

GETTING INTO THE INDUSTRY

This probably applies to anybody getting into the industry, but writers could definitely benefit from this in particular, but try to gain a little knowledge of each of the disciplines: art, programming, design, and production. That way, they can understand how their story proposals will impact scheduling and so forth. The writer should understand the artist's standpoint of how the characters will require models and animations, or know the basic principles of design or of the hardware that the story will be told on. That way, the ideas that are proposed are actually in the realm of what can be done on a project. That knowledge of what it takes to make a game can really help a writer push the limits in certain areas and thereby deliver a higher-quality story experience for the player.

7 Organizing Dialogue

In This Chapter

- Developing Dialogue
- Formatting Dialogue

Writing game dialogue requires more than just getting words down on the page. The documentation must match the development process, and the writer needs to understand how the game is produced. In this chapter we'll discuss the way the development team interacts with the writer and the active format of dialogue documentation.

DEVELOPING DIALOGUE

When writing games, it's helpful to understand the basic structure of the development cycle and to understand what the key players on the team do. The story design and the dialogue will affect designers, programmers, artists, and producers, each of whom has an agenda and a scope of work. By studying the ways in which these team members interact with the story, the writer can save the other developers time and energy. Each project is structured differently, and roles and responsibilities vary from company to company, but the core principles will remain the same.

DESIGNERS

Designers are responsible for developing the core gameplay concept, whether it originates with them or gets handed down by production or management. The game designer will have some input with regard to the story line, setting, and level structure. The game designer will also have some awareness of franchise restrictions and will probably have some input about the dialogue that's written, which may vary from comments and suggestions to flat-out veto. In either case the designer may have the most coherent vision of the overall game's feel and concept and can be a valuable resource.

As the game evolves through the course of production, the game designer may revise portions of the game, including level design, character rosters, and the sequence of events. This will all have a serious impact on the story and dialogue.

For instance, let's consider a superhero game called *Justice Unit*. The third mission begins in a bank vault, which the superteam is defending against the threat of an attack. The current mission design calls for a minute-long delay before the supervillains attack. During this time one of the player character's teammates fills him in on Overcharge, the evil supervillain who's planning on attacking the bank. His weakness is that his mechanized suit of armor slows him down, but he becomes more powerful as he leeches power from the superpowered beings around him. So, hit him hard and fast, because the longer the fight lasts, the more dangerous he becomes. This is all mixed in with banter from other teammates and nervous chatter from the security guards (Figure 7.1), the idea being that this will heighten the tension, resulting in a nerve-wracking wait for the inevitable attack.

SPEAKER	DIALOGUE
Guard	Who-- Who are these guys? The ones who are going to be attacking.
Sensei	They're called the Corporation. Their leader, Overcharge, was once the CEO of a major credit card company.
Bulletpoint	And he gave it up to be a supervillain? Why? The guy was rich, powerful-- I mean, seriously, Queenie, does that make sense to you?
Ice Queen	Don't call me Queenie. Hell, don't talk to me, period.
Bulletpoint	Ooh, someone get me a blanket, I'm getting the cold shoulder here--
Sensei	Quiet! I sense them. They're... outside!

FIGURE 7.1   In-game banter from *Justice Unit.*

During play-testing, it's decided that the bank space is too small to accommodate a huge fight with multiple opponents. Also, the minute-long wait isn't nerve-wracking; it's boring, so the designer instead opts to set the battle in the city streets, outside the bank. The fight takes place right after the robbery, and the Justice Unit is tasked with apprehending the bad guys. The load screen gives way to Overcharge thudding down the street in his armor, clutching burlap bags with dollar signs on them. This invalidates all of the dialogue that's been written. No time for banter, character development, tension, or that key piece of information about how to win this fight. This can all be scrapped, but the hint for the player needs to go in. It's not enough to just copy and paste the text; the content must be shortened into a quick burst of information that the player hears as he's diving into battle.

Designers create gameplay, and writers contextualize it. If possible, the writer should maintain close contact with the designers on his project, as their work is most closely tied to his own.

PROGRAMMERS

Writers and programmers don't usually interact all that much, but there are several key conversations that they can have, which will save time and money in the end.

In any game various technical restrictions must be taken into consideration prior to writing dialogue. For example, if the voice cues are streamed from the game disc, the writer needs to know how many simultaneous audio streams can play at a given time. On one console it may be possible to stream 20 simultaneous sounds; on another the system might only accommodate 5 sounds at a time. If one factors in the ambient room tone and music, that only leaves three tracks. Add sound effects and the report from a gun, and suddenly there's room for just one audio track of streamed voice.

To continue the example of *Justice Unit*, if the writer wants to include cries of surprise from stunned onlookers, yells from bank robbers, and dialogue from the superpowered teammates (Figure 7.2), he needs to know what the parameters are prior to starting work. This vision might require adjustment based on the restrictions of the code base and the choice of platforms.

SPEAKER	DIALOGUE
Bank customer 1	Help! Oh my God!
Bank customer 2	Look out!
Guard	Everybody get down!
Bulletpoint	Sensei, they're coming in through the floor!
Overcharge	Take them out!
Bank robber	Aaah!
Bulletpoint	Got one!
Ice Queen	Bulletpoint, watch your six!

FIGURE 7.2   Example of background chatter.

Communication with the programmers can help resolve issues before they manifest themselves; for example, the developers may decide to employ a hierarchy of sounds based on priority. If multiple voice cues play simultaneously, cues from the player's team should be given first priority, as they convey useful information. Cues from civilians on the street should be given low priority, as they're just ambient noise to flesh out the game world. If the programmer knows what's crucial to the story (early in the development cycle), it's more likely that the game will deliver the kind of audio experience the story requires.

If the project is multiplatform, the developers need to know the parameters of each version, with the understanding that they may not be able to put all the voice cues in this version, but on the next-gen or PC version, they can pretty much do it all, which means they'll want to record voice cues for all contingencies.

ARTISTS

The writer's interaction with artists will depend on how involved he is with production. Three areas in which the writer will probably rely on artists for information or materials are character models, level creation, and cinematic sequences.

If the writer is involved in the character creation process, he will no doubt have his own opinions about the appearance of the characters in the game: how they look, how they move, what they wear, and so on. It's best to have a flexible vision, since the process is a team effort, but any ideas brought to the table should have some kind of support. If it's the writer's job to determine what the characters look like, any reference images that he can furnish will help get the point across. If the writer is hoping to give an evil character some visual impact, describing him as "menacing" just isn't going to do it. It's crucial to focus on concrete details.

During the level creation process the writer may have some input, which would be a good opportunity to find places to work in the kind of in-game dialogue that creates personality for the characters (if that's a design goal for the game). The aforementioned scene in the bank didn't work out, but doubtless another chance would have presented itself during a lull between fights. However, the artists are more likely to provide such opportunities if they know the game's story line requires them. For example, if the level artist knows there's a scene at the beginning of mission 8 to establish that Ice Queen is losing her powers (creating problems later on down the line), then that artist can create an alleyway long enough for all the necessary voice cues to play without interruption. It's hard to build character and personality when the voice cues are suddenly cut short by an explosion or gunfire.

The creation of cinematic sequences may require storyboarding or animatics, in which case the writer might be partnered up with a concept artist. While working on storyboards, it's important to know what's possible beforehand. When working in-engine, the developers may have to work with whatever assets have already been created—character models, levels from existing gameplay, vehicles, and so on. If using a specific asset, such as a character model from mission 12, it's important to find out when that is scheduled to be created. If it's not going to be ready for a few weeks, but work has to begin on cinematics soon, there's no point in building a cut scene around that character. It's not going to work out in the long run unless the character artist's schedule is rearranged.

The same principle applies to prerendered cinematics, but the limitations may be more budgetary than anything else. It's not uncommon for storyboards to undergo repeated revisions in order to come in under budget. Understanding what the limitations are, and then working within them, will save the developers the trouble of multiple meetings.

PRODUCERS

Producers deal with budgets and schedules and submissions. If a writer learns to speak the producer's language, the story process won't be a burden on the game's production. This will help keep valuable character-building scenes from being cut. The more organized and thorough the writer is, and the more contingencies he's taken into question prior to presenting his work for approval, the more likely it is that creative goals will be met. For example, if the writer tells the producer that there will be over 60 speaking roles in the game, the producer may visualize a complex and expensive process. If, on the other hand, the writer says that multiple roles have been assigned to each actor, taking line counts into consideration, and that the project will require 15 voice actors to play roles delineated in a structured spreadsheet, then the creative vision has an improved chance of survival.

Producers deal with ever-changing parameters, and writers must learn to adjust accordingly. If the project leads decide to cut the bank lobby scene to create a better game, the writer must work with that new vision. In the aforementioned case it's important to focus on keeping the vital information (the voice cues that tell the player how to defeat Overcharge) and to create new lines that convey this data to the player succinctly (since the writer no longer has the benefit of the slower-paced bank lobby scene). Then the writer needs to find a way to work the banter and character development into another scene.

FORMATTING DIALOGUE

The process of recording dialogue is a complicated one, consisting of numerous moving pieces: writer, designer, director, sound designer, sound programmer, producer, and voice actor. There is also the question of a shifting story line, which is a given (unless the project is immune to changes to level design and character roster). Because of the sheer number of changes that transpire between project alpha and ship date, it's inevitable that changes to the story content will also occur, often at the last minute. This can result in reshoots, which means wasted time and money. Some of these complications can be ameliorated through careful documentation. In this section we'll examine ways to organize voice assets prior to, during, and after the voice shoot.

PASSIVE FORMAT

Much game content is written in the passive format, which resembles the format used by movies and television shows. This script is formatted to streamline the filmmaking process—Courier New font, wide margins, use of all-caps, lots of white space. It's easy to mark up during filming (see Figure 7.3 for an example). Script supervisors use the margins and white space to make necessary adjustments, and the large font and capitalized words make it easy to locate content in a hurry. This is a result of the way movies are made. The term *passive* refers to the audience's level of participation while experiencing passive media: the audience sits there and watches; they are spectators (as opposed to participants).

```
INT. FIRST CITY BANK - NIGHT

SENSEI grips his katana. ICE QUEEN and BULLETPOINT are standing
near the vault. Two guards have their pistols aimed at the door.
Everyone is waiting for OVERCHARGE to attack. PLAYER is in the
middle of the room, facing the bank doors.

          GUARD
     Who-- who are these guys? The ones who are going tobe
     attacking.

          SENSEI
     They're called the Corporation. Their leader, Overcharge,
     was once the CEO of a major credit card company.

          BULLETPOINT
     And he gave it up to be a supervillain?

SENSEI sighs and shrugs.

          BULLETPOINT
     But why? The guy was rich, powerful-- I mean, seriously,
     Queenie, does that make sense to you?

          ICE QUEEN
     Don't call me Queenie. Hell, don't talk to me, period.

BULLETPOINT shivers.

          BULLETPOINT
     Ooh, someone get me a blanket. I'm getting the cold
     shoulder here--

SENSEI holds up a hand.

          SENSEI
     Quiet! I sense them -- they're outside!
```

FIGURE 7.3   The passive format employed in filmmaking.

Most games are nonlinear enough to render the passive format inappropriate. If one relies on the Hollywood rule of thumb that one page of script equals one minute of screen time, then theoretically, a 20-hour game would require a script 1,200 pages long. If the passive format is used to create noninteractive content, such as in-engine or prerendered cinematics, it is still unfeasible. The prerendered cinematic isn't filmed in real-time; it's created over days or weeks, usually by a number of people including artists, animators, producers, and designer. Therefore, a format created to facilitate rapid changes on the fly doesn't fit the process of cinematic creation. The white space and the large font serve no discernable purpose in this context.

However, if the intention is to create a text-based narrative (as opposed to a visual narrative structure, such as the use of sequential storyboards), then a modified version of the passive format can be of some use. By removing all of the marginal formatting, and by using a more efficient font (such as 10-point Times New Roman), this format can be useful. See Figure 7.4 for an example.

INT. FIRST CITY BANK - NIGHT

SENSEI grips his katana. ICE QUEEN and BULLETPOINT are standing near the vault. Two guards have their pistols aimed at the door. Everyone is waiting for OVERCHARGE to attack. PLAYER is in the middle of the room, facing the bank doors.

GUARD: Who-- who are these guys? The ones who are going tobe attacking.

SENSEI: They're called the Corporation. Their leader, Overcharge, was once the CEO of a major credit card company.

BULLETPOINT: And he gave it up to be a supervillain?

SENSEI sighs and shrugs.

BULLETPOINT: But why? The guy was rich, powerful-- I mean, seriously, Queenie, does that make sense to you?

ICE QUEEN: Don't call me Queenie. Hell, don't talk to me, period.

BULLETPOINT shivers.

BULLETPOINT: Ooh, someone get me a blanket. I'm getting the cold shoulder here--

SENSEI holds up a hand.

SENSEI: Quiet! I sense them -- they're outside!

FIGURE 7.4 A revised version of the passive format.

ACTIVE FORMAT: SCREEN/PLAY

An accounting tool can be a writer's strongest ally on a project. Programs such as Excel are particularly useful when documenting in-game dialogue, where multiple variables can make it a challenge to keep track of all possible dialogue threads. Taking into consideration all of the aforementioned dependencies and relationships, as well as the limitations that are encountered when using the passive format, the following structure can be of use when writing content for a game.

This format is called Screen/Play. It is one format among many, but it has been tested in the field and found to be an effective method of story content documentation. Other spreadsheet formats are available, but for reasons that will be explained in the following, Screen/Play covers all of the necessary bases. See Figure 7.5 for details.

ACTOR	CUE	CONTEXT	INFLECTION	AREA	EFFECT	FILENAME

FIGURE 7.5 Screen/Play, an active format spreadsheet.

Note that the cells all feature the same faint gray grid. This is visible when using the program but doesn't appear when the document is printed (which makes it harder to read unless the settings are changed). This is the default setting, so it will be necessary to create the grid around any cells with content. See Figure 7.6 for details.

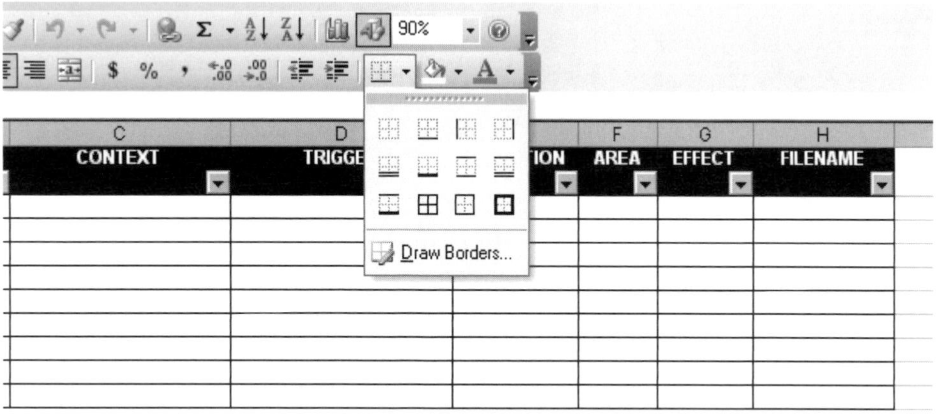

FIGURE 7.6   The grid doesn't appear on the printed page unless modified.

By highlighting the cells across the top (Actor, Cue, Context, Inflection, etc.) and selecting Data > Filter > Autofilter from the menu, it's possible to add filters to the headings. This will enable the writer to select specific kinds of data from the fields. See Figure 7.7 for an example.

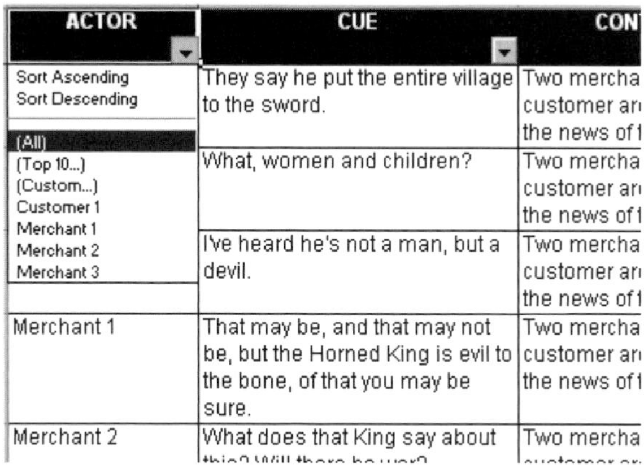

FIGURE 7.7   The filter is used to sort through the Actor column.

If, as in the above example, the spreadsheet is arranged chronologically, it will feature various actors talking to one another, but to isolate a single actor, one need only click on the small gray box in the Actor field and select that character's name. The same function can be applied to the other fields.

It's best to use the landscape format when setting up the page. This way, rather than print each row on multiple pages (Actor, Cue, Context, and Inflection on page 1; Location, Area, Effect, and Filename on page 2), one can get the whole row across a single page. This can be set up by selecting File > Page Setup/Page > Landscape. In the example below (Figure 7.8) the dotted lines indicate that the page will still be cut off at the end, and the spreadsheet will bleed over onto a second page. It will be necessary to adjust some of the row widths to get the spreadsheet to print on a single page.

TRIGGER	INFLECTION	AREA	EFFECT	FILENAME
Scripted cinematic 3A01	serious	3.1		m03-a01-mer01
Scripted cinematic 3A01	ominous	3.1	distortion	m03-a01-drg01
Scripted cinematic 3A01	serious	3.1	echo	m03-a01-nin01
Scripted cinematic 3A01	serious	3.1	on	m03-a01-drg02
Scripted cinematic 3A01	conf	3.1		m03-a01-mer02
Scripted cinematic 3A01	serious	3.1	echo	m03-a01-nin02
Scripted cinematic 3A01	serious	3.1	distortion	m03-a01-drg03

FIGURE 7.8 Adjusting the landscape setting will result in more text on the page.

Headings

Actor

In this area list the speaker. It's best to keep this as short as possible. Don't abbreviate to the point of being incomprehensible, but a last name will suffice if one is available. Make sure the heading maintains consistency throughout the document. If the script refers to a character as Jason in mission 2, he should not be cited as Jason Caldwell or Mr. Caldwell in mission 4. It's best to be meticulous in the search for typos in this field. If a name is misspelled and someone tries to select all of

Jason's lines, the results will not include Jasson or Jasn, and any dialogue attached to those typographical errors will not appear in the filtered search.

Cue

The actual spoken text appears in this field. The parenthetical notations should be kept out of this field, if possible, and should instead appear in the context field. Here, the voice actor will want to see raw text, not notations such as "(sadly)" or "(yelling)."

Context

Here, the writer should indicate the context for the line to the person reading the dialogue. It's best to keep this as brief as possible; chances are, the reader knows the basic setup (superheroes under attack in a bank lobby). The situation immediately preceding or prompting the dialogue is the issue at hand, and that's what should be conveyed in this field. Specific references to AI responses also belong in this column. For example, if the game plays a death scream when the "player_dead" A.I. state is invoked, the writer will want to cite "player_dead" in this column, along with a note for the voice actor who will be doing the screaming. The writer may also prefer to split this into two columns: one for the actors and one for the developers who will be integrating these assets into the game (scripters, programmers, and so on).

Inflection

In this field the writer should indicate the emotional state to the actor. The primary use of this field (other than the obvious) is to keep the volume level consistent across the various cues. Voice actors can read over 200 lines in a single session, and that can take its toll on the vocal cords. If the writer wants to get the most out of the voice recording session, he may want to group cues together by volume. For example, the session may start with whispers, then all conversational tones, and then proceed to any yelling or death screams.

It's best to keep an eye on the number of individual inflections. There's no need to get creative with adjectives; "angry" is good, and it's not necessary to describe the next cue as "furious" or "enraged" to avoid repetition. In fact, repetition is good, in that it's easier to use the Sort function (Data > Sort) to lump all the "whispered" cues together, then the "normal" cues, and then the "angry" cues. Unless the writer is going to direct the voice acting, it's best to give the voice actor a specific emotional state for the inflection. Any additional material should go in the Context field.

Location

Here, the writer should indicate where in the game the dialogue is taking place. This will vary, depending on the type of game. For example, in a mythocentric game such as *Morrowind* or *GTA3*, the writer may indicate a type of environment (indoor shop). For a logocentric game such as *Everything or Nothing*, the writer might indicate "Peru, The Ruined Tower."

Area

For the Area field, the writer should enter a number that can be sorted easily or arranged chronologically without too much fuss. It makes it easier to answer questions if someone asks how many voice cues character X has in mission 3, but, again, it depends on the type of game and on how rigidly structured the game experience is. The Area field might turn out to be superfluous, or it may prove necessary to add more fields to the spreadsheet. If the game is split up into multiple areas and levels and sections, additional columns may be necessary.

Effect

Here, the writer should indicate any effects that need to be applied to the voice cue. This includes radio futz, echoes, distortion, and so on. It's something that can be filtered at the end of the process and handed off to the sound designer or programmer to streamline the process for him. It can also be used by the quality assurance testers to ensure that all applicable effects have been added to the game. It's also helpful to voice actors, because there's a difference between yelling across a freeway at someone and yelling into a radio. The additional contextualization can give them more useful information during the recording session.

File Name

Once the overall number of voice cues has been established (dozens, hundreds, thousands), the writer can begin to plan a naming convention for the dialogue. If a convention was established during the development of a previous game, it might be viable to import that convention into this game. Otherwise, one will have to be created. A good naming convention possesses the following characteristics: (1) it's easily sorted in chronological order, (2) it tells the reader where the cue appears in-game, and (3) it leaves room for the additional cues that inevitably get recorded during pick-up sessions.

Character Field

When preparing for the voice shoot, it may prove beneficial to reformat the column that refers to the speaker. By renaming the Actor column to Character, and adding a Voice Actor column, the writer may be able to streamline the process of getting content into the voice actor's hands. Figure 7.9 shows the new field.

CHARACTER	ACTOR	CUE	CONTEXT	INFLECTION	AREA	EFFECT	FILENAME
King Arthur	David Johnson	Mordred, will you not listen to reason?	Mordred, Lancelot, and Arthur have gathered before the two armies to talk of a cease-fire.	anxious	1.2		m01-a02-art01
Lancelot	Mark Jones	Of course he won't, my lord. He's but a dog, a cur that--	Mordred, Lancelot, and Arthur have gathered before the two armies to talk of a cease-fire.	angry	1.2		m01-a02-lan01
King Arthur	David Johnson	Be silent. Mordred, what is your answer?	Mordred, Lancelot, and Arthur have gathered before the two armies to talk of a cease-fire.	angry	1.2		m01-a02-art02
Mordred	David Johnson	Is it peace that you want?	Mordred, Lancelot, and Arthur have gathered before the two armies to talk of a cease-fire.	curious	1.2		m01-a02-mor01
King Arthur	David Johnson	It is.	Mordred, Lancelot, and Arthur have gathered before the two armies to talk of a cease-fire.	serious	1.2		m01-a02-art03

FIGURE 7.9   Split the voice actor and character fields into separate columns.

Note that two different characters are played by the same voice actor. By using the drop-down menu for the Voice Actor, the writer can filter out all characters voiced by other actors. Filtering the list in this way can make it easier to estimate line counts and to verify the number of roles voiced by a single actor (depending on the arrangements, the developers may find that the voice actor can only voice a certain number of roles for a given fee).

In addition, by filtering the list, it's possible to print out all speaking parts from a given voice actor at one time. It's useful for the voice director to have all dialogue in hand, but an actor generally only needs his lines. Admittedly, it's good to know what the other characters are saying in a conversation, but that leads us to the Trigger field.

Trigger Field

Depending on the complexity of the game's narrative, the writer may want to divide the Context field into two fields: Context and Trigger (Figure 7.10). As explained above, Context establishes the situation for the voice actor. By adding the Trigger field, the writer can use the Context field to describe what's going on and the Trigger field to indicate exactly what has prompted the character to speak.

The Context field indicates the general situation, which tells the voice actor the overall tone and mood of this scene. The Trigger field describes a series of specific situations that fluctuate in intensity: a mumbled aside, a sarcastic one-liner, a line delivered in a normal tone of voice. By outlining the individual triggers, the writer can convey a little more information to the voice actors, further improving the chances of getting the desired delivery.

CHARACTER	CUE	CONTEXT	TRIGGER	INFLECTION	AREA	EFFECT	FILENAME
Merchant 1	I've heard rumors. They say that the lords of the realm have gathered in the capital to discuss their plans. Time will tell, I suppose.	Two merchants and a customer are discussing the news of the realm.	Player passes through trigger 3B.	serious	3.2		lev3_a2_3B6
Merchant 3	Good day, my lord. Some fine weapons we've got here. Take a look.	The player has walked into a merchant's tent.	Player enters tent 24.	normal	3.2		lev3_a2_001

FIGURE 7.10 The Context and Trigger fields are separated into two columns.

Line Choice Field

Once the developers are in the studio and the voice actors are recording their lines, there will probably be several takes the developers will need to choose among. The actors will probably record at least two or three takes for each line of dialogue, just to ensure that at least one of them fits well with the game's vision.

Depending on how many people are involved (writers, designers, producers, directors), the developers may wind up with conflicting ideas about which take was the best. In the Line Choice field (Figure 7.11), the writer can allot a small amount of space for handwritten picks.

CHARACTER	ACTOR	CUE	CONTEXT	INFLECTION	AREA	EFFECT	FILENAME	LINE CHOICE
King Arthur	David Johnson	Mordred, will you not listen to reason?	Mordred, Lancelot, and Arthur have gathered before the two armies to talk of a cease-fire.	anxious	1.2		m01-a02-art01	2
Lancelot	Mark Jones	Of course he won't, my lord. He's but a dog, a cur that--	Mordred, Lancelot, and Arthur have gathered before the two armies to talk of a cease-fire.	angry	1.2		m01-a02-lan01	3
King Arthur	David Johnson	Be silent. Mordred, what is your answer?	Mordred, Lancelot, and Arthur have gathered before the two armies to talk of a cease-fire.	angry	1.2		m01-a02-art02	1
Mordred	John Smith	Is it peace that you want?	Mordred, Lancelot, and Arthur have gathered before the two armies to talk of a cease-fire.	curious	1.2		m01-a02-mor01	3
King Arthur	David Johnson	It is.	Mordred, Lancelot, and Arthur have gathered before the two armies to talk of a cease-fire.	serious	1.2		m01-a02-art03	2

FIGURE 7.11 Developers can mark their choices in the Line Choice field.

Unnecessary Fields

Not everyone involved with voice recording is going to need access to all of the fields. For example, voice actors don't really need to see the File Name field or the Line Choice field. These aren't relevant to their work. So, once there's a master list, and the actors are ready to begin the recording process, the writer may want to create customized printouts for the principal players.

For voice actors, the Character/Cue/Context/Trigger/Inflection layout, illustrated in Figure 7.12, works best.

CHARACTER	CUE	CONTEXT	TRIGGER	INFLECTION
Odin	I will face Ymir alone.	Odin approaches the cave of the frost giants.	Player approaches Frost Gate.	confident
Vili	This is folly -- he will destroy you!	Vili is afraid that his brother will be killed.	Player moves through Frost Gate.	anxious
Odin	Then that will be my fate.	He is not afraid to die in battle.	Player moves through Frost Gate.	serious
Ymir	Who is this that disturbs my meditation?	Someone has just entered his chamber uninvited, and will probably have to die.	Player enters Hall of Ice.	angry
Odin	I am Odin. I have come here to battle you, frost giant.	He issues his challenge before attacking, because he's honorable.	Player nears Throne of Ice.	serious
Ymir	Then you shall die!	Ymir is enraged by Odin's arrogance.	Ymir stands up.	angry

FIGURE 7.12   This layout features only the information required by the voice actor.

The Character field is important, because a single voice actor can perform numerous roles at a single voice shoot. The cue is the line of dialogue that's being spoken, so that's obviously vital. Context and trigger explain the scenario, and inflection guides the performance.

For game designers or sound designers who implement the audio files into the game's editing tool, the Character/Cue/Trigger/Location/Area/Effect/File Name layout, illustrated in Figure 7.13, works well:

CHARACTER	CUE	TRIGGER	LOCATION	AREA	EFFECT	FILENAME
Merchant 1	I've heard rumors. They say that the lords of the realm have gathered in the capital to discuss their plans. Time will tell, I suppose.	Player passes through trigger 3B.		3.2		lev3_a2_3B6
Merchant 3	Good day, my lord. Some fine weapons we've got here. Take a look.	Player enters tent 24.		3.2		lev3_a2_001

FIGURE 7.13   The designer layout, which focuses on the scripting process.

In any case, the writer will want to base the customized spreadsheet on the needs of the person in question. Otherwise, he delivers a great deal of useless information that clutters up the spreadsheet, robbing it of its usefulness.

Strong and inflexible naming conventions for the spreadsheet's file name are invaluable. The writer doesn't want to accidentally copy over the master spreadsheet with one of the customized variants. It's important to be sure that the master version, with all information and fields, is given a name clearly indicating that it's the master (such as voice-cues-final_master.xls). All role-specific variants should be labeled as such (for example, voice-cues-final_voice-actors.xls or voice-cues-final_sound-designer.xls). This information needs to be communicated to all team members involved in the voice-recording process. It's also important to establish rules regarding modifications to the spreadsheet. Changing a single line of dialogue can create a ripple effect of confusion later down the line. Any changes made must be made to the master list first and then to all role-specific variants.

Formatting Text Size

The writer may want to adjust the text font, depending on who's going to be using the spreadsheet. For the master copy, it's likely that the writer will use a smaller text size, because if it's being read on a monitor, the reader can always zoom in, and if it's being printed out, all the columns should appear on a single page. Therefore, a font size of 8 or 9 is advisable.

For voice actors, the writer should use a larger font size. For one thing, there are fewer columns, so larger text will fit. Furthermore, the voice actors are going to be reading text off a page, typically while getting into character. They may close their eyes, hunch over, gesture, or recoil while speaking. It adds a lot to the performance, and it's much easier for them to do this when they can look down, glance at the line of dialogue, and immediately commit it to memory. The writer can facilitate this process and get a better delivery by using large, easy-to-read text.

After highlighting the text that needs to be formatted, the writer can right-click on a cell and select Format Cells and then click on the Font tab or use the drop-down menu (Format > Cells > Font). See Figure 7.14 for more information.

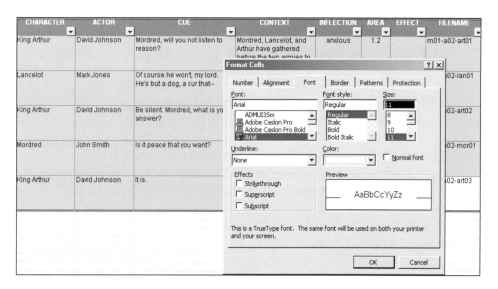

FIGURE 7.14   The text size has been formatted.

In some cases the writer may want to render the text in the cells as scalable, shrinking to fit the cell (done with Format Cells > Alignment > Shrink to fit). This way the writer can fit more information onto a page. The risk is that the text may be shrunk to the point where it's illegible. See Figure 7.15 for an example of scaled text.

CHARACTER	CUE	CONTEXT	TRIGGER	INFLECTION
Odin	I will face Ymir alone.	Odin approaches the cave of the frost giants.	Player approaches Frost Gate.	confident
Vili	This is folly -- he will destroy you!	Vili is afraid that his brother will be killed.	Player moves through Frost Gate.	anxious
Odin	Then that will be my fate.	He is not afraid to die in battle.	Player moves through Frost Gate.	serious
Ymir	Who is this that disturbs my meditation?	Someone has just entered his chamber uninvited, and will probably have to die.	Player enters Hall of Ice.	angry
Odin	I am Odin. I have come here to battle you, frost giant.	He issues his challenge before attacking, because he's honorable.	Player nears Throne of Ice.	serious
Ymir	Then you shall die!	Ymir is enraged by Odin's arrogance.	Ymir stands up.	angry

FIGURE 7.15   Scalable text may prove hard to read but will shrink to fit in the cell.

Paper Size

The writer can change the paper size to accommodate additional columns or larger font size. Click on File > Page Setup > Paper Size and select Legal to switch to 11" x 14". Don't forget to set the page to Landscape layout (File > Page Setup > Landscape). Legal-size paper can be particularly useful when printing the master list. For example, if the writer wants to go over all story content with all involved members of the development team (designers, sound designers, sound programmers, producers, and so forth), he may want to use the legal size.

Recasting On Short Notice

The developers may decide to recast some of the characters. To change the Actor field, or any other field, there's a shortcut that can save some time. First, the writer should delete one of the values in a field and add the new value. After that, he can copy the new value to the clipboard, highlight all instances of the given value, and finally paste the new value in. For example, if replacing Jack Smith with Joe Schmoe, first delete Jack from one of the fields and type Joe Schmoe. Highlight Joe Schmoe and select copy (Ctrl-C) and then highlight all instances of Jack Smith and paste (Ctrl-V).

File Name Issues

When creating file names, the writer may want to come up with something that's easy to recognize visually. It should be concise, and it should reflect the game's level structure. For instance, *King Arthur: Fall of Avalon* employs the following file names (Figure 7.16):

CHARACTER	CUE	CONTEXT	TRIGGER	INFLECTION	AREA	EFFECT	FILENAME
King Arthur	Mordred, will you not listen to reason?	Mordred, Lancelot, and Arthur have gathered before the two armies to talk of a cease-fire.	Scripted cinematic 1A02.	anxious	1.2		m01-a02-art01
Lancelot	Of course he won't, my lord. He's but a dog, a cur that--	Mordred, Lancelot, and Arthur have gathered before the two armies to talk of a cease-fire.	Scripted cinematic 1A02.	angry	1.2		m01-a02-lan01
King Arthur	Be silent. Mordred, what is your answer?	Mordred, Lancelot, and Arthur have gathered before the two armies to talk of a cease-fire.	Scripted cinematic 1A02.	angry	1.2		m01-a02-art02
Mordred	Is it peace that you want?	Mordred, Lancelot, and Arthur have gathered before the two armies to talk of a cease-fire.	Scripted cinematic 1A02.	curious	1.2		m01-a02-mor01
King Arthur	It is.	Mordred, Lancelot, and Arthur have gathered before the two armies to talk of á cease-fire.	Scripted cinematic 1A02.	serious	1.2		m01-a02-art03
Mordred	Then there will never be peace between us, father.	Mordred, Lancelot, and Arthur have gathered before the two armies to talk of a cease-fire.	Scripted cinematic 1A02.	angry	1.2		m01-a02-mor02
King Arthur	Then let there be war.	Mordred, Lancelot, and Arthur have gathered before the two armies to talk of a cease-fire.	Scripted cinematic 1A02.	serious	1.2		m01-a02-art04

FIGURE 7.16 This series of filenames is developed based on order of appearance in the game.

- m01-a02-art01
- m01-a02-lan01
- m01-a02-art02
- m01-a02-gue01
- m01-a02-art03
- m01-a02-mor01
- m01-a02-art04

Let's look at the naming convention here. First, the game consists of a series of missions, each segmented into areas (two or three areas per mission). There are numerous speakers in each mission. The filenames indicate that they're taking place in mission 1 (m01), area 2 (a02), and then each filename ends with an indication of who's talking (Arthur, Lancelot, Mordred). Since each character has fewer than 100 speaking parts in a given section, but more than 9, a two-digit number next to the three-letter identifier is necessary. The game's parameters dictate the naming convention.

Locating and Choosing Alternates

Depending on how the voice data is going to be processed, the writer may wind up with alternates. For example, during the recording of *King Arthur: Fall of Avalon* the voice actor recorded the line, "Stand your ground, knave!" three times. The team decided on the first take, but the other two were kept just in case. The first take was named m01-a02-lan01. The alternates were m01-a02-lan01A and m01-a02-lan01B. During play-testing, it was decided that the first take, which sounded great in the studio, just didn't work in the game, because it didn't sound aggressive enough. The developers decided to plug in one of the alternates, specifically, m01-a02-lan01B. There are two ways to handle a situation like this:

1. Rename m01-a02-lan01B to m01-a02-lan01–(in short, drop the B) and copy over the first take. This works well, provided that a backup of the first take is kept somewhere (and not just copied over). After all, the team might change their minds again later, and it's best to keep options open until the game is on store shelves.
2. Keep the filename for m01-a02-lan01B, but make sure both the scripting tool and the documentation reflect the change—the addition of the letter B. This requires meticulous attention to detail, because if the documentation doesn't accurately reflect the change, the game testers might flag the voice cue as a bug. If the designers don't make the change in the scripting tool, the game will pull up the wrong file, ignoring the alternate. See Figure 7.17 for details.

CHARACTER	CUE	CONTEXT	TRIGGER	INFLECTION	AREA	EFFECT	FILENAME
Lancelot	Stand your ground, knave!	Combat yell.	Player character attacked by brigands.	angry	1.2		m01-a02-lan01
Lancelot	Stand your ground, knave!	Combat yell.	Player character attacked by brigands.	angry	1.2		m01-a02-lan01B
Lancelot	Stand your ground, knave!	Combat yell.	Player character attacked by brigands.	angry	1.2		m01-a02-lan01C

FIGURE 7.17   Alternate voice cues.

SUMMARY

Each game features its own development process and documentation standards, but by studying the way other developers interact with story design and by considering the needs of the project, the writer can create an appropriate format for dialogue that will be easily integrated into the game's production process. In this chapter we examined the structure of the development team and studied active format documentation.

8 Creating Cinematics

In This Chapter

- Prerendered Cinematics
- Scripted Cinematics

The process of cinematic creation involves the entire development team: writers, designers, artists, programmers, and producers. The end result of the cinematic process is a short film that produces a narrative experience for the player, be it entertaining, informative, suspenseful, or dramatic. Therefore, the writer must be as involved as possible in the process of creation and should try to shepherd the cinematic through the stages of development.

Prerendered cinematics are animated and rendered by a team of artists, whereas scripted cinematics are generally created by game designers in a scripting editor. Prerendered cinematics are created and saved as video files, whereas scripted cinematics are produced in real time, just like scripted events during gameplay (Figure 8.1).

Prerendered	Scripted
Created using specialized program	Created using scripting editor
Graphics superior to in-game	Graphics same as in-game
May be developed in-house or by an external vendor	Created by game designers

FIGURE 8.1   Prerendered versus scripted cinematics.

PRERENDERED CINEMATICS

The overall concept should begin as a presentation of content and materials. The writer needs to consider the elements that will be necessary to create the cinematic, for example, characters, locations, objects, weapons, and vehicles. What is the scope of the scene? Who will be in it? What will they be doing? What are the core elements the player will see while the cinematic is playing? The writer must also determine the purpose of the content. Why is the player watching? What are the goals of the cinematic? It's possible that the scene is intended to elicit a mood, such as excitement or awe. For instance, the introduction to *Marvel: Ultimate Alliance* shows Captain America, Wolverine, and the other heroes tearing through an army of evil robots while hurtling through the air atop a gigantic S.H.I.E.L.D. helicarrier. The camera zooms around as the characters engage the enemy, resulting in massive explosions and satisfyingly crushing impacts. The resulting spectacle sets the tone for the rest of the game. The cinematic may also be used to establish the core narrative, which will then be continued throughout the game in installments. For example, in *SOCOM™ 3*, the intro cinematic shows General Heydar Mahmood, one of the game's villains, giving a speech to his people. The speech culminates with the execution of a civilian delegate on a mission of peace. As the game progresses, further cinematics show the depth of Mahmood's cruelty and megalomania but also establish his reactions to the player's successful completion of each mission. In this way, the player becomes enmeshed in the overall narrative.

Cinematics can also reveal information about the player character. In *Prince of Persia: Warrior Within*™ the opening cinematic reveals that the prince has undergone drastic changes since *Prince of Persia: The Sands of Time*™. Exhausted from fleeing the relentless Dahaka, the Prince is dark, sullen, and angry, a far cry from his more optimistic and cheerful persona in the earlier game (though in *Prince of Persia: The Two Thrones*™, the next installment in the series, this personality change is further explained as a result of the Prince's exposure to the Sands of Time).

It is also a good idea to begin calculating the total amount of cinematic footage. The writer should begin to consider the number of cinematics and the duration of each. If the cinematics are intended to establish the main character's persona and then build up to a dramatic personality change halfway through the game, the cinematic structure will need to reflect this design decision. It will not be sufficient for the game to begin with a 15-second intro cinematic that's followed up five levels later by another short scene. This structure won't devote enough time to establishing the main character's personality, so the expected dramatic personality change will be robbed of any impact. This doesn't meant that every level has to be accompanied by a four-minute intro, but it does mean that the developers will have to consider a lengthy intro that establishes the character's personality, along with other cinematics later in the game that continue to reinforce this identity, setting up the shocking change later.

There are no hard and fast rules for calculating the cost of cinematic sequences, because each studio has its own expenses and price. However, it's never too early to begin the discussion of budget with the game's producer. If the game is a story-driven title whose cinematic sequences are vital to the game's appeal (and therefore sales), the writer will doubtless be able to propose the kind of stunning, visually rich cinematic that opens games like *Final Fantasy XII* or *World of Warcraft*®. However, an action-driven game with a relatively simple narrative structure may only warrant a few minutes of prerendered cinematic footage, which the writer must parcel out over the course of a 10- or 15-hour game experience. If the writer wants to establish the main characters and impress the core concept of the game onto the player, then a pair of cinematics that bookend the game may suffice: one serves as the introduction and gets the player excited about the gameplay, and the other serves as a reward (and conclusion) when the player has completed all of the levels. For example, *Twisted Metal: Black®* establishes the player character's backstory in a cinematic, and the completion of the game results in another cinematic that reveals that character's fate. Because there are several player characters to choose from in the game, there are numerous intro cinematics, but the game's developers wisely reused certain resources (such as the establishing shot of Blackfield Asylum seen in all of the characters' intro cinematics). The writer may instead elect to begin every level with a brief prerendered cinematic, giving the player an opportunity to catch his breath before proceeding to the next area.

During the concept stage, the documentation of all necessary assets will save considerable time later on. If the writer outlines a concept for cinematic sequences that requires a few dozen character models, but later discovers that the cinematic team will only have the time (or budget) to create 20 models, then the writer will be better equipped to make the necessary adjustments to the documentation to achieve the stated goals. See Figure 8.2 for a sample concept document.

Title	"Wrath of the Green Dragon"
Function	Level 3 intro cinematic
Overview	While waiting for the arrival of the Green Dragon (Vexalyss), Merlin sees a trio of brigands set upon a traveler. He rushes to the man's aid, but the man transforms into the Green Dragon and kills all three men in a painful and grotesque manner. Merlin tries to stop him from devouring the third brigand while still alive, but Vexalyss says that if Merlin interrupts, they will become enemies. Merlin turns away as the man is devoured. Then Vexalyss presents Merlin with his Third Quest.
Goals	Introduce Vexalyss, establish his cruelty; show contrast between Merlin and Vexalyss.
Characters	5 character models - Vexalyss, Merlin, Brigand 1, Brigand 2, Brigand 3
Locations	A forest in the Western Reaches
Objects	4 - Merlin's staff, Brigand's sword (3)

FIGURE 8.2 A concept document for a series of cinematics.

SCREENPLAY

Once the concept has been established and green-lit, the writer needs to begin the process of creating the screenplay, which will serve as the basis for the voice-recording spreadsheet, the storyboards, and the animatics. Prior to writing the screenplay, the writer must settle on a format. Because of the linear nature of the cinematic sequence and its resemblance to film or television many writers employ the standard Hollywood script format (Figure 8.3) when writing the screenplay for a prerendered cinematic. As mentioned in Chapter 5, the Hollywood format assumes working conditions that are not applicable to the game industry, such as the need for on-the-spot rewrites (which necessitate wide margins) and the need to prompt an actor while filming (which necessitates the use of centered dialogue, headed by all-caps).

```
PLAYER passes through trigger 3B, where MERCHANT 1 and MERCHANT 2
are discussing the news of the realm with CUSTOMER 1.

            MERCHANT 1
    They say he put the entire village to the sword.

            MERCHANT 2
    What, women and children?

            CUSTOMER 1
    I've heard he's not a man, but a devil.

            MERCHANT 1
    That may be, and that may not be, but the Horned King is
    evil to the bone, of that you may be sure.

            MERCHANT 2
    What does that King say about this? Will there be war?

            MERCHANT 1
    I've heard rumors. They say that the lords of the realm
    have gathered in the capital to discuss their plans. Time
    will tell, I suppose.

PLAYER enters tent 24, where he is greeted by MERCHANT 3.

            MERCHANT 3
    Good day, my lord. Some fine weapons we've got here. Take a
    look.
```

FIGURE 8.3   The Hollywood script format.

However, owing to its relative familiarity to most members of a development team, the format is widely used despite its limitations. If the writer is trying to keep track of resources while documenting the story content in a prerendered cinematic, the Hollywood format is less than useful and will probably require an additional document to supplement the story content, such as a spreadsheet that breaks down the necessary assets used in the cinematic (Figure 8.4).

Title	"Wrath of the Green Dragon"
Function	Level 3 intro cinematic
Characters	5 character models - Vexalyss, Merlin, Brigand 1, Brigand 2, Brigand 3
Locations	A forest in the Western Reaches
Objects	4 - Merlin's staff, Brigand's sword (3)

FIGURE 8.4 An outline of necessary assets for the prerendered cinematic in Figure 8.3.

The Hollywood format also makes it harder to keep track of the number of lines spoken and the number of characters featured in a scene. This will also require the use of additional documentation so that the writer can more easily plan for subsequent voice shoots or character model creation.

By employing the Screen/Play method, or an alternate spreadsheet format, the writer can communicate all of this data to all members of the development team with a single document. The document should include the following information: the characters featured in a scene, their lines of dialogue (if any), the accompanying action, camera movements, special effects, audio content, and significance (as discussed in the concept section). If the writer is concerned that certain story elements may be risky, the document can also list alternates. For example, if one of the characters uses an expletive, and the game's rating remains uncertain, then the writer can include an alternate in the spreadsheet, along with a note about the ratings issue. The writer might also include a note about a particularly elaborate explosion that results in large-scale destruction to a building explaining that if the budget cannot accommodate the widespread destruction described in the document, then an explosion that kills a certain character will suffice. The important thing is that character X needs to die.

The description of action in this screenplay must be realistic. That is, the writer's explanation of events must be concrete and specific and must be so precise that any reader should be able to visualize the events described. Simply indicating a character's emotional state is risky, because there are many ways to interpret this information, and the end result may not be what the writer had anticipated. Instead of indicating that the character speaks angrily, the writer should document the specific actions the character takes (slamming a door, jabbing at someone's chest with her index finger). It's also pointless to discuss a character's mood in detail, unless that information is going to be communicated directly to the player in some way. For example, a cinematic screenplay that describes how the main character "turns away, overcome with remorse at the thought of his crimes" will result in confusion and complication. How are the cinematic artists supposed to know what remorse looks like to the writer? There are many ways to turn away, but there's no way to be sure that they will deliver the correct body language and posture unless the writer specifically delineates the actions or sounds that constitute the cinematic's story content. Here's a solid rule of thumb: read it out loud to someone and tell them to picture it. It's easy to picture someone turning away, or hanging his head, or slamming a door, but picturing someone being filled with remorse is subjective and therefore can't necessarily be visualized without some interpretation on the part of your listener. Purge your screenplay of all such elements, and your prerendered cinematics will be stronger for it.

When documenting your cinematics, it may prove useful to establish a single master list that can be sorted or organized according to cinematic, or level, or voice actor, or audio effect (such as radio squelch or echo). When the cinematic screenplay has been approved and production has begun, that documentation will enable the writer to put together the casting information more rapidly, thereby facilitating the voice recording process. Figure 8.5 shows a master list of resources like the one described above.

CHARACTER	LINES	DESCRIPTION
Merlin	500	Male, early thirties, strong and authoritative voice, but compassionate. English accent.
Talerios	200	Male, early twenties, sounds nervous and timid. English accent.
Vexalyss	150	Male, mid-forties, powerful voice. Sounds capable, arrogant, and a little cruel. Scottish accent.
Lady of the Lake	100	Young female, mysterious and seductive voice. English accent.
Brigand 1	50	Male, tough and nasty. English accent.
Brigand 2	50	Male, tough and nasty. English accent.
Brigand 3	50	Male, tough and nasty. English accent.
Town Guard	50	Male, thirties or forties. English accent.
TOTAL	1150	

FIGURE 8.5   A spreadsheet indicating necessary resources for voice recording.

Once the screenplays for all of the prerendered cinematics have been written, the approval process should begin.

APPROVAL

Once the concept has been established and a screenplay written, the cinematic content will doubtless go through some kind of approval stage, resulting in the green light to proceed with storyboarding or animatic creation. During the approval stage numerous developers may be involved in the evaluation of the screenplay, including leads, producers, managers, and directors. Depending on the studio's relationship with the cinematic team, they may also have some say in the process. Ultimately, the purpose of the approval stage is to ensure that the content is appropriate and that the scope is viable. If the writer has clearly established both content and scope during the concept phase, the approval stage will proceed more smoothly, although there are no guarantees that the material will pass muster on the first try. Rewrites are, after all, inevitable.

Role Definition

The roles of each participant in the approval process should be clearly defined. The writer will be receiving a great deal of review and critique during the process of creating cinematics, so it's important to decide how the feedback will be handled and who will be doing what. With numerous developers offering input, the writer will be bombarded with information and instructions, some of it contradictory. Having a single contact person who interacts with the writer, be it a lead designer or producer or other member of the development team, will help immeasurably.

Feedback

A well-defined feedback loop can save the writer much time and confusion during the approval process. Ideally, the writer is a part of the evaluation process and can serve as an advocate for the material presented (more on that later), but if the material is reviewed elsewhere, the feedback given to the writer should be succinct, specific, impartial, and internally consistent. While this is also the case with feedback presented in person, spoken feedback can be discussed at the meeting, resulting in an explicit understanding among all involved parties (those giving the feedback and the writer, who is receiving it). If the feedback is presented to the writer as a written document (not unlikely, considering the prevalence of multistudio development), the four criteria listed above (brevity, specificity, impartiality, and consistency) should guide the documentation of all evaluation and critique. See Figure 8.6 for an overview.

Brevity	Short and to-the-point
Specificity	Precise and informative
Impartiality	Focused on stated goals
Consistency	Organized into one document

FIGURE 8.6 Characteristics of good feedback.

Brevity

Complicated feedback will only delay the process by causing the writer to ask questions to clarify the key points. Feedback, like all documentation, should be as concise as possible (Figure 8.7).

It seems like the main character in this cinematic could use some "beefing up" -- what can we do to make him more "macho"? If we could add bulk to the character, giving him larger muscles, or even something as standard as stubble or a steely-eyed glare, we could make him seem a little tougher, a little more intimidating. On the other hand, we may not have time to address the visual aspect, so we might just want to consider doing something with his voice. He just doesn't sound dangerous -- he sounds a little flat, and maybe even hesitant. Can we recast at this stage? If so, we should definitely focus on a deeper, more gravelly voice.	Main character has small frame, but should be more muscular. Voice sounds flat and hesitant -- should be recorded again, possibly with another voice actor.

FIGURE 8.7 Complicated feedback versus brief and to-the-point critique.

Specificity

If the feedback does not identify the precise elements that need to be changed or give the writer a specific area to revise, it will only produce more questions and additional meetings. Feedback like "it's not dramatic enough" or "the dialogue seems inappropriate" doesn't furnish the writer with enough information to adequately guide the revision process (Figure 8.8).

Explosion is a let down	The explosion at 1:34 should be bigger
Kyla's arm looks weird	Kyla's left forearm is larger than her right
Voicework doesn't thrill me	The voice actor for Kyla should be recast
Music starts late	The music starts at 1:23, should start at 1:19

FIGURE 8.8   Specific feedback will speed up the revision process.

Impartiality

Though it's tempting to express one's own convictions during the development process, all feedback should remain as impartial as possible. The game is intended to appeal to a broad audience, not a single developer, and all notes to the writer should be as neutral as possible in order to avoid confusion and mixed messages. By focusing on the stated goals, and by presenting the feedback as a series of factual data points, the developers can ensure that the writer understands what went wrong and what needs to be improved. For example, telling the writer, "I didn't like the bad guy because he seemed kind of weak" is not nearly as valuable as pointing out that "the goal of the cinematic was to create an intimidating and monstrous archenemy, but in this scene, he asks his subordinates for advice several times, which makes him look indecisive and weak."

Consistency

If the writer receives conflicting feedback from multiple sources, this necessitates tracking down every person involved and sorting out exactly what the consensus is (which will probably require additional meetings and emails). Rather than streamlining the process, this muddies the waters and results in delays and frustration. While feedback will no doubt come from several developers during the approval process, a single person should be appointed to filter and organize the feedback into a single document. This point of contact will be able to cut down on repetition and can ensure that the notes are all consistent. Enabling a single person to serve as the intermediary between the writer and all those involved in the feedback process also makes it easier for the writer to receive information. Rather than sorting through numerous emails, looking for a necessary action item, the writer can consult the single (and final) list of feedback, using it as a checklist while making corrections, additions, or subtractions to the screenplay.

This is especially useful once the work is done, because the revised work can then be compared to the feedback, and this means that less time will be spent determining if the writer was able to complete all of the requested tasks properly.

Advocacy

During the approval process many agendas are being served. The producer will doubtless want to ensure that the cinematics are completed according to schedule and under budget, the art lead will no doubt be hoping for high-quality movies that complement the game's artistic style, and the marketing team will probably want assets that could be used to advertise the game on television or online. However, it is the writer's mission to ensure a high standard for the narrative content of the cinematic sequences, and it will be up to him to guarantee that the cinematics advance the story content correctly and that they match the core vision established during preproduction. During the loop of feedback and revision, it is easy to lose sight of what the cinematics are intended to accomplish, and not everyone shares the writer's understanding of the game's story line. Thus, it will be up to him to make certain that the final draft of the screenplay contributes something meaningful to the game's narrative.

Turnaround Time

During the approval stage the writer and the approval team must establish realistic turnaround times for feedback and for revised versions. If the process is such that the approval team gives feedback and then leaves the writer to his own devices, the only deadline that needs to be set is a timetable for the feedback. However, it's more likely that the feedback will result in a revised version of the screenplay that must be submitted for another round of review and critique and so on until final approval has been given.

To keep the machinery moving, all parties should clearly define how long it will take to receive feedback and how long the writer will have to review feedback, solicit clarification, and rewrite the screenplay. Without this information, the vagaries of game development will take their toll on the review process, and suddenly everyone will realize that it's been a month since the screenplay was submitted, and nobody knows what's going on.

Group Read-Through

It's not uncommon to read through a game screenplay, but since many games feature thousands of lines of dialogue, it's not common to do a group read-through. Cinematics, on the other hand, usually amount to a few hours of content at most, so it's much more logical to read through the screenplay as part of the review and approval process. Furthermore, much game content is nonlinear, but a screenplay is easy enough to read through sequentially, given the structure of cinematics. There are a few things to keep in mind while reading through a cinematic screenplay, and if the writer can attend that meeting, to ensure that these conditions are met, it will save time and energy in the long run.

First, if the writer is present at the read-through, he should try to remain as flexible and impartial as possible during the reading. It's one thing to receive feedback in the form of an email that can be read at one's desk. It's another thing altogether to get that feedback directly while the group is reading one's screenplay. Getting defensive, however, will not result in a better game. It will only slow down the approval process and it will earn the writer a bad reputation among the developers. Remaining neutral and stoic is the best policy.

Second, the read-through cast should be assembled carefully. While the people in attendance may be decided beforehand, by dint of the project's hierarchy, the readers should be left to the writer's discretion. For example, if the programming director needs to be on hand to review the content, so be it, but if he's a self-styled comedian, he probably doesn't need to participate as a reader (unless the game in question is supposed to be funny). By casting someone wacky as the game's villain during the read-through, it's more or less guaranteed that the desired impact of the scenes will be lost. Of course, your average group of game developers isn't trained to read screenplays dramatically, so the read-through isn't going to elicit the same sense of wonder, tension, or excitement that the finished product will evoke, but you want to minimize the damage as much as possible by making sure the right people are performing in the read-through. Assign major speaking roles to those you feel most confident about, and don't hesitate to bring character notes or story synopses to the meeting if you feel that it will help. As the writer, you are the champion of the story, and the odds aren't always in your favor. Wield whatever you've got.

Third, you may not want to have a speaking role yourself. Instead, you may want to narrate the unspoken portions of the screenplay so that everyone understands what's going on as the dialogue's being spoken.

Asset Documentation

Part of the approval process deals with content, but another aspect of the process is the calculation of cost and resources needed. The more information you can provide at this stage, the easier it will be to get the vision through the gate. By preparing lists of assets and events (Figure 8.9), you give the approval team the information they need to determine whether these cinematics are feasible given the project's parameters. Consider preparing a document that outlines the total number of character models, vehicles, locations, and special effects depicted in the screenplay.

Cinematic	Function	Characters	Objects
1A	Level 1 intro	Merlin, Talerios	Merlin's staff
1B	Level 1 outro	Merlin, Lady of the Lake	Merlin's staff, Lady's dagger
2A	Level 2 intro	Merlin, Vexalyss, Brigand 1, Brigand 2, Brigand 3	Merlin's staff, Brigand's sword (3)
2B	Level 2 outro	Merlin, Vexalyss, Town Guard, manticore	Staff of Water, Guard's sword
3	Level 3 intro	Merlin, Talerios, Vexalyss	Staff of Water, Talerios's sword
4A	Level 4 intro	Talerios, Lady of the Lake	Talerios's sword, Lady's dagger
4B	Level 4 outro	Talerios, Vexalyss	Talerios's sword, Vexalyss' book
5	Level 5 intro	Merlin, Talerios, Vexalyss, Ogre 1, Ogre 2	Staff of Earth, Talerios's sword, Ogre's club (2)
6	Level 6 intro	Merlin, Vexalyss, Undead Talerios	Staff of Wind, Talerios's sword
7	Game outro	Merlin, Horned King, Vexalyss	Staff of Fire, Horned King's trident

FIGURE 8.9   Example of cinematic asset documentation.

STORYBOARDS

After the screenplay has received approval, the next step is the creation of the storyboards. Storyboards communicate the visual aspect and user experience more effectively than mere words on a page and therefore make it easier to sell the cinematic to members of the development team. Typically, a concept artist sketches the storyboards out as a series of still images that communicate action and motion from one scene to the next. Arrows and other indicators may be used to indicate the movement of characters on screen or of the camera itself (such as when zooming or panning). Sound effects and speech bubbles may be part of the images or they may be captioned at the bottom of each image (as in Figure 8.10). However, the captioned storyboard is easier to integrate into the animatic process, as will be described later.

 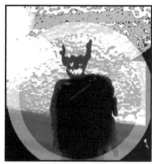 

The monster approaches Caldwell, and the beam from the flashlight throws its monstrous shadow on the wall.

Once Caldwell sees the shadow, the monster transforms into its true shape and attacks.

After it has been killed, its Apparition is Harvested by Caldwell, and the camera fades out.

FIGURE 8.10 Example of storyboards.

Storyboards are a means to an end, and not the end itself. Therefore, their schedules should be based on the amount of time needed to create a serviceable storyboard, not the amount of time needed to create an aesthetically pleasing storyboard. While it's a noble goal to ensure that the storyboards are artistic and attractive, the reality is that the first draft should simply indicate the location of characters and objects, as well as ancillary information such as motion or camera movement. It's also important to keep in mind that storyboards are not an actual game asset (though they may appear as a special feature), so their level of detail should depend on scheduling restrictions.

Cohesion

At this stage the concept art team may have already produced illustrations for the locations, characters, and objects in the game. If so, every effort should be made to ensure that the storyboards match these depictions so the development team has a more concrete handle on the game's look and feel. These storyboards will probably wind up in the hands of the cinematic team at some point, and the consistency in art styles will prove useful then as well. The more work that is done to establish continuity among the story assets, the better the finished product will be.

Review

Upon completion, the storyboards should be reviewed and approved, much like the screenplay for the cinematics. The methods of review vary from studio to studio but include the paper review, the museum-collision review, and the slideshow review. In each of these cases the writer will probably need to serve as the advocate for the story once more. Though more kinetic than the screenplay, the storyboard is still nothing more than a series of still images accompanied by text and will require a great deal of imagination on the part of the approval team. Imagine the storyboards for the jaw-dropping intro to *Onimusha 3* or *World of Warcraft*. The enthusiasm and vision of the writer and concept artist can go a long way toward selling the team on the cinematic vision.

The paper review consists of a group of developers sitting in a conference room, flipping through photocopied storyboards while the writer and/or concept artist explain the context for each panel. This approach is quick and easy and requires minimal work but lacks creative energy. It's hard to translate a series of images on a page into a dynamic short film.

The museum-collision review consists of taping the storyboards to the wall in a room and allowing the developers to walk down the wall, reading the cinematics as they go. The developers tend to become engrossed in their reading and, like clumsy museum-goers, tend to collide with one another when moving from one panel to the next (thus the name). The popularity of this review style is puzzling, as it hardly facilitates group discussion and makes it harder for the writer and concept artist to communicate with the developers. The only advantage to this style of review is that it does allow the developers to gather together and discuss panels in small clusters, a more informal approach than the paper review. However, ultimately, the museum-collision doesn't really communicate the necessary kinetic energy of the cinematic sequence.

The slideshow review requires a little bit of work on the part of the writer. First, he must get the storyboards from the concept artist in digital form and crop each panel to a uniform size (or as close as possible). Then, once the individual files are given sequential names and placed in a folder, the writer can select the first one and play it in a program like Windows Picture Viewer (which comes with most PCs). By selecting Start Slide Show, or by clicking on the forward arrow, the writer can show off the still images on a projection screen or laptop, giving the other developers a more kinetic presentation. Though probably not accompanied by any audio at this stage, the slideshow will nonetheless communicate more information about the cinematics than a mere stack of pages stapled together.

The preparation done for the slideshow review will serve the writer well in the next stage of development: the animatic sequence.

ANIMATICS

The animatic is a rough draft of the final cinematic and is intended to give the developers a more concrete idea of what the finished product will look and sound like. There are two types of animatic sequence: the flipbook animatic and the rough animatic.

Flipbook Animatic

This is a more elaborate version of the slideshow described in the preceding section. It is a movie file that is created using digital versions of the storyboards. Given the relative simplicity of the process, this is an animatic that the writer can create herself, given ample time and resources. First, the writer must get digital copies of all of the storyboards from the concept artist. After cropping each panel to a standard size (using Microsoft Paint, Adobe® Photoshop®, or some other image-manipulation program), the writer must create an animated slideshow for each cinematic sequence. The slideshows can be created with any movie-making software, such as Adobe Premiere®. Windows Movie Maker, which comes with Windows XP®, is easy to learn, and features all of the necessary functionality.

Once the writer has opened the program, he needs to insert all of the storyboard panels, in their correct order, into the file. By adjusting various options, the writer can adjust the speed of transition from one slide to the next; add effects such as pan, zoom, and blur; and even add audio to the file (more information is covered in the documentation for each software program; the help files for Windows Movie Maker are quite useful). If the writer wants to create an extremely elaborate slideshow, it's even possible to insert audio components, such as placeholder voice cues or music. The writer doesn't necessarily need the audio team's resources to achieve this goal; most computers feature a voice-recording software package of some kind, and with the use of a regular microphone, he can record placeholder voice cues and insert them into the file. Of course, if the writer has access to a sound team, as well as their library of music and sound effect files, then the audio accompaniment for the slideshow will be that much more powerful. Regardless of how far he wants to go, when the slideshow is complete, the writer can export it into a movie file, which can serve numerous purposes.

This slideshow presentation can also be used to introduce story content to other members of the development team early on. For those who are unfamiliar with a project's story line, this can deliver the idea more effectively than a written document or verbal communication. It can also help the cinematic team develop the rough animatic (described in the next section).

Once created, the slideshow animatic is easy to edit or revise, particularly when using Windows Movie Maker. Slides can be rearranged, cut, or added, and effects and transitions can be manipulated with a minimum of fuss. Exporting a new movie file requires only a few minutes, unless the number of slides is extremely high. By adjusting the time spent on an individual slide, the writer can adjust the pacing of the movie, and by adjusting the brightness, contrast, and other effects, the writer can adjust the look and feel of the movie.

As with the storyboards themselves, it's important to bear in mind that the animatic is a means to an end and is not part of the final product. Therefore, the writer should concentrate on getting the job done efficiently, not on creating an amazing movie that will wow the approval team. Of course, the higher the quality, the more impressive the flipbook animatic will be, but the writer is not a film-maker, and the slideshow is not a film. Likewise, the approval team should focus on the pacing and overall feel of the movie, as opposed to its cinematic merits. The time for critique will come later, when the cinematic team has produced a rough animatic for evaluation purposes.

The writer should also be ready to make considerable adjustments during this phase of development. Often, what sounds good on paper doesn't work when read aloud into a microphone, and if the flipbook animatic is accompanied by voice acting from members of the development team, the writer may find that some of the dialogue needs to be revised.

The dialogue should be handled as professionally as possible within the constraints of resources and schedule. If the writer works with the sound team and gets members of the development team to read dialogue for the flipbook animatic, the writer should treat it like an actual voice shoot: he should create voice notes, story summaries, and contextual documentation (as described in Chapter 9, Directing Voice Actors). Each of the speakers should be cast, and if the schedule permits, this should definitely include an audition phase. By matching each role with the best speaker possible, the writer will minimize the risk that the voice acting sounds cheesy or hokey. Admittedly, none of the speakers is likely to be a professional voice actor, but some programmers sound better than others. Commit to the high standard of quality, and the other developers will give the recording session more of their time and energy, resulting in a stronger audio accompaniment for the flip-book animatic.

Critical Elements

At this point in the process, the writer may wish to begin to introduce the concept of the critical element to the discussion. This is an essential piece of story information that's presented in the cinematic, which the player needs to know in order to complete the game. For example, in *Rise of Merlin*, the player character wields the Staff of Fire against the Red Dragon in level 9. The level 9 intro cinematic depicts Merlin receiving the Staff of Fire from the Lady in the Lake, along with instructions to destroy the Red Dragon. If this information is cut, the game's context is altered, if not outright damaged, and the writer will have to find another way to communicate this information to the player (probably requiring additional resources or changes to the schedule). By documenting this critical element, the writer gives the approval team the information they need to make the best decision possible for the game. Otherwise, they may cut portions of the cinematic later on, only to learn that they've created additional work and stress for the writer and other developers.

Other elements of the cinematic, such as the Red Dragon flying overhead (foreshadowing), Merlin's conversation with the Lady of the Lake (character development), and the pyrotechnics from the Staff of Fire (visual flair) can be sacrificed. They add something to the game, but their omission will only weaken a game's narrative—not damage it. It's important that the writer understand the difference when documenting the critical elements in a game's cinematics.

Rough Animatic

After the flipbook animatic has been created and approved, the cinematic team begins work on the rough animatic. The cinematic team may be in-house, or they may be external contractors. If they're external, it's in the developer's best interest to view their demo reel and a list of past clients. The writer may or may not be a part of this stage of the process, but if so, it will be useful to speak to past clients about creative direction and interaction with the cinematic team. In many games the bulk of the story is communicated through cinematics, so it's imperative that this process go as smoothly as possible.

The rough animatic is a video file that serves as a rough draft for the final version of the animatic. It's intended to convey the basic movement, pacing, camera work, and timing of the final product. As a result, early iterations of the rough animatic may substitute blocks and spheres for objects and characters in a game. The spaceship or dragon might be represented by a blue rectangle moving through the air, and the characters on the ground might be egg-shaped objects sliding around on a featureless plane. Once that early blocking phase has been completed, the cinematic team will begin to add more detail and specificity to the video until the cinematic is complete.

For example, later phases of the rough animatic will feature wire-frame objects and characters, then untextured models, and finally models with textures and animations. The camera will begin to zoom in and out, or pan, or change perspective as appropriate. Initially, the goal is to block out the space and give the developers an idea of the cinematic's look and feel, but with each new iteration, the cinematic team will approach the vision the developers have furnished.

The writer may find himself on the other side of the approval fence at this stage, as he may be expected to offer feedback and critique to the cinematic team. While it's important to avoid hurt feelings or misunderstandings, no one is served if the writer is too timid to give constructive criticism; the criteria for approval cited at the beginning of this chapter should inform the writer's feedback regarding the cinematics. As the work progresses, the writer should document specific elements of the animatic that accomplish (or fail to accomplish) the goals set out for each cinematic. Is the imagery exciting or funny or sad or frightening? If not, what elements are holding the cinematic back from realizing its stated objective? Attention should also be paid early on to technical issues, such as the placement of objects in the video. Are the characters facing the right way, playing the correct animations, and moving in the right direction?

AUDIO

The audio component contributes a great deal to a cinematic's effect on the player, so care must be taken during the creation of cinematic voice over. The writer will probably work with the sound design team on the audio design for cinematics. First, the team will need to replace the placeholder voice cues with actual voice cues. Second, the writer will need to verify that the cinematic studio incorporates the audio components properly and in the correct order (see Figure 8.11 for more information). Once the cinematic story components have been assembled, the voice shoot can begin. Depending on a studio's development process, the shoot for the cinematics may be combined with the shoot for other parts of the game, such as in-game dialogue, or the cinematic shoot may precede all other voice-recording sessions. More information is presented in the following chapter.

Audio Component Verification	
Are all of the voice cues audible?	Yes / No
Are the voice cues playing in the right order?	Yes / No
Were the correct versions of each cue used? In other words, make sure that the studio didn't mistakenly use an alternate.	Yes / No
Do the voice cues feature the correct effects, such as radio squelch or echo?	Yes / No
Are all of the voice cues playing at the correct volume level?	Yes / No

FIGURE 8.11   The writer should verify core information about cinematic audio.

SCRIPTED CINEMATICS

Scripted cinematics are rendered in real time, using the same scripting tools that are used to create gameplay. Their development is similar to the creation of prerendered cinematics. The key differences are resources and the scripting process.

RESOURCES

While prerendered cinematics are created using programs intended to facilitate the creation of computer-generated movies, most scripted cinematics are created using programs that were built to facilitate the creation of gameplay. This fundamental difference means the scripted cinematic is going to look a great deal like the gameplay itself (unlike the prerendered cinematic, which usually looks much more impressive than gameplay). It also means the game scripters are going to use a tool that's best suited for another purpose altogether.

Scripted cinematics tend to use existing resources, and though these new elements can be created expressly for use in a scripted cinematic, this will require additional work on the part of the development team. In other words, it's likely that the artist responsible for creating character models will be responsible for creating the models used in scripted cinematics, which is not necessarily true for the prerendered cinematics. For example, in *Rise of Merlin*, the player (Merlin) battles the Red Dragon. Both character models are part of the game's development schedule, and the character artists have created the models as instructed. However, the scripted cinematic that establishes the conflict between Merlin and the dragon also includes another character, the Seer. Since the character of the Seer is not featured in the gameplay, he was not originally part of the schedule for the character artists, and he'll have to be added to that schedule in order to appear in the scripted cinematics.

SCRIPTING PROCESS

Scripted cinematics require a dedicated team whose job it is to script the scenes according to the design document. The upshot of scripted cinematic development is that more control is given to the developers than is customary with the creation of prerendered cinematics (especially if the prerendereds are being developed externally). The downside of scripted cinematics is that the scripters may not have a background in filmmaking and may not be qualified to created dramatic or tension-filled cinematic sequences. No matter how good the scripted scenes in a game are, they usually can't compare with the prerendered content when it comes to emotional connection or drama.

Scripting Tools

The editor used to script cinematics may or may not feature all of the necessary options when development has begun. This is especially true in the case of a new intellectual property, because if the game being developed is a sequel, many issues were probably addressed and resolved during the previous iteration of the game. The writer's attention to detail during the early stages of development will help immeasurably at this stage. For example, if the writer has prepared a list of all necessary animations that will need to play during the scripted cinematics and can furnish that list to the programmers involved in developing the scripting editor, then it's more likely that those animations will be introduced into the editor in a timely fashion (meaning the designers responsible for scripting those sequences will have access to those animations when creating scripted cinematics). If the writer waits until the last minute to prepare and deliver this information, it could result in a considerable delay in the scripting process.

Other features may include camera controls (such as zoom or spline path) or special effects. By documenting the exact features that are needed and indicating which scene will require what features, the writer makes it easier for the team to determine what their priorities are. In a perfect world the scripting tool will include all of the requested features, but it's more likely that some will make it and some won't, meaning some scenes will have to be revised or eliminated altogether.

The writer may wind up learning how to script, if only to better communicate with the designers responsible for scripting the cinematics. In addition, later in the project, it may turn out that the writer will take ownership of any story defects, such as typographical errors in message text or misplayed voice cues in scripted cinematics. In either case the writer's ability to script will prove a powerful asset (for more information, see Chapter 12, Testing Story Content).

Challenges

The advantage to the scripted cinematic is that it's much easier to change and adjust content in real time, since there is no rendering process to speak of. Prerendered cinematics must be rendered before viewing, so there may be hours or days between new iterations. It's typically fairly easy to adjust a camera angle or the timing of a voice cue in a scripting editor, but there are some challenges the writer must address.

First, the writer must be able to access the scripted cinematics as needed; second, the story design documentation should match the game design documentation.

The scripted cinematics are easy enough to verify if they play at the beginning of a level. If, on the other hand, a scripted cinematic plays upon mission completion, then in order to verify that the camera angles, voice cues, and animations are all appropriate, the writer must play all the way through the level. This can be time-consuming and arduous, and the challenge is only compounded if there are numerous scripted cinematics throughout the level. It may be possible for the scripters to create temporary triggers that will allow the writer to watch all of the scripted cinematics at once without having to engage in gameplay. This is hardly the norm, however, and it is in the writer's best interest to find out from the producer if such temporary triggers could be added to the scripting editor. The time and energy required to add such a feature may save the entire development team more time and energy later on and will definitely ensure a higher level of quality for the scripted cinematics.

The story documentation may not match the game design documentation. Though the writer and designers would ideally work in tandem on aspects of game development, the reality is that the designers may leave the story content to the writer and may only make cursory mention of story events in their game design documents. The scripters may or may not be working from the story documents the writer has assembled; they may be using the design documents instead. Even if they're aware of the story documents, they may not be using the most recent versions when performing the scripting tasks. The writer should be sure to thoroughly document the content in each scripted cinematic and should be certain that all of the scripters are aware of the location of that document.

SUMMARY

The creation of cinematics requires work from all areas of game development, including story, design, art, and programming. To achieve high-quality cinematic sequences, the developers must approach the process in a methodical fashion, starting with concept and screenplay and proceeding through the stages of approval, storyboards, animatics, and audio integration. In this chapter we also discussed the differences between prerendered cinematics and scripted cinematics, as well as how writers can maximize the story potential of each type. Having covered the creation of this passive form, we can now move on to voice acting and then the integration of audio content into the gameplay experience.

DEVELOPER INTERVIEW

Erik Wolpaw, Writer, Valve
Psychonauts®, Half-Life 2: Episode One

WRITING FOR GAMES

I know that other types of writing are collaborative, but in game writing, you really need to work with designers. As you're creating the game, and it's play-tested, some things will work and some things won't work. You'll have to do a lot of spot-rewriting as you go. As a game writer, you're working in the service of the gameplay, instead of the other way around. Even on *Psychonauts*, which was story-driven, the story needed to support the gameplay, because ultimately, that's what people are interested in.

MAINTAINING PLAYER INTEREST

If you read a comic book or see a movie, you're paying for the story, but in some ways, when you're a game writer, you're almost intruding on what the audience is there for. The pressure is on to be to-the-point and entertaining.

At Valve, the story is an iterative process. If we find something that's not working, then we rewrite it and test it again, and we keep trying different things until it finally works. It's a bigger challenge at Valve than I had when working on *Psychonauts*, because *Psychonauts* had a more traditional narrative structure. You experienced some gameplay, then watched a cut-scene, then experienced some more gameplay. In that instance, it's easier to integrate story into the gameplay, because the game essentially stops while the cut-scenes are playing. At Valve the cut-scenes and gameplay are integrated, so the game never really stops. So, it's harder. One problem we've run into is that the scenes tend to go on too long. We did worry about that on *Psychonauts*, but the player can always skip a cut-scene by pushing a button. In Valve's games there's no cut-scene to skip, so you spend a lot of time iterating and evaluating the game. You bring testers in and see what they think, and you keep trying to make it shorter. You try to find the least amount of words to make the scene entertaining and informative.

PUNCH LINES

There's one piece of advice that I would offer an aspiring game writer, and there isn't much other advice that I would trust. This is something that Tim Schaeffer

→

taught me. Working on *Psychonauts* was the most depressing thing that I have ever done, because what happened was, it turned into a death grind. The game had a very troubled development cycle. So the game's supposed to be funny, and I wrote this funny stuff. At Double Fine, we all sat in this one big room, maybe 50 people in this open semi-circle.

Everyone would be playing the game, for several hours a day, and so these jokes would play again and again and again, in stony silence. After two years, the jokes that I had written two years earlier were no longer funny. After 10,000 times, they were the most hateful sound you could ever imagine. The thing is, you've got to trust yourself. If you believe that you can write something funny, then remember that, and trust your feelings. Think back on the first time that you read the joke aloud, and remember that it was funny then. After that, don't worry about it anymore. Within a month, no one in the studio will think that it's funny. But if it's not funny the first couple of times you read it, then it's no good.

Voice Acting

At both of the companies that I've been at, the game writers are really involved in the voice-casting process and in the temp dialogue recording process. I'm taking acting lessons, because you want the temp dialogue to be good, so learn how to act, and how to direct voice actors. Sometimes, lines of dialogue won't make it through the process, because during the temp voice recording, you find that the words just don't sound good when read aloud.

9 Directing Voice Actors

In This Chapter

- Planning
- Casting
- Recording

The voice actor brings life to the character, investing him with humor, rage, warmth, terror, or exuberance. Getting the right content into the game is a complex process, and the writer can get a better performance by understanding the way that game dialogue is recorded.

PLANNING

Prior to the voice shoot, the writer should try to front-load as much of the work as possible, anticipating all of the variables that will arise during the recording process. By understanding the voice recording process and by considering the needs of the voice actors, the writer can streamline the process.

CHARACTERS

The key to the voice recording process is characters. The writer must know the characters inside and out to get the most from the sessions. The work done in Chapter 5, Creating the Characters, will pay off at this point, as the writer should have a great deal of documented information to draw on while assembling the materials pertaining to casting and direction of voice actors. In addition to the screenplay, the writer needs to have access to three kinds of documents at this point: vision documents, character backgrounds, and voice notes.

Vision Documents

The writer should have compiled a document that summarizes the vision for the game's soundscape, much in the way a game designer may create a vision document for the gameplay experience. Such a document should outline what the ultimate user experience should be for the game from the perspective of voice acting and dialogue. Should the voice assets evoke amusement, excitement, empathy, or tension? How will this be elicited in the player? The writer should also assemble a document that outlines the narrative vision and delineates the ways the voice assets will contribute to that vision. What are the key moments? What are the memorable lines of dialogue?

In short, the vision document is the overall description of what the writer hopes to achieve with the words the player hears (Figure 9.1). Unless the development team has a target to aim for, there's no way to be sure they're going to hit the mark.

Character Backgrounds

Each major speaking role should have a background document outlining his or her identity, including such elements as name, personality, history, education, profes-

Title	Rise of Merlin
Genre	Third-person action
Concept	Before Merlin was the wise old wizard who taught Arthur Pendragon to be king, he was a young wizard in search of his destiny. In Rise of Merlin, the player leads the wizard on his quest to attain the four Elemental Staves and defeat the wicked Horned King.
Storyline	After the Horned King seizes power in the southern Kingdoms, young Merlin is sent on a quest to defeat him. Along with his trusty sidekick Valerios, the enigmatic dragon Vexalyss, and the sinister Dragon Queen, Merlin must overcome ogres, wyverns, and trolls as he makes his wall to the Hall of the Dead. There, he must wield the elemental staves against the Horned King and bring peace to the land.
Key Moments	* Death of Vexalyss * Treason of Valerios * Destruction of the Hall of the Dead

FIGURE 9.1   Vision document for *Rise of Merlin*.

sion, abilities, context, relationships, age, and gender. The backgrounds should also contain sample dialogue if such is available.

Name: What is the character's full name? What does he go by? Does his name have any special significance?

Role: Who is this character in terms of the story? Does he play a major role, or is he a walk-on? Good guy or bad guy? Mid-level boss, sidekick, or expendable townsfolk villager type?

Personality: What kind of person is he? Friendly, treacherous, honest, cultured, or angry? What are his likes and dislikes? What does he believe in? Frame his personality in terms of the game's central conflicts. If you're working on a game about a kingdom besieged by evil dragons, ask yourself how this character would react if attacked by a dragon. Ask what he would be willing to sacrifice to defeat the dragons once and for all.

History: Document the character's background and life story. It doesn't have to be lengthy unless the character is a major player in the story line. This section can contain information about where the character's from, what kind of education he has, and what accomplishments he's achieved thus far. Cover the basic journalistic who-what-when-where-how-and-why of this character's history as briefly as possible. If you're working on a role-playing game with a complex narrative, this section's probably going to be much longer than it would be if you were working on a sci-fi first-person shooter whose protagonist has no speaking lines.

Profession: What does this character do for a living? Why? For example, in a superhero game the character's day job (traveling salesman) might just be a cover to throw off suspicion when he disappears unexpectedly for long stretches of time.

Abilities: What sets this character apart from everyone else? Whether this character is a ninja, a wizard, or a federal agent, there's probably something interesting that he's able to do that's appropriate to document here.

Context: What context does this character occupy in the narrative? Will this character ultimately be responsible for foiling the plans of the Arch-Priest Lazago? Will he help the player escape from a death-trap? What is noteworthy about this character's contribution to the plot?

Relationships: Who is this character involved with emotionally? Is the character in love? If so, with whom? Who are his friends and enemies? Who are his allies? Whom does he suspect of treachery?

Age: How old is this character? In a nonrealistic setting, be sure to contextualize this information. For example, in a sci-fi or fantasy game, a character might live to be far older than any human, so in addition to the numerical age, be sure to indicate this character's relative age as well (young, elderly, etc.).

Gender: It should be easy to figure this one out, unless you're working on a *really* interesting game.

Dialogue: If you have some available, this would be the place to cite some of the character's more representative lines of dialogue. Two or three lines should be enough to convey his persona accurately.

Voice Notes

Each character background should be accompanied by voice notes that will help with the casting and directing processes. These notes include information about pitch, vocabulary, accent, and reference.

Pitch

Is the character's voice high or low? Nasal and reedy? A deep and rumbling bass? A mid-level baritone? Bear in mind that in games with multiple simultaneous speakers, a good mix of pitches is going to help the player identify the characters. For example, in *Star Wars: Republic Commando*, each of your three teammates (Fixer, Scorch, and Sev) has a different pitch from the others, making it easier to tell them apart.

Vocabulary

Does the character have a broad vocabulary? Does he generally use monosyllabic words? Does he employ archaic terms? A character's vocabulary can tell you a great deal about his educational level.

Accent

The more thoroughly documented this section is, the more effective the notes will be during the process of casting and directing. Merely indicating that the character has an English accent tells a voice actor next to nothing. Consider the difference between Sherlock Holmes and Oliver Twist—not the same accent at all. The more detail you furnish and the more descriptive you are, the better the chances that auditioning (or performing) voice actors are going to deliver the performance you're looking for. Also, when it comes to American accents, be sure you communicate the extent of the accent. Is the Texan accent mild or heavy?

Reference

This is one of the most useful sections in the character voice note document. Cite a reference that will help illustrate some aspect of your character's voice. For example, if your character has a deep voice, you may cite an actor with a similar voice. However, indicate what it is that the actor is being cited for (accent, pitch, diction, etc.).

PREPARATION

Prior to the voice shoot, the writer should prepare for the following:

- Casting
- Recording
- Asset management
- Document formatting

Casting

Before casting the voice actors, the writer needs to establish a vision for the sound of his game. What is the audio palette like? Are there some deep voices and some high-pitched voices? How do the characters sound? If this is a sequel, will the team use the same voice actors that were featured in earlier installments? If the game is a media tie-in, such as an adaptation of a TV show or movie, the studio may want to hire the actors to perform the voice work for the game. For example, *24™: The Game* featured the voices of the major cast members portrayed in the TV show, but both *Buffy the Vampire Slayer* video games featured a sound-alike for the role of Buffy.

The more information the writer assembles prior to the auditioning process, the better. However, the notes that are presented to each actor should be as concise as possible. It's good to have access to all of the necessary data, but it's also important to present only the required notes to each actor. Figure 9.2 shows an example of casting notes. The writer will want to document each major character's involvement in the game, along with the game's premise and various comparisons if needed. The voice actors auditioning for the role may or may not be familiar with games, so citing references to popular TV shows or movies may help when assembling audition materials. Before starting the casting process, the writer should also compile a short list of sample dialogue for each major character and include that in the audition notes.

Recording

Before recording begins, the writer needs to assemble information about sound studios, the game's context, and the schedule. It's also necessary to decide who will be attending the voice shoot.

Sound Studios

The development team shouldn't necessarily work with the first sound studio they run across. Each studio offers different resources and experiences, and it's up to the development team to partner up with the right studio. It's important to ask for a resume, portfolio, and references. Look at the games they've worked on. Are they equipped to handle a game with your particular needs? If you're working on a AAA

Casting Notes: Vexalyss	
Role	Vexalyss, the Red Dragon. Vexalyss is a brutal and merciless warrior who is drawn into Merlin's quest to defeat the Horned King. Vexalyss acts out of self-interest, and is not concerned for the lives of innocent people. He respects Merlin's combat skills, though he sees his compassion as a weakness.
Premise	Rise of Merlin tells the story of the legendary sorcerer. Set in a mythical age of dragons and monsters, it tells the story of Merlin's great battle against the armies of the Horned King.
Description	Vexalyss is ancient, but when he transforms into human form, he appears to be a mighty warrior in his forties. His voice is deep and gravelly. He sounds tough and confident. Scottish accent.
Dialogue 1	Another act of mercy, sorcerer? That will be your undoing. These pink swine aren't worth your consideration. (mood: scornful)
Dialogue 2	Merlin, there's a group of trolls headed this way! (mood: urgent)
Dialogue 3	The gate's locked. What do we do now? (mood: frustrated)

FIGURE 9.2 Casting notes for *Rise of Merlin*.

title with 10,000 lines of dialogue, and they've mostly handled small games with a few hundred lines of dialogue, you need to find out if they've got the bandwidth (and know-how) to deal with your game. In all likelihood, you're better off working with a studio that has shipped comparable titles, and even then, you're going to want to check those references. You can also play the games they have worked on or read the reviews to see what was said about the voice acting.

Game Context

At the recording studio the writer should be armed with materials pertaining to the game's context, including story documents, concept art for main characters, renders of character models, plot synopses (for the entire game and for individual levels), and a laptop with an electronic version of the script. It's also good to bring a flash drive, so that any rewrites can be shared between computers in a hurry. The game context materials serve a single purpose: they further explain the game's concept to the voice actors while they are recording dialogue. Though these resources may not be needed during the voice shoot, it's always better to have and not need than to need and not have. The voice actor may be familiar with the game already or may have completely forgotten auditioning for the part, and the more information the writer has at his disposal, the easier it's going to be to bring the actor up to speed.

It's also good to remember that not all voice actors are familiar with video games, and comparisons to *Resident Evil* or *Call of Duty* may only confuse them further. Be prepared with lists of mainstream media comparisons, such as TV shows or movies that are more likely to contextualize the game content for them. References like *Saving Private Ryan* and *Dawn of the Dead* can convey a great deal of information in a hurry, enabling the writer to skip ahead to the more immediate details (such as character motivation and the context of a particular scene). However, be sure the content you're alluding to is accurate in terms of mood as well as theme. *The Longest Day* and *Saving Private Ryan* are both films about World War II, but they are radically different depictions of warfare, and each reference carries its own connotations.

Schedule

How will the voice shoot be scheduled? All at once, or over a period of several weeks or months? Will there be long breaks between actors? What will the development team be doing during this downtime? How many lines are there, and how much time will be needed for each actor? Will all of each actor's lines be recorded at once? Is that feasible? The average actor can get through roughly 200 lines of dialogue in one four-hour session, but four hours is a long time, especially if you're screaming or impersonating a dragon. The truth is, any voice session over two hours is going to start to take its toll on an actor's voice if precautions aren't taken. Scheduling an actor for multiple sessions in a single day, or even on consecutive days, can result in a rough, hoarse delivery. It's best to talk to the actor about what will work for him, as many actors have learned (the hard way) what their vocal cords can tolerate. Depending on whether you work with union talent, there may also be restrictions on the number of voices an actor can perform in a given session. Prior to scheduling the voice shoots, discuss these restrictions with your contact at the sound studio, who should be able to help you figure out how to get the most from the voice recording process without breaking any rules.

Attendees

Who will be attending your voice shoot? Why? After all, it's fun to go and hang out with voice actors, particularly if they're celebrities, but the fact is, many cooks in the kitchen can ruin the soup. Every person attending the voice recording session should be performing a specific and necessary role, agreed-upon in advance. Directing the voice talent, interfacing with the sound director, and revising the manuscript are tasks that must be performed, regardless of how many people it takes, but a room full of aspiring voice directors will only perplex the voice actor and slow down the voice acting process. Be certain that the sound studio knows how many people will be attending. They may not be able to accommodate everyone in the studio comfortably, and it's important to know beforehand.

Asset Management

After the recording process, the sound studio will be transferring the audio content into the hands of the development team. How will this be handled? What format will the files be in? How will the files be stored? How will the development team back up the files? Where? How will these files be delivered to the development team? Via FTP, burned onto a disc, or some other way? When? In addition to researching all of these questions, the writer must also find out whether he'll be able to access the files immediately once they've been received. If not, what will it take to convert the files into a format that the writer can listen to? Is there a software package that the writer needs to install? It's important that the writer begin to verify the content of all of the dialogue as it's received. Though the sound team will also be double-checking the integrity of the content, it's the writer who must serve as the story's advocate during development, and it's the writer who must be sure the right take was delivered for each line of dialogue.

Document Formatting

What kind of document will be submitted to the sound studio? A Hollywood screenplay? A spreadsheet? Is the document ready for the recording process? It should contain all necessary information for the actors at this point. Is the document printable? If it's a spreadsheet, it should be formatted for standard landscape printing or possibly for 8.5" x 14" landscape (depending on the number of columns you've included). If you're bringing the hard copy of a 10,000-line game, you're talking about a printout of roughly 400 pages. If you try to split the document up and bring individualized printouts (one for each actor), you may actually wind up extending that page count. Then, of course, you'll want multiple copies (one for the actor, one for the director, and one for each additional person that's going to be involved in the voice shoot). How will this document be prepared and transported to the voice shoot? Are you bringing it on the plane? Seriously? If you're bringing the document in electronic format, determine where you're going to print and copy it. Remember that if you've formatted a separate version of the Screen/Play for the voice actors, you want to be sure that only pertinent information is included (see Figures 9.3 and 9.4). The last thing you need to verify during this step is the naming convention for files. If you haven't already, confirm these with the sound team and address any issues or inconsistencies that arise. Take special care to ensure that there are no duplicate file names in your document, because this may cause serious problems for the recording studio or for your own sound team.

CHARACTER	CUE	CONTEXT	TRIGGER	INFLECTION	AREA	EFFECT	FILENAME
Vexalyss	Another act of mercy, sorcerer? That will be your undoing. These pink swine aren't worth your consideration.	Merlin is rescuing the villagers from the fire.	The last villagers has been rescued.	scornful	1.2	distortion	vex_1-2_001
Vexalyss	Merlin, there's a group of trolls headed this way!	Vexalyss and Merlin are traveling across the plains.	Vexalyss sees a group of trolls.	urgent	1.2		vex_1-2_002
Vexalyss	The gate's locked. What do we do now?	The group has reached the Necropolis of Zharduim.	The Necropolis of Daurkhim is sealed.	frustrated	1.3		vex_1-3_003
Town Guard	Welcome to Khauria.	The group has arrived at Khauria.	The group nears the Town Guard as they pass through the gate.	normal	1.3		tg_1-3_001
Talerios	Death Knights approaching from the east!	Talerios and Merlin are traveling across the desert.	Talerios sees a group of Death Knights.	urgent	1.4		tal_1-4_001
Vexalyss	Ogres, advancing on us from the south!	Vexalyss and Merlin are traveling across the plains.	Vexalyss sees a group of ogres.	urgent	1.5		vex_1-5_001

FIGURE 9.3   The full version of Screen/Play.

CHARACTER	CUE	CONTEXT	TRIGGER	INFLECTION
Vexalyss	Keep silent, sorcerer. We don't want to be heard.	Vexalyss and Merlin are sneaking through the Necropolis.	The player has bumped into something, making a noise.	whispered
Vexalyss	We should make sure that we have enough arrows.	The group is purchasing supplies in town.	The player has concluded a purchase from the weapons merchant without buying any arrows.	normal
Vexalyss	Nice shot!	Vexalyss and Merlin are in combat.	The player has just killed an enemy with an arrow.	admiring
Vexalyss	Good work, Merlin.	Vexalyss and Merlin are in combat.	The player has just killed an enemy.	admiring
Vexalyss	Another act of mercy, sorcerer? That will be your undoing. These pink swine aren't worth your consideration.	Merlin is rescuing the villagers from the fire.	The last villagers has been rescued.	scornful

FIGURE 9.4   A condensed version of Screen/Play, formatted for voice actors.

CASTING

During the casting process, the writer's goal should be to make sure the voice actors who are cast are the best possible fit for each role, given the studio's parameters. Using the vision documents created earlier, the writer should stay focused on the needs of the story throughout the process of auditions and evaluations. When listening to demo reels that have been submitted by a potential voice actor, it's hard to be sure the actor can deliver unless, by happenstance, one of the recordings matches the role you're auditioning for. The odds of this are slim, so insist on an actual audition whenever possible. Furnish a broad range of dialogue for the auditions (as seen in Figure 9.5).

CHARACTER	CUE	CONTEXT	TRIGGER	INFLECTION
Vexalyss	Another act of mercy, sorcerer? That will be your undoing. These pink swine aren't worth your consideration.	Merlin is rescuing the villagers from the fire.	The last villagers has been rescued.	scornful
Vexalyss	Merlin, there's a group of trolls headed this way!	Vexalyss and Merlin are traveling across the plains.	Vexalyss sees a group of trolls.	urgent
Vexalyss	The gate's locked. What do we do now?	The group has reached the Necropolis of Zharduim.	The Necropolis of Daurkhim is sealed.	frustrated
Vexalyss	Ogres, advancing on us from the south!	Vexalyss and Merlin are traveling across the plains.	Vexalyss sees a group of ogres.	urgent
Vexalyss	Keep silent, sorcerer. We don't want to be heard.	Vexalyss and Merlin are sneaking through the Necropolis.	Merlin bumps into something that makes noise.	whispered
Vexalyss	We should make sure that we have enough arrows.	The group is purchasing supplies in town.	The group has exited the purchasing menu without acquiring any new arrows.	normal
Vexalyss	Nice shot!	Vexalyss and Merlin are in combat.	Merlin has killed an enemy with an arrow.	admiring
Vexalyss	Good work, Merlin.	Vexalyss and Merlin are in combat.	Merlin has killed an enemy.	admiring
Vexalyss	Traitor! You have betrayed us all!	Vexalyss, Merlin, and Talerios are in the Throne Room.	Talerios is revealed to be an agent of the Horned King.	angry

FIGURE 9.5   A spreadsheet of audition dialogue.

The audition should include lines of different lengths, volumes, and emotional intensities. You want some yells, some whispers, and some lines delivered in a normal tone of voice. The more information you provide about the character at this stage, the better-equipped the actor will be to deliver the sound you're looking for. Chances are, no one from your development team will be available to direct during the audition process, so be specific with the sound studio about the documents you'll be sending them and be sure to communicate that the actors should have access to these documents.

While evaluating the audition, there are a few things to keep in mind, including accuracy, variance, enthusiasm, character, and the seduction of "good enough."

ACCURACY

Compare what's being said with what's on the screenplay document. Is the actor delivering the right line? Admittedly, during the recording process, it's not uncommon for actors to ad lib when the developer has specifically asked for this. It's also possible that during the recording process, the actor may suggest an alternate line. However, during the audition process, you want an actor who is delivering the line that you have written, the way that you have written it. If that's not the case in the audition, then you may experience difficulties during the recording process. Also pay attention to the way the line is delivered. Is the actor's inflection appropriate? Does it match what's indicated on the spreadsheet? If the inflection listed is "angry," but the actor's delivery sounds more sad than upset, you want to consider that during the evaluation process.

VARIANCE

If the actor performs multiple takes, listen to each group of recordings and compare them to one another. Is there enough variance? Often, during recording an actor will deliver the same line three different ways, leaving it to the developer to pick the takes that work best for the game. If the actor delivers three identical takes during the audition, it's not a good sign. You want a dynamic range, which indicates that the actor is ready to experiment with his voice a little in order to give you more options.

CHARACTER

Does the actor fit the part? If the character is a soldier on a battlefield or a sinister demon, does the actor really bring that concept to life? It's one thing to get a good read and another thing to truly inhabit the role. Often, what the player sees on the screen is a moving image that screams just before being blasted or slashed into oblivion. It's the sound of the spoken word that helps lend personality to the character model in the middle of a hectic gun battle or swordfight. Close your eyes and try to picture the character as you listen to the auditions. Better yet, have concept art, screenshots, or a stable build available as you listen. Does the audition fit? Has the actor really nailed it? Often, the synergy is unquantifiable, the sort of thing you recognize once you've heard it.

GOOD ENOUGH

Be very wary of the seductive "good enough." The process of auditioning voice actors can be a lengthy one, and it is sometimes tempting to say a performance was good enough to get the job done. Giving in to this temptation will not result in excellence. Know in advance what you're looking for, define it concretely, and strive to find the actor who can deliver the sound you seek. If there's an actor who played a role in another game, whose work struck you as high caliber, don't hesitate to try to locate and hire that actor for your game if the role you're offering is a good match. Hold out for the best whenever possible (within reason, of course).

RECORDING

The dialogue has been written, the cast has been assembled, and you're now in the recording studio, getting ready to bring the characters to life. What next?

THE PROCESS

When recording dialogue in the sound studio, your goal is to get the best performance possible from the voice actors. To pull that off, you need the following:

- A unified vision
- Role definition
- Structure
- Confidence
- Specificity
- Flexibility
- Backloaded screams
- Air breaks
- Pronunciation

A Unified Vision

What is the story concept for your game? How does this actor's character play into that concept? In what way does a specific line of dialogue communicate that character's motivation or personality? Determine the vision for each character and make sure everyone is on board with this idea. If everyone in attendance has a different idea about how the actor should be reading his lines, you're going to experience the sort of counter-productive conflict that detracts from the game's overall quality. Consensus is important once the recording process begins. During the planning stage, it's perfectly acceptable to discuss every nuance of the characters, the casting process, and the audition reels, but once the actor is in front of the microphone, the vision must be shared by all present. If mixed signals are sent, and it's obvious that the developers themselves are in disagreement over the nature of the character or his accent or his attitude, then all hope of a stellar performance is lost.

Role Definition

During the recording process, everyone in attendance needs to know what his role in the process is and what's expected of him. If an associate producer attends the voice sessions to make sure the process is running harmoniously and that all participants have the necessary resources to complete their tasks, then it would be a grave mistake for that producer to suddenly decide to take on voice direction duties when those responsibilities have already been delegated to someone else. All members of the development team need to know in advance what tasks they will be performing at the recording studio, and they need to be certain that the entire team is working toward the same goal. If roles are poorly defined in advance, it's possible that everyone will attend the recording session with the intent of directing the voice actors or of making the final pick on every line of dialogue. Role definition is especially important when large numbers of developers are attending the recording sessions; if there are only two developers at the voice shoot, it's easy enough to reorganize in the studio, but if it's a large group, and the hierarchy wasn't clearly established ahead of time, chaos is bound to ensue.

Structure

To avoid those awkward pauses while developers rummage through backpacks for crumpled printouts, it's good to approach the recording session with the same level of organization that has informed all other aspects of the story development process. Begin by outlining the information you want to communicate to the actor. For example, you may want to divulge the story concept, as well as an outline of the major events in the game and then talk about the story cycle for his character (see Figure 9.6 for details). From there, you may want to segue into the character bio and voice notes and then proceed to a sound check and some sample lines. If you have the actor's audition reel (which is recommended), you might want to play that back at this point to refresh his memory. If there's any feedback or critique, that might come next, before the actual recording begins. If there's a different system you wish to employ, make sure you've documented it and discuss it prior to the recording session. The last thing you want is to have someone else tell the actor to begin recording while you're getting ready to explain the character notes to him. This confusion will only muddy the waters and delay the process.

TASK	MINUTES
Discuss the story concept	1
Outline major events in the game	1
Discuss story cycle for Vexalyss	1
Character bio, voice notes	3
Soundcheck	3
Audition reel playback	1
Sample lines	2
TOTAL TIME	12

FIGURE 9.6   An example of structure for a recording session.

Confidence

A lack of confidence is a deal-breaker under any circumstances, but in the recording studio, it can give the impression that you haven't given sufficient thought to the process or to the goals of the session. If there's something that needs to be said, then say it. Actors are as professional as game developers, and that means their hides are as thick. This isn't a license for rudeness; it simply means that if you want an actor to try a line of dialogue just one more time, but *this* way, then it's your obligation to say so. If it's for the good of the game and if it's going to result in a superior performance, you don't really have a choice in the matter. If there's a voice cue that's been nagging at you, and you want to go back at the end of the session and record that cue just a couple more times, then so be it. As long as you're not pushing the actor past his limits or wasting time by noodling around when there are better things to do, nobody will think less of you for being committed to excellence. Constructive criticism is an art form, however, so be sure you aren't phrasing your requests in an accusatory fashion. You're simply stating facts: you would like to hear that line again, but this time like so; or you want to take a moment to clarify the context for this line, because you think it would be helpful.

Specificity

If there's a line of dialogue that's giving the actor trouble, it may help to clarify the situation or to volunteer to read the line yourself (although you do not want to make a habit of this, as it may appear condescending, so use your judgment, and if you feel it might be offensive, don't do it). If you are going to furnish context for the actor, be as precise as possible and define the scene in concrete terms. There's a difference between "In this scene, he's afraid for his life," and "In this scene, there's a zombie gnawing on his throat, and he thinks he's going to die in great agony." The more specific your context, whether on the printed page or in conversation, the more guidance you provide the actor. This does not mean you need to furnish a *lot* of specific information. It just means the information you give should be very clear and precise. If your written or spoken context is lengthy, it's going to slow down the process and bore the actor. Keep it short and keep it real. This applies to the Context and Inflection headings on your spreadsheet, to the documents you bring to the voice shoot, and to the verbal feedback you give.

Flexibility

As the writer on a project, it's easy for you to take the story advocacy concept too far. All writers are susceptible to it to some degree. It's important to distance yourself from the project to the extent that you're able to recognize constructive criticism for what it is: an attempt to rectify an error, not an attack on your skill. It's rare for a programmer to attend a meeting where a bunch of people (some of them strangers) sit around and poke at his code for several hours. However, on a bad day, that's exactly how a recording session can feel to a writer. It's easy to get defensive, but for the good of the project (and one's reputation), such urges must be squelched. Instead, listen closely to what's being said, and evaluate it on its own merits. If a line of dialogue is clunky, or a tongue-twister, fix it. If the actor has feedback, listen to it. After many such sessions, the voice actor may have some excellent advice about how to streamline the voice cue so that it's easier to read out loud. Don't apologize excessively. If you're working on a game with several thousand lines of dialogue, and there's one line that's in need of improvement, you're not exactly a colossal failure. In fact, by demonstrating flexibility on the spot, you're contributing to the project in a positive way. Don't be afraid to offer your own input if a line is being rewritten on-the-fly. That's probably why you're at the voice session. It's not uncommon to bring the writer to the recording studio for the sole purpose of revising content on an as-needed basis.

However, though flexibility is an admirable quality, and necessary in any aspect of game development, do not forget that you're there to defend the story. If a decision is being made that would adversely impact the story line or characters, it's your responsibility to voice any concerns or reservations that you have.

Backloaded Screams

Death screams and monster growls can take their toll on an actor's voice, so reserve these for the end of the recording session and be sure all other cues have been cleared away. For example, if a long line of dialogue was skipped to give you enough time to rewrite it, be sure you get that taken care of before the high-intensity portion of the session.

The impact of screams and yells can cause damage to the vocal cords of an actor, so be reasonable. If you have a massive amount of high-intensity content, you may wind up blowing the actor's cords out halfway through if you don't plan thoroughly. It may be worth splitting those screams and growls into multiple voice shoots. The actor is probably going to have some experience with that kind of delivery and will most likely be able to tell you just what he is capable of, but if not, keep an ear out for scratchiness and cracking in the voice. From a purely mercenary standpoint, those elements will add little to your game and may actually detract from the experience. From a professional standpoint, the voice actor earns a living with those vocal cords, and there's nothing good about damaging someone else's ability to make a living. If your game features an excessive amount of shrieks and growls, do your research and consult with your voice actors before surprising them with four straight hours of high-intensity voice work that's sure to render them unemployable for several days.

Air Breaks

Regardless of the intensity of the voice work, it's good to give your actor time to breathe and drink water (which is crucial during a recording session). This time can be used to skim ahead, verify spelling and pronunciation, or stretch one's own legs. Taking short breaks to cool off can also be good for your voice actor, because it helps prevent the breathy, rushed sound caused by strenuous activity.

Pronunciation

Regardless of what kind of game you're developing, there are bound to be some place names, character names, or other elements that will strike a voice actor as somewhat foreign. Be certain that you've got the correct pronunciation listed wherever applicable.

DIRECTION

If you direct the voice actors, you're furnishing context and feedback for the reading. The exact method you want to employ is going to depend on a number of factors. The actors may have a method that they prefer, or you may want to experiment with different approaches for different types of dialogue. In general, you can give instructions for a large amount of text and then progress through it and do retakes at the end, or you can move line-by-line down the page. As a rule, when working on batches of similar cues, such as AI responses, it may be best to employ the former, and when recording instance-specific voice cues, you'll want to do the latter.

Figure 9.7 shows a batch of cues that indicate enemy movement to the player. At the beginning of this section, the writer might elect to give the actor a description of the conditions under which these cues are applicable: "At this point, your character sees ogres lumbering toward the player, and you're trying to warn him. You're not panicking, or screaming, but the situation is serious." After giving the actor enough direction to work with (which might include a description that's longer or shorter than the one above, depending on the voice actor), the writer should allow the actor to proceed through the list of cues, going back to pick up any additional takes that are needed. After that, the writer should proceed to the next block of cues. This approach works particularly well for AI-driven voice cues, which reflect a change in AI state (such as from neutral to hostile or from alert to under attack). Since there are usually many such cues, in order to ensure sufficient variegation, it's a good idea to blitz through them in large chunks, so that the actor can maintain consistency through the delivery and so the process isn't held up by direction after each take.

CHARACTER	CUE	CONTEXT	TRIGGER	INFLECTION
Vexalyss	Merlin, a group of ogres headed towards us!	Vexalyss and Merlin are traveling across the plains.	Vexalyss sees a group of ogres.	urgent
Vexalyss	Ready yourself, Merlin. A group of ogres approaches.	Vexalyss and Merlin are traveling across the plains.	Vexalyss sees a group of ogres.	urgent
Vexalyss	Ogres, advancing on us from the south!	Vexalyss and Merlin are traveling across the plains.	Vexalyss sees a group of ogres.	urgent
Vexalyss	Sorcerer, there are trolls coming from the south!	Vexalyss and Merlin are traveling across the plains.	Vexalyss sees a group of trolls	urgent
Vexalyss	Merlin, trolls are advancing on our position.	Vexalyss and Merlin are traveling across the plains.	Vexalyss sees a group of trolls.	urgent
Vexalyss	Merlin, a group of trolls is headed our way!	Vexalyss and Merlin are traveling across the plains.	Vexalyss sees a group of trolls.	urgent

FIGURE 9.7 A batch of similarly contextualized voice cues.

In Figure 9.8 the scripted banter is part of a conversation between three characters. Depending on how the writer decides to approach the voice recording process, there are at least two ways to handle the documentation: the actor could receive the text as is or he could just get his own cues. In either case, the writer will probably need to do some degree of contextualization for the actor and will probably have to do a little bit of explaining between each line.

CHARACTER	CUE	CONTEXT	TRIGGER	INFLECTION	AREA	EFFECT	FILENAME
Merlin	Then how can we defeat him?	Merlin is consulting with the Dragon Queen and the Lady of the Lake.	Scripted cinematic 3A01	serious	3.1		m03-a01-mer01
Dragon Queen	The Horned King will not be defeated.	Merlin is consulting with the Dragon Queen and the Lady of the Lake.	Scripted cinematic 3A01	ominous	3.1	distortion	m03-a01-drg01
Niniane	Banished, but never slain.	Merlin is consulting with the Dragon Queen and the Lady of the Lake.	Scripted cinematic 3A01	serious	3.1	echo	m03-a01-nin01
Dragon Queen	You will need to gather the four Elemental Staves.	Merlin is consulting with the Dragon Queen and the Lady of the Lake.	Scripted cinematic 3A01	serious	3.1	distortion	m03-a01-drg02
Merlin	Where shall I find them?	Merlin is consulting with the Dragon Queen and the Lady of the Lake.	Scripted cinematic 3A01	confused	3.1		m03-a01-mer02
Niniane	That is not known to us.	Merlin is consulting with the Dragon Queen and the Lady of the Lake.	Scripted cinematic 3A01	serious	3.1	echo	m03-a01-nin02
Dragon Queen	You must seek the counsel of Vexalyss.	Merlin is consulting with the Dragon Queen and the Lady of the Lake.	Scripted cinematic 3A01	serious	3.1	distortion	m03-a01-drg03

FIGURE 9.8   A group of cues from scripted banter in a specific scene.

While directing voice talent, the writer should always consider the following:

- Warm-up
- Getting into character
- Context
- Momentum
- Feedback

Warm-up

Prior to the recording session the voice actor may need to do warm-up vocals. Be sure to allot sufficient time in your schedule for these. Vocal warm-ups can include stretches, yawns, sighs, and the repetition of nonsensical phrases.

Getting into Character

The actor may spend a few minutes getting into character, which can include experimenting with various voices, adjusting the thickness of an accent, or getting a feel for the character's mood and attitude.

Context

Any context you furnish before the recording session will prove useful, but remember that even though you've spent the past year or two on this game, the voice actor may not even know the name of your game yet. If your contextualization consists of a stream of complex data, it's unlikely that he's going to be able to make sense of it while he's trying to focus on his Irish accent. Keep it simple and direct and don't rely on jargon or development-specific terms. If it helps to use concept art or character renders, do so, because it will help make the material more concrete for the voice actor.

Momentum

If the actor is on a roll and he's hitting his lines, then there's no point in halting the flow of the recording session to give him context for an upcoming line when he's obviously got things under control. If the actor has built up some momentum and the lines sound good, go with the flow and don't feel compelled to interrupt unless something is off. The benefit of letting an actor proceed in such a fashion is that the resulting voice sounds more consistent in-game.

Feedback

When giving feedback, remember the criteria applied during the cinematic script approval process (detailed in Chapter 8, Creating Cinematics): it's succinct, specific, impartial, and internally consistent. Feedback given to voice actors should be the same. Keep it brief, be specific about what you'd like to hear changed, keep it neutral, and be consistent.

SUMMARY

Once the dialogue has been recorded, the developers are able to give voices to their characters, making them seem more lifelike. This process requires the writer to anticipate the needs of the voice actors and of those who will be using the voice assets later on in the development process. By preparing for documentation, casting, recording, and directing, the writer can avoid many of the pitfalls that arise during the voice acting process and can thereby help the actors deliver their best work. In this chapter we discussed ways the writer can participate in the planning stage, manage the audition process, and contribute to the direction of voice actors. Future chapters will discuss how these voice assets are then integrated into the game.

10 Knowing Technical Parameters

In This Chapter

- Parameters
- Level Design
- Technical Limitations

PARAMETERS

The writer must understand the parameters that govern the implementation of voice cues to ensure that the story is conveyed properly through dialogue, or else all of the time and energy that went into preparation and preproduction will have been in vain. By familiarizing himself with the game's level design and technical limitations and by understanding the process by which NPC dialogue is implemented, the writer can circumvent many of the challenges that will arise.

LEVEL DESIGN

The level design process varies from studio to studio. In some cases a top-down map is created first. This two-dimensional blueprint for the level shows entries and exits and indicates the basic routes the player can follow as he progresses through the area. The level is based on this blueprint, with input from other developers, such as the game designer or creative director. Ultimately, the person responsible for creating maps is a level designer (sometimes referred to as a level artist). Using software packages such as BioWare's Aurora toolkit and Epic's UnrealEd, level designers build three-dimensional game spaces.

When the level designers create playable world spaces for the player to move through, they immediately define a large portion of the shape of the game experience. The design of a level can be claustrophobic (*Doom 3*) or wide-open (*Oblivion*), and the decisions made during this process can have a serious impact on a game's narrative delivery system. Through the creation of the world space, and by employing strategies such as the sneak-preview and the discovery, a level design team can work with the writer to integrate dialogue seamlessly into the game world.

WORLD SPACE

The world space that is created by a level should facilitate the flow of dialogue as appropriate. It's up to the writer to effectively communicate the level's story design and dialogue requirements to the level artist and to ensure that the world space is created with that content in mind. Otherwise, the level design may interfere with the game's narrative, resulting in misunderstood or unheard dialogue. For example, if a level begins with a lengthy conversation between the player's two AI-controlled sidekicks and then proceeds into an ambush, the level designers must be aware of the story content in question. The game level needs to begin in an area of relative safety and should proceed through another lengthy safe zone. For example, a corridor that's free of enemy characters will enable the two sidekicks to have their conversation, thereby imparting information to the player. However, if the long corridor is a straight shot, the player may sprint from one end to the next, eager to move into the next encounter. While this is not necessarily a bad thing, the length of the corridor must be such that even if the player runs the whole way, moving into the next area (where he's ambushed), the voice cues still have enough time to play. Alternatively, the corridor could be full of twists and turns, though still empty, prompting the player to move through the area more slowly while his teammates chatter. The disadvantage here is that if the player moves slowly through this area, then dies in the ambush, and has to play the level again, he's going to know that the corridor is empty and sprint through it. So, again, the writer must anticipate the user experience and try to figure out how to convey the necessary story data under different circumstances.

When creating the world space, it's possible that the level design will reflect key story elements, such as areas of the game world that are not yet available for exploration. In *Half-Life 2* the player often reaches areas that cannot be accessed until after a key conversation has taken place. For example, while in the canals, the player reaches the air boat but cannot move forward until he has spoken with the other characters in the area. At that point the gate is lifted and there is a high-speed chase through the canals. In such instances the writer must be certain to indicate to the level designer which elements of the design are inflexible. If it were possible for the player to abandon the air boat and simply proceed forward on foot, the player might have missed the conversation with the other characters and would therefore have missed all of the story content that they were designed to convey. Therefore, the developers at Valve completely blocked off all progress, forcing the player to experience the narrative content prior to accessing the air boat and the rest of the mission.

SNEAK PREVIEW

The use of the sneak preview in level design allows the player to see a distant destination that he will eventually be able to explore (once he's traversed the part of the game world that he's in right now). This glimpse of other places helps make the world seem more concrete, gives the player something to anticipate, and makes the game world seem more believable and immersive. In *Super Mario World*® the player was able to access a cliff, below which he could clearly see the Valley of Bowser. This served to clearly identify the destination, as the valley was now more than just text on a screen. It was a place the player could see from afar. It also gave the player something to look forward to, as any fan of the series would know that the game would conclude with a battle with Bowser. It also helped to make the world seem more concrete.

Once the writer has fleshed out all of the locations in the game, it may be that two locations are in close proximity to one another, or are even in the same place but separated by some barrier that can't be crossed directly. In the *King's Field®* games the player often sees a goal that is on the other side of a chasm or on a distant ledge that he can't quite reach. Later on the player is able to access this item or area. By collaborating with the level designer, the writer can add tension and anticipation to the acquisition of goals in-game. Resolving a scenario can be that much sweeter if the player has a well-developed idea of what's in store. For example, in *Rise of Merlin*, the player needs to acquire the Tome of the Ancients to complete his Quest of Knowledge. Upon entering the Crypt of Kharanthas, the player can immediately see the Tome atop the Altar of Kharanthas. However, the altar is floating overhead, and the player currently has no way to reach it. Only by playing through the entire level can the player reach the ledge at the top of the crypt, which will allow the player to hop down onto the Altar. By working with the level designer, the writer can make certain that such scenario elements are worked into the level's design.

DISCOVERY

Given the conventions of a form that players experience repeatedly, it's not uncommon for players to become quite familiar with the process of narrative delivery in games. For example, consider the colored key. If you're playing a first-person shooter and you find a Blue Key, it's pretty obvious that you should be looking for a Blue Door. That kind of knowledge just comes with the territory. In a sense the same is true for certain narrative elements. Consider the friendly character located near a sealed portal. If you are supposed to enter the Crypt of Kharanthas, and it's locked, and there's an old beggar standing near the crypt, you can bet your last piece of lembas bread that he knows how to get in. If you kill the guy, you fail the mission. If you give him some money, there's a good chance he'll help you out. Again, it's something a player becomes accustomed to over time, and it presents the writer with something of a challenge. After all, how does one overcome such obstacles without impeding the player's progress? In film the red herring is employed to prevent the audience from immediately deducing the identity of the murderer, but in games a red herring can cause more confusion and frustration than suspense (imagine finding a Blue Key and wasting time searching for a Blue Door, only to discover that there is none).

The writer can circumvent some of the established patterns of in-game narrative delivery by permitting player discovery. Rather than handing the player information, the writer permits the player to engage the information. While the crucial data must, of course, be given to the player directly (to ensure that the player has the necessary information to play the game), nonessential data can be sprinkled through the level in the form of artifacts that the player can access on a case-by-case basis. In *Doom 3* the player receives critical information from his superiors. However, the game world is full of PDAs and computers that the player can access; these contain emails that further flesh out the game world and shed light on the gruesome fates of the emails' authors. In the *Resident Evil* games the player's mission is quite straightforward: kill zombies, survive. However, the levels are full of notes and diaries the player can discover and read, fleshing out the game world and giving the impression that things are happening outside of the player's field of view. The use of discovery in these instances can help keep the narrative delivery from feeling stale. By working with the level design team, the writer can create different ways to facilitate discovery for the player: a computer lab where emails can be read, a storage room full of documents, a nightstand with a diary inside, and so on.

PITFALLS

Numerous mistakes can be made during the level design process that will hamper a game's narrative experience, resulting in confusion or frustration for the player (or, at the very least, diminishing the quality of the story presentation). These include vague instructions, incorrect specificity of location in dialogue, and the omission of critical data from NPCs (Figure 10.1).

Pitfall	Description	Possible solutions
Vague instructions	Player not sure what to do	On-screen map, text-on-screen, in-game dialogue
Incorrect specificity	Story content no longer accurate	Create generic cues that guide the player
Omission of critical data	Player moves past critical information	Work with level designers to prevent player's forward movement until data has been received

FIGURE 10.1 Pitfalls of integrating dialogue with level design and some solutions.

Vague Instructions

The player should always have an idea of what it is that he should be doing. If the player faces a problem, the tools needed to fix that problem should be discernible, given a reasonable expenditure of effort. If a game presents a challenge whose resolution remains a mystery to the player, despite his best efforts, he'll eventually lose interest and become discouraged. The same is true for navigation: if you're playing a game and you can't figure out where you're supposed to go, there should be a way to verify your position against the location of your objective. Whether that's an on-screen map or the inability to retrace your steps (meaning that you will have to go the other way), there should be some kind of feedback to indicate to the player the direction he should be moving in. The writer can communicate this information to the player in a number of ways, including text on-screen, text artifacts in-game, and dialogue.

Through text on-screen, the writer can communicate information to the player in the form of a pop-up box containing information about the player's location. This is typically accomplished through a game's scripting editor. Text artifacts are places in the game where text is visible to the player, which can be used to convey information about the player's next objective or quest. For example, a road sign can indicate the location of a city, or a sign nailed to a wall can indicate the direction of an exit. Dialogue, of course, can be the most effective tool for conveying a player's next objective or the direction the player should be moving in. However, dialogue is not without its risks.

Incorrect Specificity

During the development process it's possible that the game's scope will change, including the levels that are designed and built. For example, though the Dungeon of Despair may be located north of the village chapel in the original version of the design document, the level artist may be forced to remove the chapel to cut down on the number of polygons in the map (after all, the chapel was just for decoration, since the player can't actually enter it during gameplay). However, during the pre-production process, the writer had created (and later recorded) dialogue that referenced the Dungeon of Despair's location in regard to the chapel. The chapel was a very distinctive landmark, and the writer reasoned that since it was the highest building in the village, the player would have no trouble locating it and then proceeding north to the Dungeon. Once the artist cut the chapel from the village level, the writer faced a problem. The dialogue had already been recorded by the time the decision was made to change the map, and there was no additional voice shoot in the game's schedule (and it would certainly not be possible to schedule a new shoot for a single line of dialogue). The writer had counted on the existence of the chapel to help guide the player toward the destination, and without it, the writer would have to come up with another way to guide the player.

This problem of dialogue that's incorrectly specific is a result of the inevitable changes that accompany game development; characters get cut, maps get changed, and scenes get revised at the last minute. Unfortunately, many of these decisions are made during the final stages of a game's development, when it's discovered that there just won't be enough time to complete all of the character models because one of the character model artists just left the company or because another game with an earlier release date needed help, so developers were loaned to the other project to make sure that it shipped on time—and so forth. It's impossible to predict what challenges will occur during the process, and despite his best efforts, the writer may find that some of his work has been invalidated by the changing landscape of the project. The resolution of such challenges requires creativity and preparation. For instance, the writer may create a series of generic cues, such as "It's north of here," "You're nearly there," and "It's just a little farther this way." Couple these cues with NPCs, and the dilemma of the Dungeon of Despair is ameliorated somewhat. In many games the player becomes accustomed to receiving instructions from an external contact of sorts (Lara Croft has a team of aides in *Tomb Raider: Legend,* the SEALs in *SOCOM* receive orders from HQ, and so on). In such cases the writer can anticipate the possibility that changes to the level design will obviate some of the more specific cues and can create generic cues from the external contact to help move the player along to the next situation.

Omission of Critical Data

When designing a game with multiple paths to a single destination, it can be tricky to manage the player's movements. If there is critical data the player needs to access before moving on, the writer needs to be certain that the level designers don't permit the player to proceed past that information (particularly if it's critical to the player's success). For example, in the aforementioned example of *Rise of Merlin*, if the player approaches the Crypt of Kharanthas and finds it impossible to enter, he may search for an alternate method of entry rather than converse with the old beggar standing nearby. If it's possible to enter the dungeon through a hole in its roof (resulting in a major loss of hit points when the player falls to the ground, but nonetheless theoretically possible), then you can guarantee that players are going to try it. And if it's possible to pause the game on impact with the ground and drink all of the healing potions in one's inventory, then unpause the game, you can bet that players are going to do that too. And if this results in the player's access to the Crypt of Kharanthas without the magical password that unlocks the Seal of Dragons (which would have been received from the beggar), the player is going to be stuck in the Crypt with no way out and no idea what he's supposed to do next. If this seems like a bonehead maneuver on the player's part, ask yourself—have you never found yourself in such a predicament? It's easy, when playing a game, to feel that one has found a secret, when the truth is that one has merely exploited a mistake on the part of the developers. To prevent such problems, the writer must work closely with the level designers to establish which areas are only accessible under certain conditions. While the hole at the top of the crypt was aesthetically pleasing, because it permitted a single shaft of sunlight to permeate the darkness of the tomb, it resulted in unforeseen (and undesirable) consequences for the player and should therefore be cut from the game to prohibit the player from ruining his own experience. If there's no way into the Crypt of Kharanthas, the player will eventually have to speak with the old beggar.

TECHNICAL LIMITATIONS

During the production of the game's story and the integration of dialogue with the gameplay, the writer must work within the parameters established by the game's hardware platform, engine, and code base. Though most writers are not intimately familiar with the technology being used, the other developers on a project are, and they are available to answer questions. It's up to the writer to determine the limitations that will define the parameters for a game's story presentation and to make the most of the resources that are available. The writer should explore the areas of sound design, character interaction, and AI during all stages of production and should maintain close working ties with the developers working in these areas. Outside of cinematics, a great deal of a game's narrative context is communicated through character dialogue, and if the writer knows what is or isn't possible, he's better equipped to design the story content accordingly.

SOUND DESIGN AND PROGRAMMING

The writer's conversations with the sound team should focus on the burning question, "What can I get away with?" Ultimately, that's what a writer needs to know prior to the dialogue integration process. This question takes many forms, and the more information the writer gathers, the higher the level of polish that will be possible. Issues that the writer should explore include:

- Number of cues per character
- Variegation
- Randomization
- Nonvoice audio interference
- Distant dialogue
- Muffled dialogue
- Scripted voice process
- Interruption

Number of Cues per Character

To determine how much dialogue can be integrated into the game, the writer needs to know how many voice cues can be used for each character. This will help the writer to understand how many different ways a single phrase can be said, for example. In *Rise of Merlin* the dragon Vexalyss takes human form and accompanies the player character through the Wasteland of Yzaul. During this quest the dragon gives the player advice and informs him of dangers ("Ogres, advancing on us from the south!"). If *Rise of Merlin* is a next-generation project, the total number of cues possible will probably be quite high, but if it's a current-generation title, the number of cues may be severely limited (which will be discussed in greater detail later in this chapter). The dragon may only be able to store a few dozen cues in the game's memory at any given time, sharply curtailing the number of variations that are possible. This leads us to variegation.

Variegation

If there is a recurring element in a game experience, it's possible that any accompanying voice cues will be played each time that element surfaces. For example, in the aforementioned instance, the dragon Vexalyss informs the player each time he sights enemies. If he only has one voice cue for a specific kind of enemy, the player is going to hear that cue over and over again ("Ogres, advancing on us from the south!" "Ogres, advancing on us from the south!"). This takes its toll on a player's immersion, gradually eroding it by reminding the player that it's only a game. By employing variegation, the writer can ameliorate this somewhat. Multiple cues that say the same thing can be used to vary the audio content somewhat, resulting in a less monotonous experience ("Ogres, advancing on us from the south!" "Merlin, there are ogres to the south!"). If there are numerous enemies to choose from (ogres, giants, trolls, and wyverns), and the character of Vexalyss can only store so many voice cues in his memory, then the number of variations on each theme becomes limited, and it's likely that the character will begin to repeat himself eventually. However, each additional variation that is introduced will diminish the chances of repetition and will further change the audio landscape of the game, making it feel more natural and less monotonous.

Randomization

This, of course, depends on the game's ability to randomize content, which in most cases is a given. However, the writer should confirm the nature of the randomization with the sound team, just to be certain. For example, consider the following three possibilities based on the voice cues shown in Figure 10.2.

CHARACTER	CUE	CONTEXT	TRIGGER	INFLECTION
Vexalyss	Merlin, a group of ogres headed towards us!	Vexalyss and Merlin are traveling across the plains.	Vexalyss sees a group of ogres.	urgent
Vexalyss	Ready yourself, Merlin. A group of ogres approaches.	Vexalyss and Merlin are traveling across the plains.	Vexalyss sees a group of ogres.	urgent
Vexalyss	Ogres, advancing on us from the south!	Vexalyss and Merlin are traveling across the plains.	Vexalyss sees a group of ogres.	urgent
Vexalyss	Sorcerer, there are ogres coming from the south!	Vexalyss and Merlin are traveling across the plains.	Vexalyss sees a group of ogres.	urgent
Vexalyss	Merlin, there are ogres to the south!	Vexalyss and Merlin are traveling across the plains.	Vexalyss sees a group of ogres.	urgent

FIGURE 10.2   Randomized voice cues.

Example 1

The five cues in Figure 10.2 play one after the other, ensuring that there are no re-peats. However, if the pattern plays long enough, the player will realize that he's hearing the same five cues in the same order, over and over again. This may not be detectable if there are other cues playing in between, however. For example, if there are also similar cues for the detection of giants, trolls, and wyverns, and the appearance of those monsters is varied, then the player might never catch on to the pattern. Obviously, since there's a pattern, this is not true randomization.

Example 2

The five cues in Figure 10.2 play at random, so it's theoretically possible for the same cue to play twice in a row. Every time a voice cue plays from this list, there is a 20% chance that the player will hear the same cue twice in a row and a 4% chance that the player will hear the same voice cue three times in a row.

Example 3

The five cues in Figure 10.2 play at random, but the cue that just played is unavail-able after it's played once, until all five cues have played. This means that after playing voice cue 2, the only available cues are 1, 3, 4, and 5. If cue 5 plays next, then the available cues are 1, 3, and 4. This continues until all five cues have played, at which point the cues are reset and the cycle begins again. Though there is a chance of repetition, this is the most random of the three examples cited here.

There are other methods of randomization, but this should give you a stake in the ground to proceed from.

Nonvoice Audio Interference

The writer may need to find out how many sounds can play at a given time. Depending on the platform hardware and the game's engine, the sound team's palette of sounds may be vast or restricted. For example, it may be that only five sounds can play at any given time. If this is the case, the writer must mentally subtract one sound for ambient audio. Virtually every location in a game has some kind of ambient noise, be it room tone in an office building (fluourescent lights and HVAC systems) or natural sounds outdoors (wind in the trees, birds singing). That leaves four sounds. If the player is riding a horse into battle, the writer must subtract hoofbeats and the roar of the ogre, plus one for the clang of sword on shield. This leaves one voice cue for the Vexalyss, and if there's another level of interference (such as the ogre's death scream), then Vexalyss' dialogue may be dropped altogether. If you've ever played a game and heard a character suddenly fall silent halfway through a line of dialogue, it may be a result of such technical restrictions.

The writer may want to investigate the hierarchy employed by the audio team in the hope of establishing some rules for critical information. While it's more than acceptable to drop nonvital voice cues from the game (as opposed to suddenly dropping, then restoring, the sound of hoofbeats, which would be strange and off-putting to the player), certain voice cues are more important than other sounds. For example, it may be that voice cues from Vexalyss are judged to be more vital to the player experience than the death screams of enemy combatants, so the sound programmer may elect to drop the death screams in the case of a conflict between the two.

If the writer is working on a next-generation game with powerful resources, the point may well be moot, but development on current-generation systems and handhelds will continue well into the life-cycle of next-generation consoles, and the writer may find himself facing this challenge. It's better to establish the ground rules early on, so consult with the sound team as soon as it is possible to do so.

Distant Dialogue

The writer may have created an exchange between two characters the player overhears while moving toward them. This information may be crucial to gameplay, or it may just add color to the game. For example, in *Rise of Merlin*, the player may overhear two lords speaking to each other in a castle. While standing on a parapet near the window, the player might eavesdrop on their conversation and learn that the Council of Mages is unhappy with the Dragon King's decision to invade the Western Reaches. Though this information is not vital to the player's completion of any quests or tasks, it helps explain why the Council has begun to prepare for war. Alternatively, the player's objective might be to infiltrate the Dragon King's citadel and gather information about his plans, in which case it is necessary for the player to sneak into the citadel and listen to the conversations taking place within. In either case the propagation of audio will determine the player's ability to overhear the conversation. Audio propagation is the emanation of sound from the source of the noise in question, and in many games, this means you can hear something before you see it (and the noise gets louder as you approach the source). Good audio propagation is subtle: as you enter the radius of propagation, you can just barely hear music, a conversation, or the sound of a car engine. Bad propagation is sudden: one minute, you're creeping through a corridor in total silence; you turn a corner and are nearly deafened by loud music. If your game experience requires the player to eavesdrop on distant conversations, or if the narrative is augmented in some way by a gradual increase in sound as the player approaches the source of noise (such as the breathing of a sleeping dragon), then it's good to discuss this aspect of audio with your sound team.

Muffled Dialogue

As in the previous example, there may be times when the player needs to eavesdrop on content in the next room. For example, the player may be a spy, gathering information covertly. In an ideal scenario, the player ought to be able to hear dialogue through a closed door, but given the parameters of the project, this simply may not be possible. It's best to know in advance if this is a viable way to approach overheard dialogue in your game.

Scripted Voice Process

The writer should consider the role of the design team in the scripting process, though whether it's the audio design team or the game design team will depend on the studio. Once voice cues are recorded and processed, the scripters place them in the game by means of a scripting editor. While the writer may not be directly involved in the scripting of dialogue, he should at least be familiar with the basics of the process and should be able to script a simple conversation between two characters, so as to better speak the language of the design team.

Interruption

In film and television it's not uncommon to hear two characters interrupting each other while in the midst of a heated discussion. In games it's far more common to hear that dreadful silence between voice cues, even when it's obvious that we're supposed to believe this exchange is part of a furious argument.

"You're out of control! I want your badge and gun on my desk, or else—"

(long, awkward pause)

"Dammit, sir, they killed my partner, and they gotta pay! You can have my badge when it's over—"

(long, awkward pause)

"I'm tired of covering you, Burke! You're too close to this case! Back off!"

The culprit in this case is probably the scripting tool, though a lack of preparation doubtless played a part as well. The functionality of each scripting program varies, but in general, the scripter is able to indicate which cues play and in what order. If the scripter wants to simulate an argument, the scripting tool may or may not permit overlap between scripted cues. If not, and if it's mandatory that one cue finish playing before another begins, the scripter must time the two voice cues perfectly. For example, if the first voice cue is 2.43 seconds long, the scripter should indicate that the second cue has to begin after 2.44 seconds have elapsed. However, this level of detail may not be possible, and the scripter may have to indicate 2.5 seconds, or even 3 seconds. It's a question of what's possible with the tools available. If the issue is addressed early in the process, the audio programmer may be able to fine-tune the timing for scripted voice cues, and it may even be possible for the programmer to add the ability to overlap voice cues (which would be ideal, because then the second cue could begin while the first was still playing, adding more intensity and verisimilitude to the argument).

NPC Dialogue

The NPCs in a game seem more believable if their dialogue is consistent with what we perceive to be the reality of the game world. In other words, if you're shooting at a terrorist, and he's asking the other terrorist, "Hey, do you hear something?" the whole thing is ruined. The player's yanked out of the immersion as swiftly as if the developer had flashed a big sign on the screen reading, IT'S JUST A GAME. The awareness of the NPCs is not the bailiwick of the game writer, since it's the programmer who furnishes the AI. However, the writer can work with the programmer to ensure that the characters at least say the right thing in a critical situation. There are a number of ways that NPCs can contribute to a game's mood through their choice of words.

Awareness

Many first-person shooters include a squad of teammates who accompany the player character through a series of missions. In most cases these teammates are programmed to inform the player of any changes in status, such as calling out when they take fire from hostile characters. In *SOCOM 3* the characters even indicate which direction they're taking fire from: "Sir, taking fire from the north!" This allows the player, who has access to an on-screen compass, to reorient himself toward the source of the gunfire. In a linear game, whose enemies are typically going to appear from in front of the player, this might not be as valuable, but in a nonlinear shooter like *SOCOM 3*, this feature helps the player be more effective and it reinforces the perception that the teammates are aware of their surroundings. However, simply writing such voice cues won't be enough to guarantee that the characters perform as desired. The writer needs to communicate the requested effect to the design team so they can decide how best to approach the situation. For example, in *Rise of Merlin* when Vexalyss is telling the player of the incoming monsters, one of two things needs to happen: either the AI needs to be able to differentiate between ogres and wyverns, so that the character "knows" which voice cue to play, or the entire sequence needs to be scripted. If it's the latter case, the game scripters will spawn wyverns in and then direct Vexalyss to warn the player accordingly.

Repetition

While it's good for NPCs to reinforce player objectives and to restate information so that the player is better equipped to interact with the game world, outright repetition is always dismaying to the player.

Hostile Ambience

What is the point of enemy dialogue? In some cases it is intended to alert the player to a change in status. When the bad guys yell, "Reinforcements are on their way," it tells the player that he can soon expect heavier resistance. It can also give the player an advantage. If the player manages to get behind enemy lines and hears the bad guys discussing the location of the POWs, the player now has more information to work with. Enemy dialogue can also enhance a game by creating ambience, serving no other purpose than to establish a mood. A solid example of this is *Resident Evil 4*, which boasted some truly sinister voice acting. Players who speak Spanish will recognize some of the profanity hurled at Leon Kennedy by the villagers, but the content isn't really the point of the voice acting in this case. It's the distorted quality of the vocals, coupled with the guttural delivery, that reinforces the game's fundamental creepiness. Likewise, the Scrags in *Quake* made sounds like human whispers, and screamed "No!" when struck—again, creepy.

Alternates

When the player receives key information in the form of voice cues, the writer should always consider an alternate method of information delivery. For instance, in games like the *James Bond* and *Syphon Filter®* series, the player receives orders and information from off-screen speakers but can also access that information via an objective screen. In *Morrowind* and *Oblivion* if the player enters into an agreement with an NPC, that information is recorded in the journal.

SUMMARY

Like any other member of a development team, the writer must work within the project's parameters and must learn how to create a strong narrative experience from the available components. In this chapter we discussed the various technical parameters that the writer must be aware of when documenting a game's story content. We explored level design, the pitfalls of level design, technical limitations, audio programming, and NPC dialogue. Future chapters will discuss the integration and testing of narrative content.

DEVELOPER INTERVIEW

Mikey Spano, Artist, Epic Games
Gears of War, Ghost Recon: Island Thunder

LEVEL DESIGN

I think requisite understanding about the level design process depends on a writer's involvement in a project. Obviously, the more the writer knows about a project, the better he or she will be at their job; but in the real world, I would expect the screenplay and dialogue writers to have a solid understanding of the pacing and mood of a level and bring strong solutions to the table to combat some common pitfalls such as repetitive one-liners and jarring talking-head cinematics. I'm keeping my fingers crossed that with more of a focus on art direction and character acting, games will be able to overcome overly descriptive narratives that are usually used to set the mood of a game. Hollywood movies only have about two hours to tell some pretty epic stories, so they don't have time for long descriptions of a character's motivation or how a set should make you feel; the actors and set designers are very deliberate and can usually sell a story in no time flat. I hope that game developers continue to learn from Hollywood screen writing and cinematography.

$\rightarrow$

Story in Games

I don't think the task of improving a writer's understanding of game development falls squarely on the laps of the writers themselves. I think it's the team's responsibility to make sure everything fits together. Everyone on a development team should consider himself equally responsible for the total package and should be encouraged to share their opinions and techniques with the writers to help keep everything consistent.

Conveying story to a player while they are concentrating on a million other things seems to be the most difficult task in game design today. The player is usually bombarded with tons of micromanagement (staying safe, defeating enemies, planning what to do next, etc.), so throwing a story on top of all that either ends up being obtrusive and annoying (cut-scenes that pull you out of the game) or totally ignored by the player (radio chatter and disembodied voices).

Collaboration

In the case of story implementation, I think less is definitely more. Story is absolutely a necessity in most modern games, but the difficulty lies in how to present the story to the player without frustrating or confusing them. To combat this, writers can work with character animators and art directors to try to convey emotion that wasn't previously possible due to the limitations of last-generation character animation technology. Writers can also work with level designers to infuse story elements into levels where the player has a bit of downtime. There's nothing worse than missing a key story element because you were too busy trying not die to hear what was being shouted by some faceless voice.

Writers can improve their usage of the level design process by making sure they work closely enough with level designers to ensure that their story is being told properly without interfering with gameplay. It's up to level designers and writers to collectively make sure that gameplay is fun, while also ensuring that the story is compelling enough to keep a player focused on their overall goal.

Gears of War

I've worked on several projects where the story and design was very strong. *Gears of War* stands out as my personal favorite due to its amazing ability to really get a player emotional about all the plot twists and turns. It's hard to really

→

nail down what went right or wrong during production of *Gears of War* because the game ended up being so great in the end. I think that the writing and design staff remained steadfast with their vision, and they made sure that every little detail was right at every turn, which left very little room for error.

ADVICE FOR ASPIRING WRITERS

My advice for all aspiring game developers is to remain open to change and honest in their criticism. It's up to everyone on a team to make sure that their project is a success, so speak up if you can think of a way to improve your game!

11 Integrating Dialogue

In This Chapter

- Integration
- Scripting

INTEGRATION

Once the voice assets have been recorded and delivered, the development team must begin the process of integrating those cues into the game content. This process can take up much of the production stage of development, during which time other priorities will make their demands on the team. The writer must understand the scope of the integration process in order to effectively direct the flow of narrative content in the game. In this chapter we'll discuss how dialogue is scripted into the game, and we'll examine some of the things a writer can do to ensure a cleaner scripting process. Then, we'll look at game localization and explore the preparations that must be made beforehand.

SCRIPTING

During the scripting process the writer needs to work closely with the scripting team to ensure that they have all the resources they need to integrate the dialogue into the game. Though every studio's methods are different, the core principles are the same. The writer should be aware of the basic functions of his project's scripting tools and should be able to converse with scripters on the subject.

Scripting is, fundamentally, the process of placing objects in a game world and assigning them behaviors. While AI may govern some aspects of general behavior, individual instances are governed by scripting (see Figures 11.1 and 11.2). For example, in *Rise of Merlin*, all ogres will attack the player on sight. However, in level 4, the Ogre Chieftan will challenge the player to single combat and will then walk through the Iron Gates toward the player. This is not the behavior exhibited by the other ogres in the game; it was something that a designer indicated in a design document, and it was accompanied by recorded dialogue created by a writer and performed by an actor. The dialogue was placed in the game by a scripter, along with the animations for "taunt" and "walk." The end result is an individual instance of a specific sequence of events.

Scripting editors vary in terms of functionality and interface, but in general, they are programs that allow game designers to quickly assign behaviors to objects in-game without having to code by hand. The interface may consist of drop-down menus, or it may require the scripter to know a particular language (such as Lua), but in either case it streamlines the process of placing objects and assigning them characteristics or behaviors.

CHARACTER	CUE	CONTEXT	TRIGGER	INFLECTION	AREA	EFFECT	FILENAME
Talerios	Yes, Merlin.	Artificial intelligence response.	Merlin has given Talerios an order.	normal	n/a		tal_ai03_01
Talerios	At once, my lord.	Artificial intelligence response.	Merlin has given Talerios an order.	normal	n/a		tal_ai03_02
Talerios	Yes, Lord Merlin.	Artificial intelligence response.	Merlin has given Talerios an order.	normal	n/a		tal_ai03_03
Talerios	As you command.	Artificial intelligence response.	Merlin has given Talerios an order.	normal	n/a		tal_ai03_04
Talerios	Merlin, I'm hit!	Artificial intelligence response.	Talerios has been injured by the enemy.	urgent	n/a		tal_ai04_01
Talerios	Lord Merlin, I'm injured!	Artificial intelligence response.	Talerios has been injured by the enemy.	urgent	n/a		tal_ai04_02
Talerios	My lord, I've been hit!	Artificial intelligence response.	Talerios has been injured by the enemy.	urgent	n/a		tal_ai04_03
Talerios	Aah! I'm injured!	Artificial intelligence response.	Talerios has been injured by the enemy.	urgent	n/a		tal_ai04_04

FIGURE 11.1   Lines of AI state dialogue.

CHARACTER	CUE	CONTEXT	TRIGGER	INFLECTION	AREA	EFFECT	FILENAME
Talerios	You sound as though you fear him.	The group is approaching the Fortress of Hauzeil.	Conversation 1-4B.	curious	1.4		lev1_a4_003
Vexalyss	Bite your tongue, whelp. I fear no man. But the Horned King wields a weapon like no other.	The group is approaching the Fortress of Hauzeil.	Conversation 1-4B.	angry	1.4		lev1_a4_004
Talerios	What weapon is that?	The group is approaching the Fortress of Hauzeil.	Conversation 1-4B.	curious	1.4		lev1_a4_005
Vexalyss	A dragon.	The group is approaching the Fortress of Hauzeil.	Conversation 1-4B.	angry	1.4		lev1_a4_006
Talerios	You fear another of your own kind?	The group is approaching the Fortress of Hauzeil.	Conversation 1-4B.	confused	1.4		lev1_a4_007
Vexalyss	The dragon of which I speak is not my kind. It is an abomination. The Horned King has cast a demon into the body of a Golden Dragon.	The group is approaching the Fortress of Hauzeil.	Conversation 1-4B.	angry	1.4		lev1_a4_008
Talerios	By the gods...	The group is approaching the Fortress of Hauzeil.	Conversation 1-4B.	stunned	1.4		lev1_a4_007

FIGURE 11.2   Lines of scripted dialogue.

The designer needs to consider the following aspects of the scripting process:

- Scripting team
- Scripting schedule
- Scripting tools
- Documentation
- Dialogue prioritization
- Voice cues and animation
- Triggered cues
- False awareness
- Dependent cues

SCRIPTING TEAM

The scripting team needs to have clear, accessible information about the expected user experience. The documentation should outline precisely when and where the voice cue plays and under what circumstances. Using the screenplay, the scripters should be able to distinguish the speaker from the audience. This information can appear as part of the design documentation or in a separate document. If the data is presented in two different documents, it should be carefully aligned, because there's a substantial margin of error if the scripters are working off of multiple documents. See Figure 11.3 for details.

Talerios (to Vexalyss)
What weapon is that?

Vexalyss (to Talerios)
A dragon.

Talerios (to Vexalyss)
You fear another of your own kind?

Vexalyss (to Talerios)
The dragon of which I speak is not my kind. It is an abomination. The Horned King has cast a demon into the body of a Golden Dragon.

Talerios (to Vexalyss)
By the gods…

Guardsman (to player)
You, there. What business have you?

Vexalyss (to player)
I think you'd better handle this.

FIGURE 11.3 The screenplay clearly indicates who's communicating with whom.

For example, in *Rise of Merlin*, while scripting the Dismal Forest level, the scripters are populating the map and setting behaviors from the design documentation, which was written by the lead designer. The ogres go here, the spider-gaunts go there, and the wyverns are going to attack from the north when the player enters the Holy Glade. However, when the scripters are placing dialogue cues in the game, they're going to be working off of the story design documentation, and it's not 100% up to date with the design documents. This means the writer was still working under the impression that the Dragon Queen would be waiting for the player at the glade and that the player would have to defend her from attack. Furthermore, the scripters are confused, because the voice cues coming from Merlin's sidekick, Talerios, indicate that the wyverns are attacking from the south. This is because the wyverns originally were supposed to do so, but this was changed when the lead designer moved the Crimson Citadel to the north side of the map so that it would be visible throughout the level. This series of complications means the scripters will have to arrive at some kind of resolution on the matter; first, though, the lead designer and the writer must hash out the details, which might take a little time. Compromises will be made and solutions will be concocted. During this time, of course, the dialogue scripting for the Dismal Forest level will come to a halt, and the scripters will have to tackle other work. If there is none, valuable time is lost until the issue is resolved.

To do the best possible work, the scripting team needs a cohesive and integrated document to work from. Any gray areas should be delineated in advance and should not have significant impact on the project. That means it is permissible to leave content in the hands of the scripters, but they should not be held accountable for its interpretation at that stage.

For example, in *Rise of Merlin* the documentation may indicate that a group of ogres attacks a village, eliciting cries of panic from the villagers. Since the documentation doesn't specifically indicate which lines should be playing, the scripters should be able to use any of the "panic" voice cues that were recorded for the villagers. If the writer wants one of the villagers to mention that her child is trapped inside their home and needs to be rescued, the writer should indicate this in the document, as opposed to assuming that the scripters will just know what to do. Scripters generally have a lot to consider during the game design process and shouldn't be expected to anticipate story design decisions, regardless of how obvious they may seem to a writer. If it's worth putting in the game, it's worth noting in the design documentation.

The documentation itself can take many forms, but if it is a text document, the writer may want to include top-down maps of key areas to clarify the location of specific conversations. The top-down map, if available, can easily be added to a Word document and can help make the details more concrete. By indicating locations of trigger zones and characters with dotted lines and Xs, the writer can help pinpoint the locations of voice cues in-game (see Figure 11.4 for an example). This helps the scripters figure out where content goes, and it allows the scripter to correct the writer when necessary. If a map has changed, or if there are alternate routes that the writer is not familiar with, the scripters may be able to bring this information to his attention, giving him enough time to make revisions or adjustments to the document.

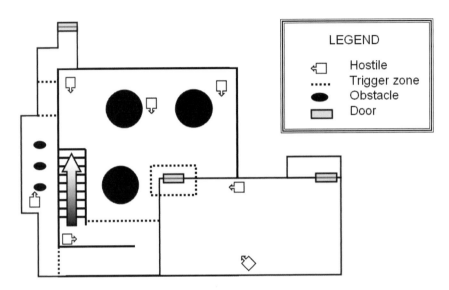

FIGURE 11.4   This top-down map helps the scripters pinpoint locations of story content.

SCRIPTING SCHEDULE

The writer needs to be aware of the scripting schedule to make sure there's enough time to integrate the voice assets. This means the writer needs to know how long it's going to take to get the scripting tool off the ground. The completion date for the scripting tools will impact the time line for the scripting of story content, and any delays in the process will cause delays for the placement of voice cues. In addition, real story testing can't begin until characters are placed and active in-game. The writer needs to factor these aspects of the process into his schedule, as they will determine how soon placeholder voice cues can be integrated into the game-build.

The number of scripters available and the dates of their availability will determine the amount of man-hours that can be dedicated to scripting, of which only a fraction will be set aside for voice cues and story content. In some cases the demands on game scripters exceed mere gameplay scripting, as they are also responsible for creating levels. Some level designers create maps and place objects and characters in those levels and then assign behaviors and characteristics to them using the scripting editor. It is only after all these tasks have been accomplished that the scripters turn their attention to story content.

At different studios different personnel are responsible for the placement of voice cues in the level. If it's the scripters, then the writer needs to coordinate his efforts with them. However, it may well be the sound designer or the writer who winds up placing voice cues in the map. In this case the scripters place characters and assign them behaviors, and then someone else accesses the file and plugs in the voice cues. Further work is done on the game scripting and the voice scripting until the map is completed. Since it's passing through multiple hands, the potential for mistakes is raised with each new round of scripting. Extra attention must be paid to detail if multiple scripters are working on a map, to ensure that one doesn't undo or corrupt the work of another.

If the scripting process is robust enough, there may be time to insert place-holder voice cues in the map. Assuming that the map has been created, and is relatively bug-free, and that the characters and objects have been placed in the game fairly early in the production process, it may be possible to record placeholder voice cues and integrate them into the map prior to the actual voice shoots. If this is the case, the writer has an excellent opportunity: he can experience the game as a work-in-progress during the development stage and can refine and revise his dialogue to further match the gameplay. Through iteration and critique, the writer can polish his screenplay until it gleams, resulting in a much more productive recording session and a higher-quality story experience for the player. This requires excellent communication between all parties (designers, scripters, audio personnel, and the writer), and it means some time will be spent recording and processing the place-holder voice cues. However, the payoff is priceless, given the advantage that it provides the writer. Some of the material that is written in the form of placeholder voice cues will probably be cut, and it's equally probable that the writer will wind up writing a great deal of new content after the first round of placeholder cues is integrated into the game. This means that if the writer had waited until after the voice shoot to integrate assets, some of the cues would have been cut, and some additional cues would have been written after the voice shoot (which would necessitate a pickup shoot later in the project, at additional expense). By avoiding all of this complication, the writer has saved the project time and money and has improved the quality of the story content.

Time should be included in the scripting schedule for the process of testing the story content. Typically, this sort of testing is left to the writer, unless the game is heavily story-focused. As a general rule, scripters are more concerned about testing the actual gameplay, which is understandable. The writer may want to allot time in his own schedule for playing through the game and verifying the accuracy and efficacy of the dialogue and other story content.

SCRIPTING TOOLS

Once the scripting tool is ready for use, it's inevitable that members of the development team will request additional features, each of which will require time to implement. For example, the scripters may request a drag-and-drop feature, which they insist would be more efficient than the drop-down menu system they're currently using.

During the planning stages, as the story design is starting to take form, the writer should begin to investigate the scripting tools and to determine whether they'll be able to accommodate the needs of the story content. The writer may want to explore the scripting tool's ability to handle special-case dialogue, such as interruptions, conversations, and simultaneous speech. If the game features a lot of spoken dialogue, it's likely that NPCs will interrupt each other, engage in two- or three-sided conversations, or try to talk over one another. If the scripting tool is not currently equipped to handle that kind of functionality, the writer needs to request such features.

The procedure for requesting features will vary, but typically, the writer would submit a request through the team's producer or design lead, who would convey that request to the programming lead. Should the need be demonstrable, and the schedule flexible, it's possible that such a request would result in a new feature being added to the scripting tool. However, there is always competition for new features, and a new feature that enhances gameplay is likely to take precedence over a feature that enhances the scripting of story materials. Therefore, the writer may not see that functionality added to the scripting editor until much later in the project.

Likewise, it may be that some of the requested changes to the scripting editor are simply not possible. This may result in some adjustments to the story content, which the writer should try to prepare for. For instance, in *Rise of Merlin* the team may be requesting a feature that would allow the scripters to create alternating dialogue for conversations between NPCs. In Figure 11.5 the two columns show the dialogue options for each NPC.

In practice, the scripting editor would randomly select one line from each row, resulting in a randomly generated conversation each time. This means that if the player is sneaking up on a pair of Imperial Guardsmen, he's going to hear a com-

GUARD 1	GUARD 2	GUARD 1
Have you heard about the Prince of Hispanya?	No, I haven't heard anything.	He gambled away the crown jewels.
Did you hear that the Prince of Hispanya is stepping down?	No. What's the story?	The fool got drunk and lost the crown jewels while gambling.
Did the captain tell you about Prince Hamiro?	No. What happened?	He can't hold his liquor, it seems. Lost the crown jewels while playing at dice.

FIGURE 11.5   The requested alternating-dialogue feature.

pletely different set of dialogue. Some lines may be repeated, but with enough variables, a great deal of randomness could be created.

Because of time constraints, it turns out that the programmer in charge of the scripting tools won't be able to integrate this feature. Since the feature is no longer available, the randomization will have to be scripted by hand. Because of the scripting schedule, that's just not feasible. Therefore, the writer is going to have to revise the plan. In all likelihood, the writer will have to create a series of regular conversations, such as that shown in Figure 11.6.

GUARD 1	Have you heard about the Prince of Hispanya?
GUARD 2	No, I haven't heard anything.
GUARD 1	He gambled away the crown jewels.
GUARD 3	Did you hear that the Prince of Hispanya is stepping down?
GUARD 4	No. What's the story?
GUARD 3	The fool got drunk and lost the crown jewels while gambling.
GUARD 5	Did the captain tell you about Prince Hamiro?
GUARD 6	No. What happened?
GUARD 5	He can't hold his liquor, it seems. Lost the crown jewels while playing at dice.

FIGURE 11.6   Standard conversation instead of alternating dialogue.

If the writer is already aware of the various dependencies (the work load of the scripting tool programmer, the scripting schedule), he may be able to develop a satisfactory alternative that still allows for some randomization. Otherwise, these exchanges of dialogue will have to be scripted as normal conversations, and that means that each time the game is played, the dialogue in a given section will be exactly the same.

DOCUMENTATION

During the planning stage the writer should be communicating with the scripters, either directly or indirectly (such as through the team's design lead or producer). To furnish the scripting team with the documentation best suited to deliver the information they need, the writer should find out what their needs are. For example, the writer needs to know which fields would be most helpful for the scripters. Figure 11.7 shows one example of the Screen/Play format geared toward streamlining the scripting process.

CHARACTER	CUE	CONTEXT	TRIGGER	INFLECTION	AREA	EFFECT	FILENAME
Name of character who's speaking.	Words spoken by the character.	The current situation.	The event that prompted the character to speak.	The character's mood.	Part of game.	Sound effect, if any.	Name of audio file, including extension.

FIGURE 11.7   The fields listed here include Area, Context, and File Name.

The writer should meet with the scripting team to discuss file names, context detail, level organization, and character citation.

Filenames

In the example in Figure 11.7 the writer has settled on a file-naming convention out of necessity, but before implementing it on a broad scale, the writer should discuss it with the scripting team. Based on their experience, they may have an idea about what kind of file-naming convention works best for them. They may prefer to indicate as much data as possible in the filename (Evil_Knight_death_scream_002.wav) or as little (kds001.wav). Their criteria may be obvious (such as the width of the drop-down menu in the scripting editor) or inscrutable.

Context Detail

How much information should appear in the Context field? The scripters probably have a preference, and since the document is intended to simplify their work, the writer should take that into consideration when documenting the context for each line of dialogue. The scripters may prefer a lengthy explanation, as it helps them make sure the line is playing precisely when it should. On the other hand, they may prefer a simple, straightforward context, written as concisely as possible. Figures 11.8 and 11.9 show two different approaches to context.

CHARACTER	CUE	CONTEXT	INFLECTION	LOCATION	EFFECT	FILENAME
Lancelot	Arthur, beware!	Combat	urgent	1.2		m01-a02-lan01

FIGURE 11.8   Short, concise context doesn't give the scripters much to work with.

CHARACTER	CUE	CONTEXT	INFLECTION	LOCATION	EFFECT	FILENAME
Lancelot	Arthur, beware!	In combat, one of the Dark Knights rides up to Arthur and strikes at him from behind, prompting Lancelot to warn him.	urgent	1.2		m01-a02-lan01

FIGURE 11.9   Detailed context gives more information but is time-consuming to write.

Level Organization

At this stage the writer should know how the levels in the game are organized. In some titles levels are loaded in stages. In others they're part of one large, contiguous world that's cordoned off as a series of areas in the design documentation. In some cases the screenplay document should include a reference to the game level. In other cases there should be a column for the level, a column for the area, and a column for the section. It depends on the size of the game and how it's organized. See Figure 11.10 for details.

CHARACTER	CUE	CONTEXT	TRIGGER	INFLECTION	AREA	SECTION	EFFECT	FILENAME
Lancelot	My lord, someone approaches.	Player is riding along the Western Reach.	Player crosses Trigger Zone F4.	serious	4	1		m04-a01-lan01

CHARACTER	CUE	CONTEXT	TRIGGER	INFLECTION	LOCATION	AREA	EFFECT	FILENAME
Lancelot	My lord, someone approaches.	Player is riding along the Western Reach.	Player crosses Trigger Zone F4.	serious	Western Reaches	4.1		m04-a01-lan01

CHARACTER	CUE	CONTEXT	TRIGGER	INFLECTION	AREA	EFFECT	FILENAME
Lancelot	My lord, someone approaches.	Player is riding along the Western Reach.	Player crosses Trigger Zone F4.	serious	4.1	m04-a01-lan01	

FIGURE 11.10   Different kinds of level organization in various spreadsheets.

Character Citation

Do the scripters have their own way of referring to the characters in the game? For example, if your spreadsheet refers to Doctor Miles Dillahunty, but the scripting editor drop-down list cites him as Dr. #3, or as Civilian_doctor_3.mdl, the scripters will probably come to you for clarification. Multiply this by the number of characters in the game and the number of scripters on your team, and you can see how it would be much more efficient to use the terms the scripters are familiar with. Meet with them to discuss the character citation and consider either using their citation style for the Speaker field or adding a separate field for their benefit.

Documenting Special Cases

If you're employing more complex forms of exchanged dialogue, it's good to discuss this with the scripters beforehand to find out how best to indicate these special cases in the spreadsheet. For example, if there is a conversation in the game between two NPCs, the writer should know in advance how to communicate this information to the scripters. While it might be easiest to just tell them, there might be over 10,000 lines of dialogue in the game. Verbal communication isn't viable at that point. In the case of a conversation there might be a separate field in the spreadsheet that's labeled Conversation (or some abbreviation thereof), which would receive a check-mark if it is part of an extended dialogue between two characters. Alternatively, lines of dialogue could be marked as such in their filenames. For example, conversational dialogue might end with 1A1, 1A2, 1B1, 1B2, and so on. See Figure 11.11 for more information.

CHARACTER	CUE	CONV.	CONTEXT	TRIGGER	INFLECTION	AREA	EFFECT	FILENAME
Merchant 1	They say he put the entire village to the sword.	3B	Two merchants and a customer are discussing the news of the realm.	Player passes through trigger 3B.	serious	3.2		lev3_a2_3B1
Merchant 2	What, women and children?	3B	Two merchants and a customer are discussing the news of the realm.	Player passes through trigger 3B.	shocked	3.2		lev3_a2_3B2
Customer 1	I've heard he's not a man, but a devil.	3B	Two merchants and a customer are discussing the news of the realm.	Player passes through trigger 3B.	nervous	3.2		lev3_a2_3B3
Merchant 1	That may be, and that may not be, but the Horned King is evil to the bone, of that you may be sure.	3B	Two merchants and a customer are discussing the news of the realm.	Player passes through trigger 3B.	serious	3.2		lev3_a2_3B4
Merchant 2	What does that King say about this? Will there be war?	3B	Two merchants and a customer are discussing the news of the realm.	Player passes through trigger 3B.	anxious	3.2		lev3_a2_3B5
Merchant 1	I've heard rumors. They say that the lords of the realm have gathered in the capital to discuss their plans. Time will tell, I suppose.	3B	Two merchants and a customer are discussing the news of the realm.	Player passes through trigger 3B.	serious	3.2		lev3_a2_3B6
Merchant 3	Good day, my lord. Some fine weapons we've got here. Take a look.		The player has walked into a merchant's tent.	Player enters tent 24.	normal	3.2		lev3_a2_001

FIGURE 11.11 An example of conversational dialogue.

In the case of a single-instance one-liner the writer needs to communicate to the scripting team that it's just a comment made by the player character or an NPC in a specific part of the game and then is never heard again. Again, this may be something that's indicated in a special field, in the filename, or even in the Context field, so long as the scripters know that the line isn't repeated each time the player performs a certain action.

In other cases a group of lines might be triggered by player action and play over and over again (at random) until a specific criterion has been met. For example, as illustrated in Figure 11.12, the player is on a training mission and is expected to cross to the other side of the river and attack the troll. Numerous alternates have been recorded for this scenario, and one voice cue is played every minute until the player attacks the troll. The writer has set it up this way because the player may choose to wander around for a few minutes or may not be paying attention because he's playing around with the inventory system. Still, play cannot continue until the troll is dead, so the player must be reminded. To avoid monotony, several versions have been recorded, and their randomization further helps avoid repetition.

CHARACTER	CUE	CONTEXT	TRIGGER	INFLECTION	AREA	EFFECT	FILENAME
Niniane	Now cross the river and attack that Troll.	The player is going through the training mission.	The player has mastered the use of the Staff, and must now use it in combat.	serious	0.1	echo	lev00_a01_nin01
Niniane	When you're ready, get across the river and fight the Troll.	The player is going through the training mission.	The player has mastered the use of the Staff, and must now use it in combat.	serious	0.1	echo	lev00_a01_nin02
Niniane	Now, get across that river. You must defeat that Troll.	The player is going through the training mission.	The player has mastered the use of the Staff, and must now use it in combat.	serious	0.1	echo	lev00_a01_nin03
Niniane	There's a Troll on the other side of the river. Once you cross the river, fight that Troll to the death.	The player is going through the training mission.	The player has mastered the use of the Staff, and must now use it in combat.	serious	0.1	echo	lev00_a01_nin04

FIGURE 11.12 A message repeats during a training mission.

It may prove useful to include a standard text document to accompany the spreadsheet, where the writer can list all of the conversations as they're meant to be heard. For example, look at the spreadsheet in Figure 11.13 and see how the text is presented in Figure 11.14.

CHARACTER	CUE	CONTEXT	TRIGGER	INFLECTION	AREA	EFFECT	FILENAME
Merlin	Easy, Vexalyss. If she wanted us dead, we'd be dead. My lady, we come in peace.	Merlin has finally come face-to-face with the Dragon Queen.	Scripted cinematic 3A04.	serious	3.4		m03-a04-mer01
Vexalyss	But we are prepared for war.	Merlin has finally come face-to-face with the Dragon Queen.	Scripted cinematic 3A04.	grim	3.4		m03-a04-vex01
Dragon Queen	I can see that, as I can see your true nature. Did you think you could fool your own Queen?	Merlin has finally come face-to-face with the Dragon Queen.	Scripted cinematic 3A04.	ominous	3.4	distortion	m03-a04-drg01

FIGURE 11.13 A conversation in Screen/Play format.

Merlin
Easy, Vexalyss. If she wanted us dead, we'd be dead. My lady, we come in peace.

Vexalyss
But we are prepared for war.

Dragon Queen
I can see that, as I can see your true nature. Did you think you could fool your own Queen?

FIGURE 11.14   The same conversation in a more linear presentation.

Version Control

The scripters should always be working from the most recent story documents, so prior to the audio integration process, the writer and the design team should agree on the version control standards for the screenplay document. Typically, a program like Visual SourceSafe® is employed to keep track of versions; members of the team "check out" a document, make any necessary changes, and then check it back in, at which point it's updated for all users. It's also possible to simply view the file, which means no changes can be made. The writer needs to know where the document is located and how to access it. In addition, the development team needs to agree in advance on the following: access, updates, tracked changes, and check-ins.

Access

Though everyone on the team should be able to view the story documents, it may be a good idea to limit the number of people who will have the authority to make changes. This reduces the risk that someone will check the document out and inadvertently alter or delete content.

Updates

A procedure should be established for sending the team updates when changes have been made. These updates can be automatic (blast-emailed to the team every time someone changes a document and checks it in) or they can be sent out by the user. In either case there needs to be some kind of repository indicating what's new.

Tracked Changes

In the document itself it should be easy to figure out what's been changed. In some cases that means tracked changes, while in others the user may need to highlight key areas. This way, scripters (and other developers) will be able to figure out where changes have been made. A summary of changes posted at the beginning of a document also serves this purpose.

Check-ins

It's possible to check a document out, work on it for days, and forget to check it back in. The team needs a clear system for check-ins, such as checking in all work at 5 p.m., regardless of what progress has been made. In this way, a computer crash won't set the team back as badly. If, however, a computer crashes after several days of work (none of which has been checked in), then all of that time is lost. It's easy to avoid such calamity by checking in work often.

DIALOGUE PRIORITIZATION

Numerous issues must be resolved before the scripters place voice cues in the game. If the voice cues interrupt or interfere with gameplay, the game experience will be adversely affected, so the writer must be sure that the following questions have been addressed. Some of these issues are strictly script-based, while others involve the work of the AI programmers who work with character awareness states.

- Interruptions
- Player movement
- Dead conversationalist
- Retriggering
- Pausing the game

Interruptions

What if the NPC is talking when the player opens fire? Should the NPC react? If it's a hostile NPC, should he return fire or call for help? In any of these cases, how will the scripted cue be affected? Will it automatically cut off, or will the dialogue continue? What if two hostile NPCs are talking, and one of them sees the player trying to sneak by? Will they stop talking, or will they continue their chatter as they open fire? It sounds very basic, but this issue crops up in many games. It's worth investigating early on.

Player Movement

What if the voice cue plays, but the player is already walking away? In real life, the speaker might trail off or might get annoyed. If the player leaves the immediate area and the speaker continues to chatter away, it reminds the player that it's only a game and that the NPCs are oblivious to what's going on. Instead, the NPC might follow the player's movements or might issue another voice cue intended to convey irritation at the player's behavior.

Dead Conversationalist

This one's a no-brainer. If two characters are having a conversation and one of them dies, it should end. However, there's no reason to assume that this is the case for your project. Find out. It may be that the conversation will continue to play, despite the death of one of the speakers. It may also be that the deceased will fall silent, but the other character will continue to play voice cues with long, awkward gaps in between.

Retriggering

If the player leaves an area and then returns, will the NPC repeat that line of dialogue? Is the dialogue worth repeating? That is, does it contain information that's important enough to justify hearing it more than once? If the game is supposed to be taken seriously, won't it sound awkward if the same exact line, voiced in exactly the same way, is spoken by the same character? It may be worth recording alternates, but in most cases, it's sufficient to simply shut down the trigger once the voice cue has played.

For example, in *Rise of Merlin*, as the player enters the city of Khauria, the guard nods and says, "Welcome to Khauria." If the player turns around and walks away, then comes back, he triggers the zone again, resulting in the exact same voice cue. If the player takes on several missions and each time returns through the same gate, he's going to hear that cue again and again. It's not critical information, and it doesn't really add much after the first iteration, so this is a cue that shouldn't play a second time.

Pausing the Game

What happens when the game is paused? Will the voice cue continue to play, or will it be paused until the player resumes the game? Or will it just stop halfway through? What if the player accesses the main menu, adjusts an option, or presses the Select button to view the objectives? Ideally, the voice cue should be paused and should pick up where it left off when the player unpauses the game, but if not, some contingencies must be developed if it's possible for the player to pause during critical information (such as key locations or objectives).

VOICE CUES AND ANIMATION

The writer may be sufficiently involved in the design process to document the movement of characters in-game during scripted gameplay sequences. In such a case the writer needs to delineate the animations that are played, possibly in the same spreadsheet that lists the voice cues. This will require communication with the animation team, as they will be able to tell the writer both what animations are available and what filenames correspond to those animations. The writer should be as familiar as possible with the actual animations, because file names and brief descriptions don't always get the point across. For example, there may be three different "retreat" animations: a steady backwards walk with gun at the ready, a hasty run, and a full-on sprint with head down. If the writer doesn't know which version of retreat corresponds to which animation, he might cite the wrong one in his documentation, resulting in an awkward scene.

TRIGGERED CUES

If a cue is scripted to play when triggered by the player character, the developers need to document the exact conditions that will trigger the response. For example, if the trigger is a proximity trigger, such that the voice cue is heard when the player enters a certain area, what happens if the player keeps moving? If the cue is long enough, can the player walk out of earshot, possibly missing key information? What if the player has allies or a squad of AI teammates? Can one of them trigger the voice cue through proximity? If so, what happens if the player orders a teammate to move into an area but doesn't enter himself? Is it possible that the cue will play even if the player isn't around to hear it?

Sometimes the cue is triggered by player interaction, so that when the player approaches an NPC and pushes a button, a conversation is triggered. What happens if the player engages more than one character? Will the cues play simultaneously, or will one drop off? What happens when a character's AI state changes?

FALSE AWARENESS

There are instances during gameplay when the NPCs are scripted to behave in a way that suggests that they're aware of their surroundings. The illusion is broken when this awareness is proven to be false, whether it's because they're unaware of an obvious condition or because they've incorrectly identified that condition.

For example, as Merlin is riding across the Plains of Doom (Figure 11.15), a group of Death Knights attacks from the east. Merlin's sidekick, Talerios, cries out, "Death Knights approaching from the east!" The player charges across the plains and immediately gets killed by enemy arrows. The player reloads from his last save point and continues riding across the Plains of Doom. This time, the player cuts south after crossing the bridge, then heads north, so that when the Death Knights charge, the ruins of the Temple are in the way, giving the player some cover from their arrows. Merlin's sidekick, Talerios, cries out, "Death Knights approaching from the east!" However, because of the large compass in the top-right corner of the screen, the player can plainly see that the Knights are approaching from the north. If the player looks to the east, there are no enemies. Just trees. The player's circumstances were altered in a way that the developers hadn't anticipated, and the scripted dialogue ceased to be applicable.

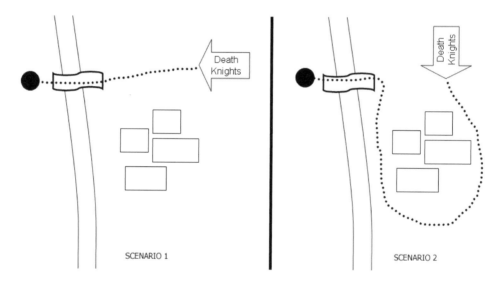

FIGURE 11.15 Merlin rides across the Plains of Doom.

There are several solutions to the problem of false awareness. Obviously, creative play-testing is a must, because if the developers always play the game "the way that the player is supposed to play," the development team isn't going to discover these issues, which tend to arise in the real world once the game has shipped. The developers must do their best to break the game, because that's exactly what the customer is going to do.

Another way to circumvent the problem is to create generic alternates for some of the more specific lines of dialogue in the game. For example, if one looks over the spreadsheet for *Rise of Merlin*, certain categories of dialogue become apparent: there are greetings, warnings of impending enemy attacks, cries for help, and instructions. Given that some of the circumstances of the game may change through the development process, the writer can create some generic cues for each of those categories. For example, in the greetings category, instead of "Welcome to Khauria," the writer can create a few generic lines such as, "Welcome, traveler." Should place names change toward the end of the project, or should new areas be created after the voice shoot, such generic lines can be substituted without disrupting the game (or its development). The same goes for enemy attacks. In addition to the more specific cues ("Merlin, beware! A manticore!"), the writer can add a few generic lines, such as "Merlin, look out!" or "We're under attack!"

DEPENDENT CUES

These voice cues only play in certain areas or scenes and are dependent on larger events within the context of the game. For example, if a building explodes, a number of voice cues might play before and after the explosion. Dependent cues can enhance the game experience, but if played at the wrong time can detract from it. The difference is generally a question of timing or of player interaction.

Timing

Often, to build suspense, characters in a game will alert the player to a critical event, which (unbeknownst to the player) is actually inevitable. The timing must be calculated precisely, or else one of two things will happen: the player will expect to have some impact on the scene or the player will be put off by the slow reaction time of the speaker. In the first case, if the voice cue plays too early ("Sir, they're getting away!"), the player may see a window of opportunity and try to take action. If the enemy is boarding a helicopter on a rooftop, the player may open fire or throw some grenades, thinking that it's possible to resolve the problem. The player's inability to affect the outcome of the events will become obvious when his weapons have no effect on the enemy or the helicopter.

In the second case the voice cue may play a little too slowly, and the speaker will assert that the enemy is getting away long after the enemy has actually gotten away. This, though not as disappointing as the first issue, is nonetheless awkward. The ideal timing gives the player sufficient warning to prepare for an event, but not so much time that the player perceives an opportunity to influence the outcome of that event. Other examples include a warning that large numbers of enemies are converging on the player's position (no time to escape), or that a nearby structure will become unstable or damaged soon ("Sir, the catwalk's going to collapse!").

It is also important that speakers not identify problems or situations before they become apparent. If someone off-screen indicates that trouble is on the way, there's no problem. But if someone who shares the player's perspective is able to discern an oncoming crisis before it's apparent, this can confuse the player. For example, if the player character is a police officer and is receiving radio calls that indicate a hostage has been taken in a nearby shopping mall, then the player will assume that the person on the other end of the radio has access to that information somehow. But if the player is told by his partner that a hostage crisis is taking place, this can be a little off-putting. How would the partner know? Characters who are moving with the player, or who share the player character's perspective, should only be able to see or hear things that the player can see or hear (unless they're clearly connected to the information in some other way, such as by receiving a phone call).

Player Action

In some instances dependent cues play as intended but are obviated by some action on the part of the player. For example, in many squad-based games the player's teammates provide updates and enemy sightings ("Sir, there are hostiles at ten o'clock!"). Sometimes, these cues are code-based, meaning that they are driven by AI. Other times these cues are scripted to play in specific situations. For instance, in a squad-based shooter, one of the enemies might attack with an unorthodox weapon, such as a rocket-propelled grenade (RPG) launcher. In such a case the teammate might play a scripted voice cue when passing through a trigger zone: "Watch out, RPG!" However, the player noticed a fire escape and decided to climb it. Once on the rooftop, he saw the enemy with the RPG launcher standing near a window (just out of sight for those on the ground), and the player shot him. Then he climbed back down and rejoined his team, and now that they've passed through the trigger zone, he hears the RPG warning and thinks that perhaps there's another hostile with an RPG launcher. After a while, he realizes what happened, and the immersion is broken. In such a case, the scripted voice cue needs to be tied to the condition of the RPG-wielding enemy; if he dies, the voice cue shouldn't play. However, the scripter probably reasoned that the player wouldn't even see the enemy until he had gotten in range, so there was no reason to suspect that the player would be able to kill the shooter and break the scripting.

In order to avoid complications brought on by player action, the development team must anticipate all of the different ways that players can break scripting. This means playing the game often and playing the game "incorrectly." That is, the development team must play the game as though they were unaware of what was expected of them (which is how most players approach gameplay).

SUMMARY

Once the dialogue has been recorded and processed, the design team can begin to script the content into the game, lending voice to the characters and creating the in-game narrative. This chapter discussed the process of dialogue integration, including the scripting team, their schedule and tools, the necessary documentation, and the triggers that are used to structure the integration of voice cues. In the next chapter, we'll examine the testing process that's used to verify the integrity of scripted content.

DEVELOPER INTERVIEW

Matt Dohmen, Designer, Mythic Entertainment
Warhammer® Online: Age of Reckoning™, Ghost Recon: Island Thunder™

STORY DESIGN

There is a gulf between "design" and "story." Many people harbor a misconception about the game creation process beginning with story, where the ideas for gameplay are born out of the story created for the game world. This is, by and large, not the way things work. A game's proposed features and the idea of how the game itself would play usually come before a game's story. Once the way a game plays is figured out, then a story that enhances and reflects that gameplay can be established.

That being said, a good groundwork for the overall story and story arc should already be in place to help guide the feature design process. But the story doesn't need to be fleshed out at that point; characters don't really need names, nor places; motivations don't need to exist yet, etc. The general story arc doesn't need to exist at that point, but it helps.

Once a game has an established set of features and a pretty robust story, and these two things complement each other, then the ways the gameplay can bring

→

the story to the player will improve. The quality of the presentation of exposition that has little in the way of interactivity will improve, and the quality and quantity of ways the player can interact and change the story will increase. Next-generation is increasingly meaning "complexity of elegant gameplay systems" more than it means "quality of graphics." Don't take "complexity" the wrong way. It is used here meaning the number of variables in any system the player can influence at one time.

Story Scripting

Scripting is limited to the tools and features given to the scripters. There are things the people scripting can do to improve the quality of something in a game without having the tools that directly enable them to do so, but the increase of quality will be limited. If, as a game writer, someone wants high-quality interaction in a scripted environment, they must champion the idea that the tools need features that allow scripters to implement those interactions in quick, efficient, and supported ways. Nothing will chafe a scripter faster than being given an assignment the tools can barely handle and not having anyone else realize that limited tools provide limited results.

If the tools are set in stone, a game writer can try to modify their story and the interactions they want to see in the game to complement the limits of the tools. If a player is supposed to have a part of a game where a number of people are talking to each other, animating at the same time, and all of it captured in motion-picture quality camerawork, the tools better have a way to elegantly implement audio, matching animations, and realistic camerawork or else that's going to be a pretty crappy moment in the game.

Challenges

It's extremely difficult to find the right place for dialogue to happen during gameplay. Most games, no matter how limited that game is in unscripted player interaction with the world, still have more places where dialogue is inappropriate than where dialogue fits well. Being able to identify those places during gameplay is difficult, and even when one person thinks they have it figured out, the next person will see it differently. It requires total cooperation between design and art to make sure the appropriate places exist within the game, and the total cooperation between design and engineering to make sure the scripter has the appropriate tools to make the dialogue happen correctly.

$\rightarrow$

Writers need to be able to change not only the actual dialog that is going to be in the game at various points, but also be able to change the timing of the dialog and the placement of the dialog while keeping the spirit of why that dialog exists. If there's, say, a bit of dialog that is supposed to occur between firefights, but the way the area is laid out and the way the computer AI works there isn't a big pause between those fights, the writer has to be prepared to change the dialog to make it fit what is actually there, even if in the end people find a way to extend that pause.

THE WORKING WRITER

The cooperation between design and art requires the writer's input. Quite often, level design will occur between people concerned only with gameplay flow and art resource budget requirements. These people aren't thinking of the optimal places for the plot to present itself; they're thinking only of the game flow. The insight the writer could provide would go best at this stage, where there are only a few people conceptualizing a game space. If a space is made with no regard to the flow of the story, it's then extraordinarily difficult to retrofit in places that are purely story-driven.

WRITING FOR AN INTELLECTUAL PROPERTY

I worked on one game whose entire project team and the management were trying to capture the minds of players with an engrossing story. The first thing that was written was the story line, which had to adhere to the intellectual property (IP), which featured over 20 years of material. I didn't envy the writers during that initial part of development, as they had to be creative, do new things that would engross longtime fans and new players at the same time, and also appease the owners of the IP at the same time. But they did it.

Once the story was in place, the maps were designed to complement that story. But, before the story was written, we already knew what kind of game we were going to make. That knowledge and constant communication between different disciplines resulted in maps that complement the story, while the story complements the game. The gameplay complements both the story and the maps. It's not an easy balance to strike, but it worked. Communication is the key.

$\rightarrow$

ADVICE FOR ASPIRING WRITERS

A great story in a bad game is still a bad game, while a bad story in a great game is still a great game. However, a great story in a great game makes that game unforgettable. Those are the games that can influence people's lives for the better and prove that video games are a legitimate art form. Just remember that it's like cheating—if your story is good and you're a good writer, you'll be able to preserve the soul of the story despite changes you have to make so that the story supports and complements the gameplay, and if you communicate well, the rest of the game will complement your story.

12 Testing Story Content

In This Chapter

- Testing Process
- Testing Materials
- Defects
- Evaluation

The testing process typically begins as soon as there's something to test. Once the game is stable enough to launch and play, quality assurance (QA) testers begin to examine it for defects, reporting their findings to the development team. As each new build is assembled, the testers find more and more problems, resulting in an ever-increasing number of bugs whose resolution will eventually require the help of most of the development team: artists, designers, programmers, and even writers. Though the majority of QA resources are devoted to the documentation of buggy code or art assets, it's also becoming quite common for QA testers to focus their energy on testing the integrity of story content. Without the meticulous process of testing and evaluation, the quality of a game's narrative will be questionable at best. Therefore, the writer should make every effort to understand the testing process and to anticipate the needs of the QA team. By understanding the QA lab process, the stages of testing, and the evaluation period, the writer can make the most of this crucial phase in a game's development.

The writer's participation in the QA process will depend on his role on the project and his involvement with the development team. Should the writer take an active role in QA, there are a few things that he can prepare for in order to be of maximum use to the project. The preparation of a test plan for story testing will come in handy later in the project, as the lead testers will doubtless be occupied creating test plans for other areas of the game, such as the interface, installation process, and gameplay. By assembling story documentation, the writer can help the QA team understand what story elements should appear in the game and where. Finally, the documentation of contingencies can be extremely useful if QA reveals an irreparable defect that requires an alternate plan.

TESTING PROCESS

Depending on the game and studio, the testing process may consist of several QA leads and analysts scrutinizing a game's story content, or it might mean that the writer plays through the game, verifying that all of his hard work has been integrated into the game. To make the most of the process, the testing schedule and necessary personnel must be discussed in advance.

SCHEDULE

While testing usually begins as soon as there's a build with sufficient functionality, the writer needs to know when (or if) story content will be tested. The more detail the writer has about the timetable, the better equipped he will be to conduct his own testing, if needed, or to request additional assistance from the QA lab.

PERSONNEL

The testing lab may contribute testers, or the story content may be tested exclusively by writers or designers. Of course, all members of the development team are likely to play through the game at some point and may submit defects as they're found, but the rigorous testing that constitutes most testing will have to be performed by a dedicated team. If there's no one in QA available to proofread the in-game text, verify the functionality of scripted events, and ensure that all dialogue is playing as designed, then the writer must take on this task.

TESTING MATERIALS

QA personnel use test plans when reviewing game content. These documents list every aspect of the game that needs to be tested and evaluated, from the stability of the multiplayer mode to the legibility of the on-screen text. Testing materials for story content should be similarly broad in scope, from the large-scale functionality, such as the cohesion of the narrative, to the small-scale detail, such as correct spelling of proper nouns.

The writer can expedite this process by assembling and organizing all pertinent story material for the QA staff in the test lab. If the documents cited throughout this book (and collected in Appendix A, Documentation) are completed by the writer, it should be easy to locate and deliver the necessary content. Some preparation will be required, of course. The writer should deliver story documents, content lists, and information about cinematics. We'll cover each of those in turn and will then explore the writer's role in the testing process and the creation of contingency plans.

STORY DOCUMENTS

The information furnished by the writer should include the basic information the test lab will need to test the game's narrative. These documents should present the bare-bones outline of the story content, such as plot, major characters, major events, conflicts, and resolutions. By this time, the writer has probably assembled several different story design documents, including plot synopses, narrative vision documents, and scenario design documents. Any of these can help contextualize the content being tested in the QA lab.

While playing the game, the primary goal for the test lab should be to determine whether the story is coherent or not. Coherence is harder to quantify than correct spelling or the correct placement of a voice cue. It's not the type of either/or function that's easily checked off of a list. Coherence is like overall gameplay difficulty. Often, during the course of a game's development, the testers and developers become so familiar with the game that they can play through the game with one hand, or without wasting a single bullet. They know where all of the enemies are, and they know exactly what to do in each situation. As a result, veteran developers are usually able to complete the game quickly and easily. This may cause the team to question the game's challenge level, and they may conclude that the game is too easy. Later, someone not directly involved with the game's development picks up the controller and gets slaughtered immediately. "This game is hard," he says. Which it is, if you're playing it for the first time.

In much the same fashion, developers can become accustomed to a game's narrative. At first, the context for the game is something that's discussed, as opposed to an actual feature in the game. Gradually, as the gameplay evolves, story elements such as dialogue and cinematics are introduced, and the narrative begins to take shape. After a year or two, many members of the development team have become intimately familiar with the game's story line and screenplay and can probably quote passages of dialogue at length. The problem is that this constant contact can make it hard for the developers to be objective about the game's narrative design, much like the aforementioned issue of game difficulty. The testers are quite familiar with the story and dialogue, but someone playing the game for the first time might find the story overly convoluted or otherwise unsatisfying. To maintain objectivity, testers should be furnished with documents that outline the exact intentions of story material and the expected results and provide a place to indicate the actual results. With this structure in hand, testers are better equipped to give the writer concrete, objectively presented information about the effect of story content on the player.

The presentation of story documentation to the testers in the QA lab can take many forms, including the following:

- Vision
- Summary
- Major events
- Levels
- Scenarios

Vision Document

The vision document outlines the core of the game's narrative. It defines the goals of the story line, the emotional response that should be elicited (fear, amusement, exhilaration), and the various ways the game evokes these emotions (shocking surprises, jokes, stunning visuals). The vision document should describe the purpose of the game's narrative, and that explanation may be as simple as, "Provides basic context for player action." Not every game is going to feature an emotional narrative.

Summary Document

The summary document relates the plot in the simplest terms possible, devoid of artistry or drama. The purpose of the document is to say what happens, to whom, and when. The summary is told in chronological order, even if the game isn't (some games, such as *Max Payne,* make use of flashback sequences). The summary document tells the test lab what the beginning, middle, and end of the story are. It also includes the main characters in the game and gives a brief description of each.

Major Events Document

This document lists the significant events in the game, such as the death of a main character, a climactic battle between the player character and his arch-enemy, or the revelation that a trusted associate is actually a traitor. The major events should be listed in chronological order and contextualized as concisely as possible. The purpose of this document is to identify the areas of the game that are intended to be narrative highlights for the player.

Level Document

The level document lists the levels of the game in order. It identifies the location of each one in terms of the game world and gives a brief description of the structure of each level. For example, the level document for *Half-Life* would begin by describing the introductory monorail sequence and then delineate the research facility at Black Mesa, as well as the various rooms and areas found therein.

Scenario Document

This list of the scenarios is particularly useful in games like *Morrowind* or *King's Field*, which present the player with an open world that isn't presented in the form of discrete levels. The scenario document outlines key scenarios in the game.

CONTENT LISTS

Often, QA analysts test content against a checklist, verifying that each item on the list is present and accounted for. Unlike the story documents, which present content to make the QA testers knowledgeable and familiar with the materials, the content list is created to serve as a list of items that can be checked off by an analyst during the testing stage. The items featured on a content list include characters, places, objects, spells, monsters, and pronunciation. These lists should be verified prior to presentation to QA, as they will be the standard for spelling and presentation.

Characters

List every character in the game, in alphabetical order, from major characters to the nameless walk-ons (Police Officer 4). The list should include the complete in-game name of the character (Merlin Ambrosius) as well as the name most commonly used in-game (Merlin) and the name of the character model (Player_Merlin.mdl).

Places

This list should cite all proper names of locations in the game. Generic locations such as Village #3 can be left off, but if it has a name, it should be presented here, in alphabetical order. A short context should be furnished for each entry. For example, next to "Castle of Despair," the writer should indicate that it's located to the east of the Kingdom of Almuria, and that it is the lair of the Silver Dragon.

Objects

The writer should include any items with proper names, particularly if the spelling is difficult or technical. For example, this list could include the names of modern weapons, such as the L86A1 LSW, or of fantasy weapons, such as the Scimitar of Xángliax.

Spells

This list should include any spells or effects that are available in the game. The list can be used to verify the spelling of all such effects and their inclusion in the game. Many RPGs feature lengthy spell lists, and a single alphabetical repository can help streamline the verification process.

Monsters

Much like the aforementioned spell list, this can help the testers verify that all of the content has been included in the game (and spelled correctly).

Pronunciation

Prior to the development of this list, the writer should consult with the QA testers involved in the process. While a pronunciation guide will no doubt prove useful, the writer should know whether the pronunciation should be "official," such as "wI-vern," or phonetic, such as "WHY-vern." In most cases a phonetic pronunciation is the easiest to interpret but will require more work than simply copying the official pronunciation from a dictionary.

CINEMATICS

When testing the cinematics, the QA team will need to know what they're looking at and what they're looking for. The cinematic test plan should include information about the number of cinematics in the game, the order they play in, the sequence of cinematics and gameplay, and the summary of events.

Scripted Cinematics

The testing of scripted cinematics is a special case. As discussed in Chapter 8, Creating Cinematics, a prerendered cinematic is usually much easier to access than a scripted cinematic. Because several scripted cinematics may play during the course of a single mission, requiring the tester to play all the way through a mission to verify them all, it's a more time-consuming and laborious process. Every time a tester dies while playing a level, he has to start over until he's viewed all of the scripted events. For that reason, the QA lab may need specially scripted versions of the levels that permit viewing of all the cinematics in a row, without having to play the game. If this is not a viable option, then the use of cheat codes such as invisibility, invulnerability, and speed can help expedite the testing process for scripted cinematics.

CONTINGENCIES

Forewarned is forearmed, and if the writer has planned for the cutting of content, he's more likely to salvage the story content and find another way to communicate it to the player. While it's always frustrating when story content is planned, designed, produced, and integrated, only to be left on the cutting room floor because of a programming or art issue, it's an inevitable aspect of game development that the writer needs to be aware of.

Cutting Content

There are many reasons for cutting content from a game. For example, it may be that a scripted cinematic is cut from the game because the animator wasn't able to create all of the required animations in time, or the scripted cinematic might be cut because the programmer wasn't able to develop the camera controls that the scripters had requested. It's also possible that scenes might get cut from the game owing to problems with voice cues. For example, it might turn out that some of the voice cues are useless because of a poor recording or because they refer to content that has changed during the development cycle (and are therefore no longer applicable to the game). The cues might simply be missing, somehow overlooked during the recording process. Whatever the case, if alternates are not available, the material must be adjusted in some way, usually by simply cutting the scene from the game.

Backup Plan

If crucial story content is cut, the writer should have some kind of plan for communicating the requisite information to the player. There are numerous ways that a writer can get such materials to the player, including text on screen, generic dialogue, and pickup voice overs.

Text on Screen

Story content, such as objectives and directions, can be provided to the player in the form of text on screen, which requires comparatively little preparation or work on the part of the scripters. Though not as compelling as a scripted cinematic or as immersive as dialogue, text on screen can get the message across to the player with a minimum of disruption.

Generic Dialogue

If the writer has recorded generic dialogue cues, such as "Investigate this area," "Proceed to your next objective," or "Get to safety," these may prove useful if more specific cues have been eliminated for some reason. The writer may want to record some generic cues from each of the major characters in the game, just in case. Generic dialogue will require some work on the part of the scripters, as it involves adding additional script work to existing levels.

Pickup Voice Overs

If time and schedule permit, the development team may opt for a final voice-over shoot (also known as a pickup shoot). This shoot, typically scheduled for the tail end of the development cycle, is used to record any last lines of dialogue that may be necessary. Sometimes this pickup session is scheduled from the beginning of the project, and other times it's scheduled only after it becomes apparent that it is needed. The number of actors and lines for a pickup shoot will be lower than a typical recording session, and it's possible that the direction may be provided to the actors over the telephone, via a conference call, rather than in person.

DEFECTS

The goal of game testing is to find and catalog all defects or problems. Though story content is important, for reasons detailed elsewhere in this book, the fact remains that a missing line of dialogue will not impact a game's sales as drastically as a multiplayer crash bug. The QA tester doesn't just find and catalog bugs; he also assigns priority to them, based on a number of factors. It's important that the writer maintain a realistic outlook about the testing process. When bugs are found and require attention, resources are typically allocated to the highest-priority bugs first. Should the writer have the means and the inclination to fix story bugs himself, he will be able to contribute more effectively to the project. By learning about the classification, reporting, and verification process, the writer is better equipped to resolve bugs himself.

CLASSIFICATION

All bugs are classified according to a number of factors, including category, severity, and priority. For the purposes of this book, we'll concern ourselves with story-related bugs, though there are bugs for every aspect of a game's development (because any element of the game, from its code base to its menu system, can be implemented incorrectly). After classification has been determined, each bug is assigned to a member of the development team for resolution.

Category

Each bug has a category. For example, a misspelled character name may be considered an editorial bug, whereas a cinematic that crashes halfway through might be considered a programming bug. Should the writer become involved in the bug-resolution process, he'll probably spend most of his time dealing with editorial bugs, such as spelling and grammatical errors, or scripting bugs, such as missing or incorrect voice cues.

Severity

Once a category has been established, the tester will need to indicate the severity of the defect. The ranking system for severity will depend on the bug-tracking software that's employed by the development team, but the highest severity will most likely be reserved for deal breakers such as crash bugs that render the game inoperable. Cosmetic defects such as mispronounced names in dialogue will be considered low severity.

Priority

Prioritization helps developers decide which bugs to tackle first and usually represents a combination of a defect's category and severity. Generally, the highest-severity editorial bug is not going to be as high priority as a low-severity gameplay bug. If the game isn't playable, the development team is going to concentrate its efforts on resolving those defects before moving on to story content. On the other hand, since the writer is usually not qualified to fix multiplayer crash bugs, he may have the necessary time in his schedule to fix those editorial and scripting bugs.

Assignment

Each bug is assigned to a member of the development team, who then becomes responsible for resolving the bug, reporting it to be a nonissue, or forwarding it to someone else for further investigation. Defects are accompanied by bug reports that describe the nature of the bug and the conditions required to reproduce it. If the writer is a full-time member of the development team and isn't currently tasked with any asset-creation responsibilities, then the writer may have story-related bugs assigned to him for resolution. This is dependent upon the writer's skill set, since a writer who is unfamiliar with the scripting editor will not be able to correct scripting bugs.

Dialogue Bugs

While testing the in-game dialogue, the QA analysts should employ a test plan based on the screenplay format that's used. A modified version of Screen/Play can be useful, provided that the testers are familiar with the contents of each column. The following is a list of problems that might be encountered while testing in-game voice cues.

- Missing cue
- Duplicate cue
- Bad recording
- Bad timing
- Missing effect

Missing Cue

The voice cue is not audible. There are several possible explanations for this bug: the cue may be missing from the database, the scripting could be pointing to the wrong cue, or the file name may be incorrect.

Duplicate Cue

A voice cue plays twice for some reason. The most likely culprit is an incorrect file name. For example, consider the exchange shown in Figure 12.1.

CHARACTER	CUE	CONTEXT	TRIGGER	INFLECTION	AREA	EFFECT	FILENAME
Talerios	You're too late, you fools!	Talerios is furious with them for killing the Horned King. However, he thinks that he can still defeat them.	Player enters Trigger Zone 11-2B.	angry	11.2		lev11_a02_tal01
Vexalyss	He is the traitor! Beware, Merlin!	Vexalyss has just realized that the enemy among them is actually Talerios.	Player enters Trigger Zone 11-2B.	desperate	11.2		lev11_a02_vex01

FIGURE 12.1   The exchange of dialogue, as designed.

The scripter mistakenly entered "lev11_a02_tal01" twice in the editor, resulting in the audio file being played twice.

It's also possible that there's a technical defect of some kind or that the file lev11_a02_vex01 is an accidental duplicate of lev11_a02_tal01.

Bad Recording

Though the file plays when it's supposed to, it's a bad recording. The dialogue may be garbled, there may be feedback or other background noise, or the file may only be audible through one speaker. Whatever the case, the file is unusable. The easiest solution is to use one of the alternate cues that were taken during the recording process. If none is available, other methods (such as generic voice over) may be called for.

Bad Timing

A cue plays at the wrong time, resulting in a large gap between cues in a conversation or prematurely alerting the player to a situation that hasn't transpired yet (such as telling the player to watch out for an approaching tank when no tank is visible). This is typically a scripting error and can be remedied by adjusting the script.

Missing Effect

In this case the voice cue plays and is clearly audible but is missing an effect. Perhaps the scene takes place in an underground cavern, and an echo effect has been applied to all voice cues save one. Possibly the voice cue is supposedly coming through a radio but lacks the radio squelch that's heard in other such cues. This bug is typically handled by the sound designer, who applies all such effects to dialogue files.

CINEMATIC BUGS

When testing the core function of prerendered cinematics, it may be possible to forego the process of loading the game build; the testers might just access the folder where the cinematic files are stored as movies and launch them directly. In this way, the tester can see if the cinematic displays all of its core functions: it shows everything that it should, all the sounds play correctly, the cinematic is neither extremely bright nor dark, and the lip-synch is correctly lined up. Once core functionality has been established, the tester still needs to be sure that the cinematic has been integrated into the game properly. The checklist delineated in Figure 12.2 is a good starting point for testing cinematics.

Questions	Yes	No
Does the cinematic play?		
Is it playing in the correct order?		
Does it play before or after the gameplay, as designed?		
Is it consistently visible?		
Is the audio track consistently audible?		
Do all of the voice cues play properly?		
Are there any missing voice cues?		
Are there any missing voice effects?		
Is the lyp-synch correctly lined up?		
Does it last as long as the documentation indicates it should?		
Is the story content in the design document clearly represented on-screen?		

FIGURE 12.2   A checklist for the cinematic testing phase.

ANIMATION BUGS

When playing through a game, the tester should pay attention to the animations displayed by the characters in-game. Are their movements matching their voice cues? Because of technical restrictions, some games can show more sophisticated animations than others, but if a character is clearly performing the "shooting" animation when there's no weapon in his hands or enemy to shoot at, it's clearly a bug. The tester should pay attention to the following:

- Does the animation match the voice cue?
- Is the character's body language appropriate for the scene?
- Is the character facing in the right direction?

EVALUATION

During the evaluation process the tester must decide if an issue is actually bug or if it's just a feature request. The difference is that a bug is a problem or mistake, a deviation from the way that something *ought* to work (see Figure 12.3). A feature request is an attempt to improve the quality of something that already works (see Figure 12.4). For example, in *Rise of Merlin* the design documentation describes the ability of the player character to heal other characters in the game. If this feature doesn't work (the player pushes the Heal button but nothing happens), then it's a bug. If the feature works, but the tester thinks this function should be accompanied by a voice cue of some kind, then that's a feature request.

Summary	Duplicate voice cue
Status	Open
Type	Voice bug
Severity	3 - Mild
Details	When the player crosses Trigger 11-2B, the audio cue "lev11_a02_tal01" plays twice, so the player hears Talerios saying "You're too late, you fools!" twice. As a result, Vexalyss' line ("He is the traitor! Beware, Merlin!") does not play.

FIGURE 12.3   An example of a story bug.

Summary	Insufficient feedback for healing
Status	Open
Type	Voice bug
Severity	3 - Mild
Details	When the player heals Talerios, the character doesn't say anything. It would be good for Talerios to give the player some kind of indication other than just the change in status in the HUD. A voice cue would probably accomplish this goal.

FIGURE 12.4 An example of a feature request.

Sometimes the line becomes blurred when it comes to story elements. It's easy to have an opinion, and once content has been integrated into a game, the entire development team has access to that content and can begin to critique it. Sometimes developers have a background in narrative; sometimes, they don't. Unfortunately, because a line of dialogue is not the same as a line of code (the former is subject to interpretation, whereas the latter is either correct or it isn't), there's a gray area that can cause complications during the testing phase.

A bug should not be based on opinion, although that's perfectly acceptable for a feature request. A bug is a deviation from what's been documented in the story design, and aesthetic considerations are not usually grounds for logging a defect into the database. During the testing stage anyone responsible for evaluating story content in the game should be mindful of impartiality and of the stated goals of story design. Otherwise, the testing and evaluation process can rapidly degenerate into a free-for-all in which all story content is subject to endless loops of revision.

While quality is always paramount, realism must eventually rear its ugly head. Once story content has passed through the evaluation stage and has been approved, it should only be altered if there's an actual defect, or else the game simply won't ship on time. The evaluation of story content should be based on formal criteria, not the personal opinions of the tester. The bug report should reflect this. Simply disliking a line of dialogue or a cinematic's camera angle aren't sufficient at this stage and should be regarded as the basis for a feature request, not a bug report.

By consistently evaluating story content against the goals delineated in the core design documents, the tester can determine whether the stated goals were achieved.

If not, the bug report should explain, as explicitly as possible, how the story content fell short of the mark.

WALK-THROUGH

Once the story content has been written, produced, and integrated, the writer should make time for the walk-through process. It's likely that the QA lab will also be performing walk-throughs, but their focus will most likely be on gameplay and functionality. The writer's goal during the walk-through stage is to gauge the overall effect of the story content and determine areas that require additional attention and polish. This process can begin as soon as there's any type of story content in the game, though it's most useful once there are voice cues and functioning cinematics.

When walking through a game, the writer essentially plays through the game as a player would, attempting to remain as objective as possible. It's difficult to pretend that one doesn't know about the attack that's just around the corner, but it's important to approach it as a player would: suspicious, perhaps, but unaware. While playing the game in this fashion, the writer should evaluate the story content in the short-term and the long-term.

Short-Term Narrative

This element of the game's story content is in the here and now. The writer should ask himself how that voice cue sounded, how that cinematic looked, and how the timing on that conversation went. The purpose of this aspect of the walk-through is to get an overall feel for the game's quality from scene to scene and level to level. Are there weak spots? If so, where? Which conversations rang false? Are there alternates that could be used? Overall, how was the timing? Meticulous note-taking will prove most useful during this stage, as it's unlikely that the writer is going to remember every detail. It may be a good idea to print out the entire screenplay and make notes in the margins while playing.

Long-Term Narrative

This element of the story content is the big picture. The writer should analyze the game's narrative presentation as a whole. Does the plot unfold logically over the course of the game? Do the characters develop and change over the course of the 10-hour or 20-hour experience as they were designed? Overall, does the story line make sense, flow dramatically, and draw the player in? This is a very difficult aspect of game design to evaluate, because it's so unquantifiable. The writer must maintain a distance from the work and should try to be as objective as possible.

SUMMARY

By preparing for the testing process and working with the QA personnel, the writer will help ensure a high level of polish for all story content, including dialogue, cinematics, and overall narrative. In this chapter we covered the testing process, testing materials, story documentation, defect reporting, evaluation, revision, and the walk-through. Once the testing phase is over, the game is ready to ship, which means there's nothing left to cover except postproduction.

DEVELOPER INTERVIEW

Jon Schweitzer, Quality Assurance Analyst, TAKE Solutions
Ghost Recon: Advanced Warfighter, Splinter Cell: Pandora Tomorrow

TESTING STORY MATERIAL

Late in development, it's an unfortunate fact: testers don't care much about typos. Those are automatically categorized as low-priority, low-severity bugs. But they are time-consuming to report, and this is something that I'd push for on my next project: in terms of spoken dialogue in the game, and the on-screen text, and the map descriptions—before any of that content is integrated into the game, there should be a way that someone in the lab can look at that content as a text file or Word document. It's so much more efficient to make corrections earlier, because once the content is in the game, the tester is proceeding screen by screen, trying to find a handful of misspellings across several different screens. Once a bug is found, the tester has to take a screenshot and enter the information into the bug-tracking system before moving on to the next one. It requires 10 times as many man-hours as it would to just proofread a text file directly. It's not always typos, either. Other times it's consistency among details, or among story elements. If that content can be evaluated before it goes into the game, it doesn't mean that it won't be tested later on. It just means that fewer bugs will be found. That's going to cut down on the time that it takes to report and fix those relatively minor defects and allow developers to focus on major game issues.

It's important to know when there are a variety of cues that could play in a given game scenario. For one thing, variables like that require more testing time. Sometimes you have to play a portion of the game repeatedly to make sure that

→

every variation of dialogue or action is properly scripted and accounted for. It just comes back to making sure that everything is documented and that there's a flow written for the level that describes what happens between points A, B, and C. There should be an outline that says, in this room, this is what's going to happen. Every possibility should be documented, and that information should be compiled into a test plan. Having that knowledge or data will make a world of difference to QA.

THOROUGH DOCUMENTATION

A lot of the time, testers focus on a narrow part of the game. You test multi-player, or a specific level, over and over again. You might not even be paying attention to the way that the story develops. You see the text on the screen, but you're not thinking about that. You're looking for defects, not the big picture. Having access to a document that describes the plot from beginning to end can help the QA team know what's going on in the game and whether the story works.

You don't want to step on toes as a QA tester. You respect the writers and designers, because they're experts at what they do, but quality assurance is often the first play test of the game. In many cases testers can see story elements that are off or that could be fleshed out more or that don't make sense.

PITFALLS

I worked on one project that featured a lot of in-game text—weapon descriptions, armor descriptions, map descriptions—and there were hundreds of little text bugs, scattered all over, and it took forever to find them all. Unfortunately, the necessary information wasn't delivered to QA until late in the project lifecycle. It helped me realize that the process needed changing, but it was just frustrating, because we didn't have anyone specifically assigned to that particular task. It fell to me by default, because I was in charge of the certification requirements process, and text fell under the terminology requirements. But it would have been good to have someone designated the text person earlier, to make sure that the text was up-to-snuff.

THE WRITER AND QA

Writers should be aware that, whatever the story line is, the QA lab only knows what's communicated to us. It sounds basic, but it's very important that the

→

vision be committed to paper. The story design should be documented and communicated to the QA team before testing begins. Once that content is down on paper, the QA lab can review it and base their test plans on it. Whether the testers are evaluating scripted cinematics or triggered events in-game, the lab needs to know where the story material will be presented. More often than not, this information is documented and presented to the lab, but then the content changes during development, and that change isn't relayed to the QA lab. When it finally gets to QA, the story content might be very different from what was documented originally. It's really important to make sure that QA knows what the designers know, as far as story is concerned.

13 Understanding Postproduction

In This Chapter

- Postmortem
- Lessons Learned
- Closing Documentation
- Additional Writing

The postproduction phase is a time to evaluate the overall development of a project from beginning to end and to discuss what steps should be taken to maximize the potential of the studio's next game. The postproduction phase is an opportunity for the writer to analyze what went right, what went wrong, and how this process can be improved. After this postmortem process, the writer should compile all available data in the game's closing documentation to streamline the preproduction phase of future games in the series. Generally, this stage of development follows the release of the game and may even take place after a number of reviews have been written. While such feedback can be useful, it is not always necessary, particularly if the focus of the postmortem is on the processes that drove development.

Once the postmortem has concluded and the lessons learned have been documented, the writer may be tasked with assembling a legacy document, which collects all story design documents into a single repository for use on future projects. In addition, the writer may contribute to additional writing, such as user manuals or marketing materials. In this chapter we'll discuss those postproduction writing assignments.

POSTMORTEM

The postmortem, despite its ghoulish name, should be a very positive experience for a development team. After all, if the team is analyzing what methods did or didn't work during the development of a game, it probably means the team is finished and the game actually shipped. In a business rife with closed studios and cancelled games, this feat alone is an accomplishment and something to be proud of. During the postmortem the members of a development team discuss the game's production and then evaluate the specifics of the process. For the purposes of this book, we'll confine discussion of the postmortem to narrative content.

The postmortem meeting is a group discussion featuring any member of the development team involved in the story design process, including writers, designers, leads, and the producers (and possibly members of the audio or art departments). The discussion should be governed by objectivity, decorum, and structure.

As with all other aspects of development, the process should focus on facts and data, not personal opinion or subjective criticism. The goal of the postmortem is to improve processes and create a working agenda, not to work out bad blood or disappointments.

Whenever possible, critique should be phrased in the passive voice. Instead of saying, "The character artists spent too long on the enemy character models and had to rush through the other NPCs toward the tail end of the project," the speaker should say, "Too much time was spent on the enemy character models, and there wasn't enough time for the other NPCs at the tail end of the project." It's not a huge difference, but it removes the accusation from the critique and therefore avoids the casting of blame. If the postmortem is to be effective, this is crucial.

The postmortem, like any other meeting, should be governed by an agenda. The person leading the discussion (the writer, perhaps, or the lead designer or producer) should keep the meeting moving along and should know what core questions should be asked of the participants. Without structure, the meeting may turn into an unproductive complaint session that leads nowhere and resolves nothing.

The person leading the meeting must appoint someone to document all lessons learned and action items for future reference.

DISCUSSION

During the discussion questions such as the following should be asked and answered by the participants:

- What went wrong?
- What went right?
- What didn't turn out as expected?
- How was the story?
- How were the cinematics?
- How was the dialogue?
- How were the scripted events?
- How was the character development?
- What additional resources would have helped?

These are open-ended questions whose answers will serve as the groundwork for the action items that will follow.

PROCESS

Once the assets themselves have been evaluated, the discussion should move to the topic of the process of asset creation. The question during this portion of the postmortem is "How did our methods work out, and what could have gone better?" The areas of discussion are:

- Story design
- Documentation

- Cinematics
- Approval
- Casting
- Voice acting
- Scripting
- Testing

Story Design

How did the story design process work? Was there enough time to explore all options? Did the story design match the gameplay? Were all of the right developers part of the story design process?

Documentation

Did everyone have access to the appropriate documents? Was the game's documentation thorough? Did it furnish all necessary information to the different developers on the team? Was the documentation process understood by everyone on the team? Was version control implemented properly?

Cinematics

Did the process of designing and creating the cinematics go as planned? Were there any technical or conceptual roadblocks that slowed down the development? Did the cinematics convey all necessary story information to the viewer?

Approval

Did the approval team get feedback to the developers in a timely fashion? Was the feedback useful and specific? How could the communication between developers and the approval team have been expedited?

Casting

Was the audition process organized well? Did the actors have access to the right casting materials? Were the right actors cast for the roles? Was there enough time to audition the appropriate number of voice actors under optimal conditions, or was the process rushed?

Voice Acting

Was there sufficient time to prepare for the voice recording process? Did the actors have enough context to provide the best performances possible? Were there enough people at the recording session? Too many? Were enough alternate and generic cues recorded? Was the voice acting sufficiently emotional? Did it sound appropriate once integrated into the game? Did the sound team have sufficient time and resources to manipulate and prepare the audio files?

Scripting

Was the scripting tool adequate to the task of integrating voice assets and creating scripted cinematics? Were the scripters properly trained on the tool set prior to the production phase? Was the turnaround time for requested features sufficient? Was the scripting tool robust enough to handle on-the-fly revisions during the testing phase, or did revisions take an inordinate amount of time?

Testing

Was the QA lab furnished with all necessary documentation? Did they have enough time and resources to test and proofread all applicable content? Was the story design documentation provided to them in a timely fashion, or did it arrive late in the game's development cycle?

LESSONS LEARNED

The next stage of the postproduction process is the lessons learned phase, in which the developers discuss and then document mistakes that were made and the ways that these mistakes can be avoided in the future.

PROCESS

During the lessons learned discussion and during the creation of the lessons learned document, developers should focus on the areas of the game's development process that need improvement during the creation of the next game. The lessons learned document should be specific, focusing on the exact nature of the mistakes that were made. It should be explicit, pointing out exactly what went wrong and why this proved to be a problem. The document should be neutral, focusing on the issue and not the names or the job titles of the developers involved. It should be prioritized, focusing on only the major issues that were uncovered during the postmortem. Cosmetic problems and minor details should be ignored. Last, the lessons learned document should be focused, dealing only with story-related issues.

Resolution

Once the document has been completed to the team's satisfaction, a task list should be created. This task list should be based on the lessons learned document and should indicate the steps that will be taken on the next project to avoid similar mistakes during that game's development. The tasks should be assigned to roles, not employees. The lead designer of the project that just wrapped up might be working in a different capacity on the next game, or he might be working somewhere else. The applicable tasks should be assigned to the role of the lead designer, so that whoever winds up in that position will inherit the tasks.

The tasks themselves should take the form of specific instructions, not guidelines or areas for investigation. For example, tasks assigned to a writer might include "Begin working on QA documentation prior to the first voice shoot, and make sure that the QA lead is copied on all emails pertaining to the voice integration process." If the task assigned to a member of the team begins with the words *explore* or *consider*, it's likely that nothing will come of that task. For the lessons learned document to be productive, it must contain explicit instructions that will inform the decision-making process for the studio's next game.

Closing Documentation

The final stage of postproduction is the creation of closing documentation. Since many games are followed by sequels and spin-offs, it's a good idea to establish a repository for information about the narrative content of a game. The writer may work on the sequel himself, or he may move on to something else, but for the benefit of whoever writes the next game, a legacy document should be developed and stored someplace safe.

Legacy Document

The legacy document is a collection of all the story design information from the project that was just completed. It's a collection of all dialogue, scenarios, main characters, and design documents pertaining to narrative. Assembling this material can help streamline the process for the next game, since the writer will be able to refer to the legacy document during the planning stages (when researching the story lines of past games, for example, as we did in Chapter 2, Creating the Concept). If time permits, the writer should try to collate this data into a short list of documents by integrating all documents of the same type (such as creating a single Word document and inserting all other Word documents into it). This can be a tedious process, particularly if each of the documents is formatted differently, but it is far more useful to have a single organized document that can be searched and bookmarked than it is to sift through a dozen such documents in search of a single data point.

Some games feature multiple endings. If the player completes the game under certain circumstances, there may be an ending that shows the hero victorious and the villain dead; if the player completes the game but doesn't acquire the Golden Sword of Metonymy, the closing cinematic shows the villain escaping, though the hero remains victorious. If a game features multiple endings, the writer may want to make a note of the canonical ending, if such exists. The canonical ending is part of the official story line of the series, and any alternate endings found in the game are considered unofficial. For example, in *Metal Gear Solid* series one of the endings features the death of a major character. Because this character returns in a later installment of the series, this ending is not considered canonical. It's good to know which ending is official, so that the story lines of future installments will remain consistent.

STORAGE

Once the story data have been assembled, they must be stored. Though it's easiest to save the file to one's hard drive, this is a risky proposition. Over time, hard drives can be erased, corrupted, or misplaced. It's safer to back the data up on a CD or DVD (multiple copies are preferable) and then archive them on a network drive. The more copies exist, and the more precise the labels affixed to them, the harder it will be to lose them.

ADDITIONAL WRITING

While a contract writer's obligations are usually concluded when the game's story content has been created, a full-time writer still has to put in 40-plus hours a week while waiting for the next game to begin. In addition to research and competitive analysis, the writer can contribute additional writing to a project, including marketing materials and manuals.

MARKETING COPY

Marketing materials can take many forms. Some of this content is generated during the production stage, when the game is announced, and some of it is released just before the game's release. Typically, the writer will interface with the marketing department or the producer during the creation of this content.

Back-of-the-Box Bullets

These include game summaries, feature descriptions, and the short, one-line bullet points that are found on the back of game packaging. The game summary is a summary, usually a single paragraph long, of the story line and major characters. The feature descriptions can be a short as a single word or as long as a few sentences. The bullet points can be listed together or appear as captions for screenshots. It's likely that the lead designer or producer will provide the key information to the writer, whose job will then be to assemble the material and write the copy to go with it. In some cases the marketing copy verges on hype, and in other cases it's deliberately understated. It's best to find out what the desired style is before working on the material.

Site Content

Content written for the Web can take many forms, including articles, interviews, developer blogs, and character blogs. In general, the writer will interface with an intermediary (such as the producer), rather than communicate directly with marketing.

Articles

The writer can create articles for a game's Web site or for industry-related sites. Such articles can be retrospectives, game histories, or interviews with developers. The marketing team or producer will probably furnish the writer with guidelines and goals for the article. The writer will need an estimated word count, a delivery format for the article (for instance: text file, Word document, or HTML file), and contact information for any interviewees.

Developer Blogs

Often, the marketing department will task a member of the development team (such as a producer or a lead designer) with writing a blog that will be featured on the game's Web site. However, usually, producers and lead designers are busy getting the game finished and don't have the time or resources to write a regular feature. Moreover, they're not necessarily going to feel comfortable writing for public consumption. The writer may be tasked with ghost-writing developer blogs, which discuss the state of the project, challenges encountered, milestones reached, and new features that have been added to the game. The purpose of the developer blog is to put a human face on the project and to communicate marketing materials to the public without being perceived as marketing copy—after all, it's coming directly from the people making the game. However, the marketing department will no doubt furnish the writer with a list of topics that must be discussed in each blog entry and will probably have final say over what is written.

Character Blogs

Character blogs are fictional journals, supposedly written by a character from the game. Developers use these to build interest in the character prior to a game's launch, and they can be particularly useful when introducing a new character whose motives and background remain a mystery to the general public. The "voice" of such a blog depends on the character and the type of game, but if the writer has already written game dialogue, the transition to writing blog content should be an easy one.

Media Tie-Ins

Some publishers employ media tie-ins, such as comic books, to market their games in unconventional ways. For example, both the *Metal Gear* series and the *Silent Hill* series have had numerous comics written about them, and novels have been published about Master Chief, the hero of the *Halo* games. It's possible that the game writer may become involved in such projects, but the more research that's done into these alternate media beforehand, the better-equipped the writer is to land such a deal.

USER MANUALS

When writing a user manual, the writer's goal is to communicate as much information as possible in as clear a manner as he can. This kind of writing is informative, not persuasive, so flowery speech and "good writing" aren't really necessary. If the player needs to know how to access the Spell List, well-written prose isn't going to make it any easier (and it might actually slow things down). User manuals are best written when the configuration and options for a game are more or less set in stone (after beta, for example).

First, the content needs to be organized in sections. Typically, the manual begins with some obligatory information, such as health warnings. After a brief summary of the game's plot and main characters, the manual usually moves on to cover the menu system, controls, and heads-up display (the HUD). Additional information can include tactics and strategies, overviews of weapons and items, lists of enemies the player will encounter, and hints and tips. Most companies also list the development team credits in the back of the manual.

Usually, the content in a user manual is intentionally dry and to-the-point. There are occasional exceptions, however, such as in *Saints Row*, which features a manual resembling the notebook of an undercover officer (complete with scribbled notes in the margins). Such manuals require additional time and preparation.

SUMMARY

During the days that follow the release of a game, memories of the development process are still fresh in the minds of the developers. By discussing and documenting the lessons learned during the production cycle, the development team can improve their methods and ensure smoother development for the next game. The writer should then write and assemble the closing document, listing all story-related information for the benefit of the next game's writer.

14 Working in the Industry

In This Chapter

- Introduction
- Additional Resources
- Award-winning Game Writing

INTRODUCTION

Now that we have covered the process of writing a game, from planning to testing, the question remains: how does one get work as a game writer? The process of finding a writing job can be challenging, but there are ways to make it easier. By networking at industry events, preparing a solid portfolio, and utilizing all available resources, you can position yourself as a more appealing candidate.

GETTING A JOB

When visiting a company's Web site, one typically sees job postings for programmers, artists, designers, producers, and testers. However, it is very rare to find a job posting for a game writer or story designer. In part, this is a result of supply and demand. After all, a project may require the work of dozens of programmers or artists, but one writer is usually sufficient. Some companies employ in-house talent, and until that writer moves on to another company or position, there will be no vacancy.

It is also important to understand that many companies do not post game writing jobs on their Web sites, or even on the industry sites detailed later in this chapter. In many cases, game writers find out about potential clients through referral or word-of-mouth. Therefore, the aspiring game writer needs to employ strategies such as networking at industry events, and getting involved in associations like the IGDA.

INDUSTRY EVENTS

At industry conferences, seminars, and expos, prospective game writers can hand out business cards, meet potential clients, and network with publishers and developers. For example, the Game Developers Conference (*www.gdconf.com*) is a trade event where developers gather to lecture, discuss, and network. The 300+ sessions are broken into tracks such as Design, Production, and Programming, and include lectures, roundtable discussions, and panels. The Austin Game Conference (AGC), managed by the CMP Game Group (*www.cmpgame.com*), focuses on the development of multiplayer, mobile, and console games. The Game Writers Conference, which is a part of the AGC, is a great place to meet other writers in the industry.

IGDA

The International Game Developers Association (*www.igda.org*) is a professional society dedicated to networking, professional development, and developer advocacy. There are over 70 IGDA chapters which gather regularly to share best practices, demo their games, or simply to network. Though membership requires an annual fee, attendance at the chapter meetings is often free, and this is an excellent way for a writer to meet game developers.

CONSTRUCTING A PORTFOLIO

There are many ways to present a potential employer with writing samples, but as a general rule, the submitted work should be appropriate, protected, accessible, and brief.

APPROPRIATENESS

Try to tailor the writing samples being submitted to the project or company in question. Though an article on game development, or a poem, or an act from a play might well constitute "good writing," they're not usually appropriate if one is interested in writing a gore-soaked survival horror game. If samples of game writing are not available, then a sample of prose or screenplay writing can serve to illustrate a writer's abilities. Again, the material submitted should be as close as possible to the theme and content of the game in question. If you don't know what kind of game a company is working on, study the types of games that they've developed in the past.

PROTECTION

Always try to submit published work. If none is available, then be sure that any writing sample you submit is copyrighted and marked accordingly. Some game developers may be wary of reading material that hasn't been copyrighted, for fear that if they develop similar content down the line, the writer may accuse them of stealing his ideas. Of course, if submitting a hard copy of a writing sample, never send the original.

ACCESSIBILITY

The document should be accessible, meaning that no special software should be required to view the writing sample (unless specified by the developers, which is addressed in the following paragraph). The writing sample should be formatted neatly and legibly, and should bear the writer's name and contact information on each page. If the writing sample includes multiple formats, then try to consolidate them into a single document; for instance, if submitting a few pages from a movie screenplay, along with 50 lines of in-game text in an Excel spreadsheet, then embed the Excel file in the Word document. The developers will be less likely to miss important information if the writing sample consists of a single document that can be easily opened and printed.

Some companies require a writer to submit writing samples using proprietary software tools. For example, BioWare's web site indicates that writers should submit samples using the *Neverwinter Nights* toolset. In such a case, having a 5-page writing sample in MS Word is not going to suffice; the writer must install a copy of *Neverwinter Nights* on his computer, learn to use the program, and then construct a module according to the guidelines on the site.

BREVITY

Though it may be tempting to include as much content as possible in a writing sample, it's important to consider the needs of your potential client. How long is it going to take to sift through a thirty-page excerpt from your novel? Is it worth it? Would a five-page excerpt communicate your writing ability as effectively? There is no rule of thumb here save common sense: ask yourself if you would read the entire writing sample if you were a game producer or lead designer, looking for a qualified writer.

ADDITIONAL RESOURCES

Gamasutra (*www.gamasutra.com*), the sister publication to print magazine *Game Developer,* features industry news, columns, interviews, and job postings. Games Industry (*www.gamesindustry.biz*) features news, contact information for game companies, and job postings. The IGDA message board (*www.igda.org/forums*) includes a Bulletin Board section, where jobs are posted on a regular basis, and a Writing section, where writers discuss issues and where developers occasionally post jobs. The IGDA Game Writers Special Interest Group (*www.igda.org/writing*) features a mailing list, where jobs are posted, as well as resources like the Game Writers Quarterly, a publication that focuses on issues of game writing and narrative. Sloperama (*www.sloperama.com/advice.html*) is the Web site of Tom Sloper. Since 1979, Sloper has worked as a game designer, producer, and creative director. His Web site is full of valuable advice about breaking into the game industry (as well as information about game development). Be warned: Sloper pulls no punches.

AWARD-WINNING GAME WRITING

It is always worthwhile to examine the successful endeavors in one's field, but there are hundreds of new releases each year. It may be helpful to consider those games which have been singled out for recognition. The following is a list of games that have received awards for excellence in game writing. Though these are not the only such awards in the industry, they serve as a good starting point.

Game Developers Choice Awards

The Award for Game Writing (*www.gamechoiceawards.com*) is voted on by regular IGDA members in good standing. The winners are announced at the Game Developers Choice Awards, which are conducted at the Game Developers Conference. Past nominees and recipients include:

2006
Recipient
- Psychonauts

Nominees
- Freedom Force vs. The 3rd Reich
- God of War
- Indigo Prophecy
- Jade Empire

2005
Recipient
- Half-Life 2

Nominees
- Grand Theft Auto: San Andreas
- Leisure Suit Larry: Magna Cum Laude
- Paper Mario: The Thousand-Year Door
- Star Wars: Knights of the Old Republic II: The Sith Lords

2004
Recipient
- Star Wars: Knights of the Old Republic

Nominees
- Beyond Good and Evil
- Broken Sword: The Sleeping Dragon
- Deus Ex: Invisible War
- Fire Emblem

2003
Recipient
- Tom Clancy's Splinter Cell

Nominees
- Eternal Darkness: Sanity's Requiem
- Grand Theft Auto: Vice City
- Mafia: The City of Lost Heaven
- No One Lives Forever 2: A Spy in H.A.R.M.S. Way

The Academy of Interactive Arts and Sciences

The Award for Outstanding Achievement in Story and Character Development (*www.interactive.org*) is voted on by qualified members of the Academy of Interactive Arts and Sciences. Members of the Academy are selected based on experience and industry credits. Past nominees and recipients include:

2007
Recipient
- The Legend of Zelda: Twilight Princess

Nominees
- 24: The Game
- Dreamfall: The Longest Journey
- Saints Row
- Sam & Max Episode 1: Culture Shock
- The Legend of Zelda: Twilight Princess

2006
Recipient
- Call of Duty 2: Big Red One

Nominees
- Brothers in Arms: Earned in Blood
- Gun, Peter Jackson's King Kong
- Sly Cooper 3: Honor Among Thieves

2005
Recipient
- Fable

Nominees
- Forgotten Realms: Demon Stone
- Grand Theft Auto: San Andreas
- Half-Life 2
- Psi-Ops: The Mindgate Conspiracy

2004
Recipient
- Star Wars: Knights of the Old Republic

Nominees
- Beyond Good and Evil
- Prince of Persia: The Sands of Time
- Ratchet & Clank: Going Commando
- The Legend of Zelda: The Wind Waker

2003
Recipient
- Eternal Darkness: Sanity's Requiem

Nominees
- Grand Theft Auto: Vice City
- Kingdom Hearts
- Syberia
- The Mark of Kri

2002
Recipient
- ICO

Nominees
- Black & White
- Metal Gear Solid 2: Sons of Liberty
- Myst III: Exile
- Conker's Bad Fur Day

2001

Recipient
- Baldur's Gate II

Nominees
- Final Fantasy IX
- Shenmue
- Skies of Arcadia

2000

Recipients
- Age of Empires II: Age of Kings
- Thief: The Dark Project

Nominees
- NOX
- Omikron: The Nomad Soul
- Planescape: Torment

1999

Recipient
- Pokemon

Nominees
- Grim Fandango
- Half-Life
- King's Quest: Mask of Eternity
- Metal Gear Solid
- Sanitarium
- The X-Files Game
- The Legend of Zelda: Ocarina of Time

Summary

In this chapter, we discussed ways to get a foothold in the game industry, including resources like the Game Developers Conference, Gamasutra.com, and the International Game Developers Association. Though many writing jobs are not posted publicly, by networking and becoming involved in the community, it is possible to find job leads. The chapter ended with a list of games that have been recognized for excellence in writing. Hopefully, this book has provided you with information about the process of game writing, and with a clearer understanding of how story content is integrated into the game development process. Good luck!

Appendix

A Documentation

I n this chapter you'll find templates, spreadsheets, examples, and checklists. This should serve as a quick reference for you on your next project.

CHARACTER	CUE	CONTEXT	TRIGGER	INFLECTION	AREA	EFFECT	FILENAME

FIGURE A.1   The template for Screen/Play, an example of dialogue documentation.

Screen/Play (Figure A.1) is a form of active documentation and can be used to document dialogue assets for cinematics and in-game action. The spreadsheet is formatted in such a way that it can be used by writers, designers, scripters, testers, sound designers, and testers. For more information, read Chapter 7, Organizing Dialogue.

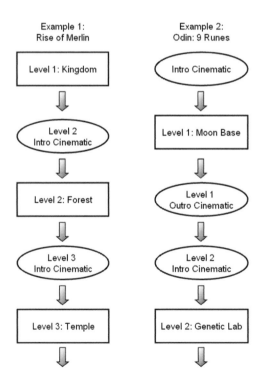

FIGURE A.2   Story-driven narrative design.

In story-driven narrative (Figure A.2) the narrative sequence furnishes the structure of the entire game experience. For more information, read Chapter 4, Developing the Context.

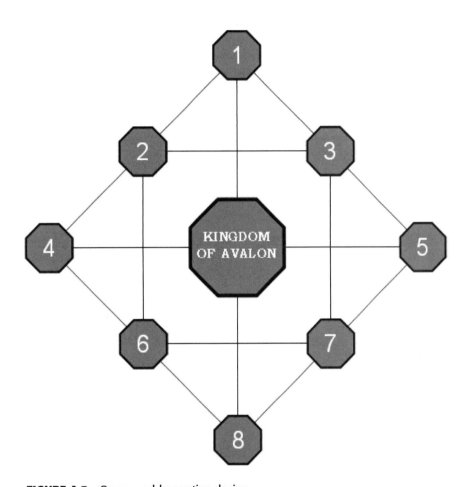

FIGURE A.3   Open-world narrative design.

Open-world narrative (Figure A.3) allows the player to explore the world at his own pace. For more information, read Chapter 4, Developing the Context.

The character web (Figure A.4) is a technique that can be used by the writer during the process of designing characters. More information can be found in Chapter 5, Creating the Characters.

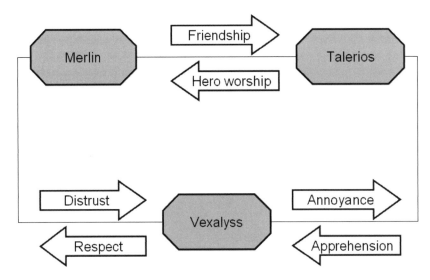

FIGURE A.4   An example of a character web.

Logocentric design (Figure A.5) is specific and precise and is primarily authored by the developer. For more information, read Chapter 6, Structuring the Narrative.

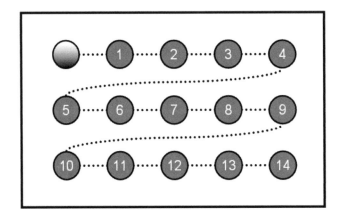

FIGURE A.5   An example of logocentric narrative structure.

Mythocentric design (Figure A.6) is wide-open and subject to interpretation and is therefore player-authored. For more information, read Chapter 6, Structuring the Narrative.

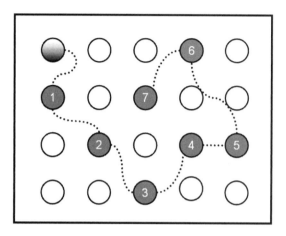

FIGURE A.6   An example of mythocentric narrative structure.

The concept document (Figure A.1) presents the necessary materials for the cinematics in a game. For more information, read Chapter 8, Creating Cinematics.

Title	"Into the Abyss"
Function	Mission 4 Intro Cinematic
Overview	Odin and Vili are in the Caverns of Midgard, where they are attacked by four of the reptilian servants of the Midgard Serpent. Odin destroys two of the enemy with his sword, but Vili is dragged into a dark pool by the other two. Odin jumps after his brother and swims into the darkness.
Goals	Show loyalty between Odin and his brother Vili; set up Dark Abyss mission.
Characters	4 character models -- Odin, Vili, Serpentman A, and Serpentman B.
Locations	Cave structure
Objects	2 - Odin's sword, Vili's hammer

FIGURE A.7   A concept document for a series of cinematics.

The spreadsheet in Figure A.8 outlines all the materials that will be required to develop a cinematic. For more information, read Chapter 8, Creating Cinematics.

Title	"Into the Abyss"
Function	Mission 4 Intro Cinematic
Characters	4 character models -- Odin, Vili, Serpentman A, and Serpentman B.
Locations	Cave structure
Objects	2 - Odin's sword, Vili's hammer

FIGURE A.8 An outline of necessary assets for a prerendered cinematic.

The document in Figure A.9 outlines the number of actors and lines that will be needed to record the voice cues for a game. For more information, read Chapter 8, Creating Cinematics.

CHARACTER	LINES	DESCRIPTION
Odin	800	Male, early thirties, strong and authoritative. Deep voice. British accent.
Vili	250	Male, mid-twenties, intelligent and clever. Tenor voice. British accent.
Ymir	100	Older male voice, deep and powerful, rumbling and menacing. British accent.
Fenris	100	Male voice, mid thirties, nearly unrecognizable growl. Monster voice (will be subtitled).
Serpentman A	150	Male voice, hissing monster voice (will be subtitled).
Serpentman B	150	Male voice, hissing monster voice (will be subtitled).
TOTAL	1550	

FIGURE A.9 A spreadsheet indicating necessary resources for voice recording.

Figure A.10 shows the total number of character models, vehicles, locations, and special effects depicted in the screenplay. For more information, read Chapter 8, Creating Cinematics.

Cinematic	Function	Characters	Objects
0	Game intro	Odin (old), Loki, Thor	Thor's hammer
1	Level 1 intro	Odin, Vili, Kuul	Odin's sword, Vili's hammer, Kuul's trident
2	Level 2 intro	Odin, Fenris	Scepter of Midgard
3	Level 3 intro	Odin, Vili, Thelfi	Odin's sword, Vili's hammer
4	Level 4 intro	Odin, Vili, Serpentman A, and Serpentman B	Odin's sword, Vili's hammer
5	Level 5 intro	Odin, Heimdall	Odin's sword, Heimdall's sword

FIGURE A.10   An example of cinematic asset documentation.

Storyboards are developed by artists as a two-dimensional representation of the content that will be appearing in the cinematic. For more information, read Chapter 8, Creating Cinematics.

The monster approaches Caldwell, and the beam from the flashlight throws its monstrous shadow on the wall.

Once Caldwell sees the shadow, the monster transforms into its true shape and attacks.

After it has been killed, its Apparition is Harvested by Caldwell, and the camera fades out.

FIGURE A.11   An example of storyboards.

With the list in Figure A.12, the writer can verify that the cinematic studio incorporated the audio components properly and in the correct order. For more information, read Chapter 8, Creating Cinematics.

Audio Component Verification	
Are all of the voice cues audible?	Yes / No
Are the voice cues playing in the right order?	Yes / No
Were the correct versions of each cue used? In other words, make sure that the studio didn't mistakenly use an alternate.	Yes / No
Do the voice cues feature the correct effects, such as radio squelch or echo?	Yes / No
Are all of the voice cues playing at the correct volume level?	Yes / No

FIGURE A.12 Checklist for audio component verification.

The vision document (Figure A.13) is the overall description of what the writer hopes to achieve with the words the player hears. For more about voice acting, read Chapter 9, Directing Voice Actors.

Title	Rise of Merlin
Genre	Third-person action
Concept	Before Merlin was the wise old wizard who taught Arthur Pendragon to be king, he was a young wizard in search of his destiny. In Rise of Merlin, the player leads the wizard on his quest to attain the four Elemental Staves and defeat the wicked Horned King.
Storyline	After the Horned King seizes power in the southern Kingdoms, young Merlin is sent on a quest to defeat him. Along with his trusty sidekick Valerios, the engimatic dragon Vexalyss, and the sinister Dragon Queen, Merlin must overcome ogres, wyverns, and trolls as he makes his wall to the Hall of the Dead. There, he must wield the elemental staves against the Horned King and bring peace to the land.
Key Moments	* Death of Vexalyss * Treason of Valerios * Destruction of the Hall of the Dead

FIGURE A.13 An example of a vision document.

Voice notes help with the casting and directing processes (Figure A.14). These notes include information about pitch, vocabulary, accent, and reference. For more detail, read Chapter 9, Directing Voice Actors.

Casting Notes: Fenris	
Role	Fenris, the Wolf. Fenris is a murderous wolf-demon that seeks to destroy all of Asgard. He has allied his forces with his despised enemy, the Midgard Serpent, and together they seek to kill Odin and Vili to cripple Asgard's forces.
Premise	Odin: Nine Runes tells the story of the god Odin, who begins the game as an old warrior telling his son of the legendary Nine Runes. Throughout the game, Odin quests for the Nine Runes that will prevent Fenris and the Midgard Serpent from starting Ragnarok prematurely.
Description	Fenris is an ageless demon that appears as a gigantic wolf with burning red eyes and smoking breath. His voice is a deep, inhuman growl. The distortion will ultimately be so severe that subtitles will be necessary, so the focus should be on a menacing delivery.
Dialogue 1	True, godling. But while you walk the land of men, you are both mere mortals. This will be your undoing.
Dialogue 2	You should probably kill yourself now. The serpent's offspring will toy with you for hours before ending their sport.

FIGURE A.14   An example of casting notes.

Figure A.15 is the full version of Screen/Play, including all applicable fields. For more details, read Chapter 9, Directing Voice Actors.

The version of Screen/Play in Figure A.16 only features information that the voice actor will need in the recording studio. For more about voice acting, read Chapter 9, Directing Voice Actors.

CHARACTER	CUE	CONTEXT	TRIGGER	INFLECTION	AREA	EFFECT	FILENAME
Odin	Wait, I hear something.	Cinematic 2B. Odin and Vili are in the Northern Forest when they see what appears to be a large wolf.	A branch snaps off-camera.	whispering	2BC		M2b_0c_001
Vili	Over there, a wolf!	Cinematic 2B. Odin and Vili are in the Northern Forest when they see what appears to be a large wolf.	Vili points to a large wolf walking past them.	whispering	2BC		M2b_0c_002
Odin	That's no mere wolf.	Cinematic 2B. Odin and Vili are in the Northern Forest when they see what appears to be a large wolf.	The wolf turns to look at them. Odin realizes that it's Fenris.	serious	2BC		M2b_0c_003
Fenris	True, godling. But while you walk the land of men, you are both mere mortals. This will be your undoing.	Cinematic 2B. Odin and Vili are in the Northern Forest when they see what appears to be a large wolf.	He's loping over to Odin and Vili, and is preparing to kill them.	ominous	2BC	distortion	M2b_0c_004
Odin	We shall see, mongrel.	Cinematic 2B. Odin and Vili are in the Northern Forest when they see what appears to be a large wolf.	He draws his sword and prepares for battle.	confident	2BC		M2b_0c_005

FIGURE A.15   An example of Screen/Play documentation.

CHARACTER	CUE	CONTEXT	TRIGGER	INFLECTION
Odin	Wait, I hear something.	Cinematic 2B. Odin and Vili are in the Northern Forest when they see what appears to be a large wolf.	A branch snaps off-camera.	whispering
Vili	Over there, a wolf!	Cinematic 2B. Odin and Vili are in the Northern Forest when they see what appears to be a large wolf.	Vili points to a large wolf walking past them.	whispering
Odin	That's no mere wolf.	Cinematic 2B. Odin and Vili are in the Northern Forest when they see what appears to be a large wolf.	The wolf turns to look at them. Odin realizes that it's Fenris.	serious
Fenris	True, godling. But while you walk the land of men, you are both mere mortals. This will be your undoing.	Cinematic 2B. Odin and Vili are in the Northern Forest when they see what appears to be a large wolf.	He's loping over to Odin and Vili, and is preparing to kill them.	ominous
Odin	We shall see, mongrel.	Cinematic 2B. Odin and Vili are in the Northern Forest when they see what appears to be a large wolf.	He draws his sword and prepares for battle.	confident

FIGURE A.16   An example of Screen/Play, formatted for voice actors.

The top-down map (Figure A.17) can help to make the details more concrete for scripters. By indicating locations of trigger zones and characters with dotted lines and Xs, the writer can help pinpoint the locations of voice cues in-game.

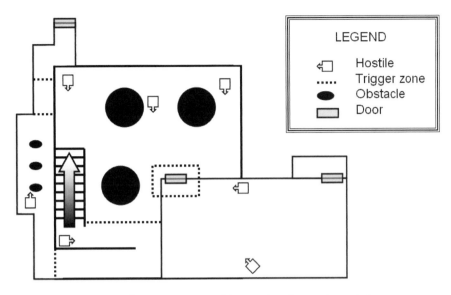

FIGURE A.17   A top-down map created by a writer for use by scripters.

The checklist in Figure A.18 can help the QA testers during the testing of cinematic assets. For more information about testing, read Chapter 12, Testing Story Content.

Questions	Yes	No
Does the cinematic play?		
Is it playing in the correct order?		
Does it play before or after the gameplay, as designed?		
Is it consistently visible?		
Is the audio track consistently audible?		
Do all of the voice cues play properly?		
Are there any missing voice cues?		
Are there any missing voice effects?		
Is the lyp-synch correctly lined up?		
Does it last as long as the documentation indicates it should?		
Is the story content in the design document clearly represented on-screen?		

FIGURE A.18   A checklist for the cinematic testing phase.

Figure A.19 shows a story bug like those found by the QA analysts during the testing phase. For more about QA, read Chapter 12, Testing Story Content.

Summary	Missing voice cue
Status	Open
Type	Voice bug
Severity	3 - mild
Details	When the player enters area 31A, the audio cue "m3a101a" doesn't play. The player should hear the voice of Vili calling out, "Stay back, brother, it's an ambush!"

FIGURE A.19   An example of a story bug.

Appendix
B Resources

BOOKS

Chandler, Heather. *Game Localization Handbook*. Charles River Media, 2004.
Chandler, Heather. *Game Production Handbook*. Charles River Media, 2005.
Freeman, David. *Creating Emotion in Games*. New Riders Publishing, 2003.
Friend, Christy, Maxine Hairston and John Ruszkiewicz. *The Scott, Foresman Handbook for Writers*. Addison-Wesley Educational Publishers, 1999.
McKee, Robert. *Story: Substance, Structure, Style, and the Principles of Screenwriting*. HarperCollins Publishers, 1997.

ARTICLES

Chandler, Rafael, "Active Storytelling in Games," available online at *http://www.gamasutra.com/features/20050707/chandler_01.shtml*, July 2005.
Chandler, Rafael, "Breaking In: Video Game Markets," *Writer's Digest*, May 2006.
Chandler, Rafael, "Character Development Techniques in Games," available online at *http://www.gamasutra.com/features/20050810/chandler_01.shtml*, August 2005.
Chandler, Rafael, "Organizing and Formatting Game Dialogue," available online at *http://www.gamasutra.com/features/20051118/chandler_01.shtml*, October 2005.
Chandler, Rafael, "Pull Together: Getting Team Buy-In," available online at *http://www.gamedev.net/reference/articles/article2258.asp*, June 2005.
Chandler, Rafael, "Screen/Play: Documenting Voice Assets," available online at *http://www.gamasutra.com/features/20060608/chandler_01.shtml*, June 2006.
Chandler, Rafael, "Screen/Play: Technical Narrative Design," available online at *http://gamasutra.com/features/20061004/chandler_01.shtml*, September 2006.

Appendix C

Developer Biographies

Chris Avellone

Chris started his career by freelancing for a number of pen-and-paper role-playing game companies in high school before Interplay hired him as a game designer in 1996. He worked on most (if not all) of Black Isle's internally developed projects, including *Planescape: Torment* (lead designer), *Fallout 2*, the whole *Icewind Dale* series, *Baldur's Gate: Dark Alliance™*, and a number of canceled titles, including *Baldur's Gate 3* and *Fallout 3*. Chris was the lead designer on *Star Wars Knights of the Old Republic II: The Sith Lords*, moved on to a senior design role on *Neverwinter Nights 2*, and is currently the creative lead of the *Aliens* RPG at Obsidian Entertainment.

Rob Brown

Rob is a senior lead designer at Edge of Reality. Prior to that, he worked as a senior lead designer at Red Storm Entertainment and a lead designer at Microsoft Game Studios. His credits include Activision's *Over the Hedge* and *Microsoft Combat Flight Simulator, 1, 2,* and *3*.

Mary DeMarle

Mary is a narrative designer at UbiSoft Montreal. Prior to that, she worked as a freelance writer on *Myst 3: Exile*, *Myst 4: Revelation*, and *Homeworld 2*. Mary graduated from Syracuse University with a BS in Television, Radio, and Film Production. Shortly after graduation she moved to Hollywood and began working for the cartoon studio Hanna-Barbera (creators of *The Flintstones®*). She began freelance writing for the entertainment industry four years later; then in 1997, she switched to games by joining up with the now-defunct game development studio Presto Studios. It was at Presto that Mary designed and wrote the award-winning story for *Myst 3: Exile*.

Matt Dohmen

Matt Dohmen was born in western Pennsylvania and met boredom immediately thereafter. After video games saved him from a life of mining or hunting beavers for pelts or whatever people do in Pennsylvania to pass the time, he decided to return the favor by entering the game industry and making sure more games are fun. He's scripted for a number of iterations of the *Ghost Recon* franchise on the PC and Xbox as well as other games using that engine, including *The Sum of All Fears* and *Rainbow Six: Lockdown*. He is currently working on *Warhammer Online: Age of Reckoning* at EA Mythic and is very much enjoying being married to a gamer while playing games and making games.

Randall Jahnson

Randall Jahnson is a Hollywood scriptwriter who has worked on movies such as *Sunset Strip*, *The Mask of Zorro*, and *The Doors*. He's also a freelance game writer on projects such as Neversoft's 2005 western shooter, *Gun*.

Susan O'Connor

Susan has been writing stories for games since 1998. Her client list includes Activision, Atari, Epic Games, Irrational Games, Microsoft, Midway, SOE, THQ, Ubisoft, and Take-Two Interactive. Her portfolio features over a dozen titles in a variety of genres, including first-person shooters, RTS titles, action-adventure games, RPGs, and MMOs. Recent projects include *Gears of War* (Epic Games/Microsoft) and the forthcoming *Bioshock* (Irrational/2K).

Jon Schweitzer

Since entering the game industry in 1999, Jon Schweitzer has worked in quality assurance for Electronic Arts and Ubisoft in positions ranging from tester to department manager. He has shipped titles that include the *Ghost Recon*, *Rainbow Six* and *Splinter Cell* franchises, as well as massively multiplayer titles such as *Ultima Online* and *Air Warrior III*. His platform experience includes PC, Mac, and consoles from Nintendo, Sony, and Microsoft. In his spare time Jon can be found reading books to his children or hanging out with his wife. He can be reached via email at *jonschweitzer@gmail.com*.

Mikey Spano

Mikey works as an artist at Epic Games. Prior to that, he was a lead artist at Red Storm Entertainment. His credits include *Gears of War*, *Rainbow Six 3: Raven Shield*, *The Sum of All Fears*, and *Ghost Recon: Island Thunder*.

Mac Walters

Mac Walters began writing at BioWare in 2003. Since then he has written (and rewritten) thousands of lines of dialog for *Jade Empire* and the upcoming Xbox 360 title, *Mass Effect*. As a writer and designer at BioWare, his duties entail everything from story and character development to writing of all shapes and styles (documentation and item descriptions may not be sexy, but they are necessary).

Erik Wolpaw

Erik Wolpaw was one of the two writers behind the influential and now-defunct Old Man Murray video game commentary Web site. Today he works for Valve Software in Seattle. In 2006 he won the Game Developers Choice Award for Best Writing for his story and dialog contributions to *Psychonauts* while working for Double Fine Productions.

Appendix

D Glossary

AAA title: A high-profile, big-budget game with high-quality production values.

Active media: Content that's presented in-game during the action. This content is directly engaged and affected by the player.

Asset: An element of the game, such as a character model or a line of recorded dialogue.

Brick-and-mortar design: In this kind of game the play experience is created as a series of discrete levels, missions, or installments, and the story content is used as mortar to cement the game experience into a coherent narrative.

Build: A software executable that can be run by a user. Typically, once game production gets underway, the programmers will release new playable builds on a regular basis, allowing the other developers to see what changes have been made to the game.

Cinematic: A computer-generated movie that can communicate plot and character information, reward the player, or serve as a pacing device.

Content: The material that's created during production, which can take the form of characters, dialogue, or cinematics.

Context: An explanation for interaction, and the idea behind the game. Context is present in all games and is usually outlined in the design documentation.

Development team: The group of people who create a game, including writers, designers, producers, artists, programmers, and testers.

Logocentric design: A series of specific moments that are determined in advance. It's linear and controlled and has been plotted out and documented by the designer.

Mythocentric design: An open space whose numerous moving parts afford the player the opportunity to create specific moments. It's wide-open and free-ranging and consists of arenas for player action that have been created by the developers.

Open-world design: Allows the player to explore the world at his own pace. While the story may be linear in its progression, the game experience is nonetheless authored in great part by the player and is nonlinear.

Passive media: Content that is appreciated or observed but not influenced by the player, such as cinematics and briefings.

Prerendered cinematic: A computer-generated movie that's created and recorded and then inserted into the game.

Production: The process of a game's development, typically divided into three stages: preproduction, when story concepts are developed and decisions are made; production, when assets are created and integrated; and postproduction, when the team discusses the project and prepares for the next game.

Screen/Play: This format for dialogue documentation is a specific type of screen-play, though there are many others.

Screenplay: A screenplay documents a game's dialogue and may also contain other information, such as notes on inflection, sound effects, and location.

Scripted cinematic: A computer-generated movie that's created using the game's scripting tool and that plays in real time.

Scripting: The process of placing objects and characters in a game and/or assigning them characteristics and behaviors. When the artists have created models for characters, weapons, and vehicles, the scripter uses the scripting tool (also known as a scripting editor) to place these elements in the game and to tell them what to do. The scripting tool may use a drop-down menu, or it may require knowledge of a scripting language, such as Lua.

Story-driven design: When a game's design is driven by story, the narrative sequence furnishes the structure of the entire game experience. The story arc is significant, even epic, and can span the entirety of the game.

Voice cue: A line of recorded dialogue.

Index